D1488885

Reforming Financial Institutions and Markets in the United States

Reforming Financial Institutions and Markets in the United States

Towards Rebuilding a Safe and More Efficient System

edited by
George G. Kaufman
Loyola University of Chicago

Kluwer Academic Publishers
Boston / Dordrecht / London

Distributors for North America:
Kluwer Academic Publishers
101 Philip Drive
Assinippi Park
Norwell, Massachusetts 02061 USA

Distributors for all other countries:
Kluwer Academic Publishers Group
Distribution Centre
Post Office Box 322
3300 AH Dordrecht, THE NETHERLANDS

Library of Congress Cataloging-in-Publication Data
Reforming financial institutions and markets in the United States
   towards rebuilding a safe and more efficient system / edited by
   George G. Kaufman.
     p. cm.
   Includes index.
   ISBN 0-7923-9383-X
   1. Banks and banking--Government policy--United States.
   2. Financial institutions--Government policy--United States.
   3. Deposit insurance--United States.   I. Kaufman, George G.
   HG2491.R415   1993
   332.1'0973--dc20   93-2298
                                            CIP

Printed on acid-free paper.

Printed in the United States of America

Contents

Preface

Since the late 1970s, financial institutions and markets in the United States have been on a rollercoaster ride. Between 1980 and 1992, some 1,150 savings and loan associations with more than $400 billion in total assets— or about one-quarter of the total number of associations in 1980 with 40 percent of the average total assets over this period—failed at an estimated aggregate present value cost of near $135 billion in 1990 dollars. Another 100 were in receivership at the Resolution Trust Corporation (RTC) in mid-1993, awaiting final resolution at an additional present value loss of more than $40 billion. These losses greatly exceeded the resources of the Federal Savings and Loan Insurance Corporation (FSLIC), which was declared insolvent and closed in 1989. Because the FSLIC was widely perceived to have the full faith and credit support of the U.S. government, Congress assumed the burden of the remaining losses to insured deposi- tors, which is estimated to be about 80 percent of the total, as an obliga- tion of the taxpayer in the Financial Institutions Reform, Recovery, and Enforcement Act (FIRREA) of 1989. At the same time, the FSLIC was replaced first by the Resolution Trust Corporation and then in late 1993 by the new Savings Association Insurance Fund (SAIF) of the Federal Deposit Insurance Corporation (FDIC). By 1993, fewer than 1,900 savings and loan associations were in operation, compared to some 4,500 asso- ciations in 1980. Failures accounted for some 45 percent of the reduction and mergers for most of the rest. A few associations converted to savings bank charters.

Although starting somewhat later and not as severe, commercial banks also experienced trying times. Between 1980 and 1992, some 1,300 com- mercial and savings banks insured by the FDIC failed. These banks had assets of $260 billion, or about 8 percent of the average total assets in the industry. The associated present value losses were near $40 billion in 1990 dollars, about one-quarter those of the S&L industry, but when combined with adjusting for probable future bank failures and losses, still large enough to wipe out the reserves of the FDIC. The fund was recapitalized through additional borrowing authority from the Treasury Department in the Federal Deposit Insurance Corporation Improvement Act (FDICIA) of 1991.

In October 1987, the New York Stock Exchange suffered its greatest monthly decline since the onset of the Great Depression in the early 1930s. On Monday, October 19, alone, the Standard & Poor 500 stock index declined 20 percent. Other markets both in the United States and worldwide declined by roughly similar amounts.

But by early 1993, the picture had changed substantially. For a number of reasons, including sharply lower interest rates, an unusually steep upward-sloping yield curve, a bottoming out of the real estate market, and pressure on surviving institutions to increase their capital ratios both by the marketplace and by the newly enacted FIRREA and particularly FDICIA legislation, depository institutions had, on average, regained profitability and greatly improved their solvency, at least temporarily. Bank earnings in 1992 were a record $32 billion and averaged nearly 1 percent of assets, the highest level since the creation of the FDIC. Book value capital ratios rose to 7.5 percent, the highest since 1965, and market value ratios were even higher. The number of banks on the FDIC's problem list declined to 787 from a peak of over 1,500 in 1987 and the lowest since 1983, and their assets declined from $535 billion early in 1992 to $408 billion, the lowest since 1985. However, a substantial number of banks achieved their improvement only through accounting trickery and assuming greater interest rate risk and remained in a precarious position.

Similarly, S&L profits in 1992 were at record levels, the return on assets the highest since 1979 at 0.57 percent, and the number of new failures slowed substantially. The U.S. stock market reached record levels in early 1993.

As a result of these improvements, the financial condition of the FDIC also improved. At year end 1992, its reserves were only slightly negative, compared to a deficit of $7 billion one year earlier at year end 1991. In early 1993, the FDIC downsized its estimates of bank failures for the year from 120 with $75 billion in assets projected in late 1992 to about 80 with only $25 billion in assets and revised these figures down again at midyear. Moreover, losses from failures were also shrinking, in large measure from enforcement of the prompt correction action and least cost resolution provisions of FDICIA. Thus, the FDIC projected that it would have positive $1 billion of reserves at year end.

The Shadow Financial Regulatory Committee had been in the forefront both in warning about the pending difficulties in the banking and thrift industries in the mid-1980s and in developing solutions to correct the problems at minimum cost to taxpayers and healthy institutions in the late-1980s. Some of the Committee's statements and underlying analyses from that period are published in *Restructuring the American Financial System* (Kluwer, 1990). That volume also contains a history and description of the Committee. Since then, the Committee members have continued to monitor and analyze developments in financial markets and make recommendations for improving their safety and efficiency. The Committee's statement "An Outline of a Program for Deposit Insurance and Regulatory Reform" (No. 41, adopted February 13, 1989) spelled out a program for structured early regulatory intervention and resolution (SEIR) for troubled institutions and served as the basis for the prudential and deposit insurance reform provisions in FDICIA.

The essays by members of the Shadow Financial Regulatory Committee published in this volume focus on constructing a safer and more efficient financial system based on the lessons learned from the debacles of the 1980s through early 1993. The two essays by George Benston and George Kaufman (chapters 1 and 7) describe the intellectual history of the deposit insurance reform provisions of FDICIA, arguably the most important banking legislation since the Banking Act of 1933, discuss the weaknesses and strengths of these provisions, and make recommendations for improving the effectiveness of the reforms. In chapter 2, Kenneth Scott and Barry Weingast discuss the economic and political forces both propelling and opposing widespread banking reform. Edward Kane and Richard Aspinwall (in chapters 3, 5, and 6) analyze the why's and how's of privatizing federal deposit insurance in the event that the reforms in FDICIA prove ineffective. In chapter 4, Robert Eisenbeis and Paul Horvitz summarize and evaluate the theoretical and empirical evidence with respect to the costs and benefits of regulators granting forbearance to economically insolvent institutions. Richard Herring (chapter 8) examines the causes and consequences of the Bank of Credit and Commerce International (BCCI) debacle of the early 1990s and the implications for the supervision of foreign banks in the United States and elsewhere. Finally, Franklin Edwards moves away from banking and discusses the broader issue of whether U.S. financial markets affect the behavior of U.S. corporate managers, particularly whether they encourage managerial myopia. Without concluding whether such myopia exists, he then examines policy options that would make financial markets more conducive to long-term planning, including permitting banks to invest in corporate equity and thus monitor firms as owners as well as creditors.

Except for Barry Weingast, all the authors in this book are members of the Shadow Committee. Although all the topics discussed in the essays were discussed at committee meetings, the views of the authors are their own and represent those of the committee only when reference is made to specific policy statements.

George G. Kaufman

Reforming Financial Institutions and Markets in the United States

1 THE INTELLECTUAL HISTORY OF THE FEDERAL DEPOSIT INSURANCE CORPORATION IMPROVEMENT ACT OF 1991

George J. Benston and George G. Kaufman*

The Federal Deposit Insurance Corporation Improvement Act (FDICIA) was passed by Congress in November 1991 and signed by President George Bush in December. The act promises to be the most important banking legislation since the Banking Act of 1933. Yet it is also one of most misunderstood and controversial laws enacted in recent years. As is true for much legislation, the act is long, sweeping in coverage, and complex. It may be divided into five major parts: (1) deposit insurance reform to correct the previous perverse incentive structure, (2) recapitalization of the FDIC, (3) consumer and related regulations, (4) supervision of domestic offices of foreign banks, and (5) "bank bashing." In this chapter we trace

* Paper presented at a Conference on "FDICIA: One Year Later" at the Brookings Institution, Washington, D.C. on December 16, 1992. The authors are indebted to Herbert Baer and Philip Bartholomew for comments and suggestions on earlier drafts. As in any brief history, a number of persons who have made contributions and should be recognized are likely to have been inadvertently omitted. The authors apologize for any such omissions. This chapter is a revised version of a paper published by the Brookings Institution in *Assessing Banking Reform*, edited by Robert Litan, 1993. Printed with permission from the Brookings Institution.

the intellectual history of the underpinnings of only the deposit insurance reform provisions of the act, which may be classified under the heading structured early intervention and resolution (SEIR). These provisions are significantly different from most deposit insurance reform proposals suggested at the time the act was being considered. Because they are not as well understood as most of the other proposals, which have been circulating longer, and shall affect banking for years to come, it is useful to trace their history to determine, why and how they might be expected to work.[1]

Deposit–insurance reform is achieved in the act through a combination of four provisions: (1) higher capital ratios, (2) timely, prespecified, and structured corrective actions by regulators in the affairs of financially troubled institutions, (3) prompt resolution of failing institutions before their capital becomes negative (closure rule), and (4) risk-based deposit insurance premiums. By themselves, these provisions are neither new nor likely to be effective. What is new and what makes the act different and potentially effective is the combination of all four.

Weaknesses in Deposit Insurance

Before federal deposit insurance, capital was seen as the primary protection for depositors, and banks held significantly higher capital ratios (Kaufman, 1992). Indeed, banks prominently displayed signs in their front windows stating "Capital and Surplus $XX million." After enactment of insurance, this was replaced by "Member FDIC or FSLIC." Bank capital as a percentage of assets declined as depositors became less concerned that it was needed to protect their funds. Timely intervention has always been the responsibility of the supervisors and regulators. But after deposit insurance reduced the fear of runs and thereby also reduced market discipline, regulators did not pick up the slack fully. Penalties were not imposed on the regulators for delayed or ineffective intervention.

Nor were there provisions for the prompt resolution of institutions that failed to respond to the intervention. Regulators had long understood that if an institution could be resolved before its economic or market value net worth became negative, there would be no loss to depositors or the FDIC. But the decision to close an institution rested with the chartering agency, which did not bear the cost of the financial losses to the FDIC of delaying resolution. Furthermore, regulators could not effectively resolve institutions until the book value of their net worth was negative. Nevertheless, until the early 1980s, at least commercial bank regulators generally resolved institutions near the time they became economically insolvent with small if any losses to the FDIC. This practice was abetted by two factors. One, until interest rates increased dramatically in the late 1970s, the market and book values of bank assets and liabilities did not differ greatly. Two, the small number of insolvencies in this period did not bring strong political pressure to bear on the regulators to delay resolution.

Premiums on deposit insurance were set as a fixed percentage of a bank's total deposits. This did not penalize banks for risk taking to the same extent as interest rates charged by uninsured depositors. Risk-based deposit-insurance premiums, similar to the premium structure of private insurance companies, had been prominently suggested at the time that federal deposit insurance was first enacted in 1933, but were not adopted. In the late 1960s, Professors Thomas Mayer and Kenneth Scott published articles in favor of such a structure (Mayer, 1965; Mayer and Scott, 1971). Thereafter, risk-based premiums were supported by most academics and in studies sponsored by both the FDIC and the Federal Home Loan Bank Board. (Federal Deposit Insurance Corporation, 1983; Federal Home Loan Bank Board, 1983).[2]

Unfortunately, neither effective timely regulatory intervention and failure resolution nor risk-adjusted insurance premiums were in place in the early 1980s . As has been well documented, the federal deposit-insurance agencies had underpriced their insurance and permitted banks to operate with lower capital ratios and riskier asset and liability portfolios than they would have maintained in the absence of insurance. Consequently, banks could not absorb large adverse shocks without depleting their capital. Moreover, the sharp increase in the number of seriously troubled institutions in the mid-1980s changed the regulators' resolution practice substantially. As they became overwhelmed by the extraordinary number of troubled and failing institutions, regulators increasingly failed both to impose their discretionary sanctions either sufficiently harshly or sufficiently timely and to enforce even the weak closure rule of zero book value capital. They frequently found it in their best interests to deny the existence of serious bank problems in the hope these would reverse or not explode until later on someone else's watch.[3] As a result, some economically insolvent or weak institutions were provided with both the incentive and the time to gamble for resurrection. But many of these gambles did not pay off and instead created losses for the insurer and, in the case of the thrifts, also for taxpayers (Congressional Budget Office, 1991).

At the same time, the regulators also came under increasing political pressure from some of their constituents, Congress, and the administration to delay closing "important" institutions in the belief that credit availability and employment in local communities would be disrupted. Indeed, some forbearance was legally mandated by the Competitive Equality Banking Act (CEBA) of 1987. In an environment in which the federal deposit insurance protected depositors from losses if they maintained or even increased their deposits at troubled institutions, resolution frequently occurred only after the banks' net worths were substantially negative for a considerable period of time.[4] In sum, the institutions succumbed to problems of moral hazard and regulators to problems of agency.

As a result of these deficiencies, when the magnitude of adverse macroeconomic shocks increased sharply in the 1980s, bank failures and losses also increased sharply. Between 1980 and 1991, some 1,400 insolvent banks and 1,100 insolvent savings and loan associations were resolved, and many more awaited resolution. Losses at resolved institutions equaled nearly 30 percent of their assets, and aggregate losses to the insurance funds totaled almost $250 billion. For savings and loans, the losses at resolved institutions exceeded the resources of the insurance fund (FSLIC) and were shifted to the taxpaying public. For commercial banks, the losses also appeared to have exceeded the existing resources of the bank insurance fund (BIF) and, at minimum, would be financed by borrowing against projected future premium income.

The Scholarly Antecedents of SEIR

The first analysis that examined the importance of a closure rule in minimizing FDIC losses and distinguished between bank failure per se and losses to the FDIC appears to have been published by Paul Horvitz (1980). He argued (p. 656) that the appropriate role of bank examination was not to prevent failures but to detect them early enough "so that the bank can be closed before its losses exceed the amount of its capital." This idea was expanded and developed into a closure rule by G.O. Bierwag and George Kaufman in a 1983 paper prepared for a Federal Home Loan Bank Board Task Force that, pursuant to the Garn-St Germain Depository Institutions Act of 1982, analyzed federal deposit insurance and prepared a report to Congress. Horvitz also served as a member of the Task Force.

Bierwag and Kaufman (1983b) noted that if institutions could be resolved before their market-value net worth became negative, losses to the FDIC effectively would be zero and insurance premiums could be reduced to amounts required to cover only monitoring and operations costs. Moreover, they argued that deposit insurance was not like most other types of insurance, such as life or accident insurance. Losses to the insurer were not largely "an act of God" that was outside its control. The deposit insurer could control its losses by controlling the timing of when insolvent institutions were resolved. Losses to the insurer occur only if it resolves an institution after the institution's net worth becomes negative. The insurer can avoid or, at minimum, minimize losses by resolving the institution on a more timely basis. Thus, resolving an institution no later than when its capital declined to zero was a desirable closure rule. This closure rule was also recommended by an American Banking Association Academic Task Force in 1986 (Benston et al., 1986).

The question was how to implement a zero-net-worth closure rule effectively. As noted earlier, largely because of deposit insurance, banks held extremely low levels of capital and it would not take very large adverse shocks to quickly turn a bank's capital negative before the regulators could resolve it. Moreover, deposit insurance eliminated the role of deposit withdrawals in closing insolvent or near insolvent institutions. This was the problem faced by George Benston and George Kaufman as members of an American Enterprise Institute Task Force on financial regulation reform in 1986–1987. They searched for a solution that effectively could be achieved within the existing basic banking and safety net structures and was politically as well as economically feasible. Thus, they rejected solutions that involved reregulation or severe structural changes, such as eliminating deposit insurance and narrow banks.[5]

The Benston-Kaufman Proposal

Benston and Kaufman "solved" the problem by superimposing on the closure rule a structure requiring higher capital levels and early intervention by the regulators on a progressively harsher and more mandatory basis as a bank's condition deteriorates through a prescribed series of capital tranches. The system of structured early regulatory intervention was designed to change the incentives confronting both banks and regulators. In an environment of limited market discipline, capital-impaired banks would be discouraged from deteriorating further by increasing the cost to them of poor performance and, at minimum, slowing their deterioration, if not reversing it altogether.[6]

By requiring progressively more mandatory and timely sanctions as an institution deteriorated through the capital categories, the proposal effectively codified actions the regulators generally undertook, but too frequently on a delayed and leisurely basis that reduced their effectiveness. The regulatory sanctions substituted for similar market sanctions that would have occurred absent deposit insurance. If, however, these sanctions failed to stem a bank's decline, the regulators would be required to resolve it at some low but positive level of capital, before its market value net worth reached zero. Federal deposit-insurance coverage would remain at the existing $100,000 level and would be enforced de facto to intensify market discipline by larger depositors. Subordinated debt would be counted fully as capital to reduce the cost of capital to institutions, to strengthen market discipline, and to provide early warnings of problems to both bankers and regulators.

The small positive capital level would provide protection to the FDIC in case of inadequate monitoring, abrupt losses and deteriorations in a bank's capital, or miscomputation of a bank's economic capital. Current shareholders would be accorded first right to recapitalize their bank when its capital declined to the resolution tripwire. If they did not exercise this right, presumably because they believed the bank to be economically worth less than this amount, and chose to have the bank taken over by the FDIC, they would be paid the net value the FDIC received for the institution from a sale, merger, or liquidation. Thus, there would be no expropriation of private capital.[7] Moreover, to the extent the structured regulatory intervention was effective, few banks would be expected to deteriorate through all the tranches, so that there would be few new failures and FDIC takeovers.

In their proposal, Benston and Kaufman proposed four capital tranches and developed hypothetical examples of the appropriate sanctions when each tranche was breached. The lower thresholds of each tranche were tied to the current (market) value of a bank's capital at 10, 6, and 3 percent of total assets. Resolution would be required at 3 percent. The sanctions included restrictions on growth, interaffiliate transactions, dividend payments, interest payments to subordinated debt holders, and product powers, and would be harsher in the lower capital tranches. The sanctions would be mostly discretionary with the regulators in the higher capital tranches and become progressively less discretionary as a bank's capital fell into the lower tranches.

SEIR was designed to introduce a "carrot" as well as a "stick" approach to bank behavior. There were not only penalties for poor performance, but rewards for good performance. Banks maintaining sufficiently high capital levels would be rewarded with broader product powers, less intense supervision, and greater managerial freedom. Thus, institutions would be encouraged to achieve and maintain the top capital tranche. As summarized by Benston and Kaufman, the advantages of SEIR included:

1. improved bank performance and a much smaller number of bank failures;
2. lower losses to the FDIC from failures;

3. lower insurance premiums to pay for FDIC losses;
4. equal treatment of depositors at failed banks of all sizes and importance, thereby ending "too big to fail";
5. reduced need for prudential regulations in the long-run;
6. reduced need for restrictions on bank activities that could be
   adequately monitored by the insurer; and
7. discipline exerted by market forces through uninsured depositors,
   subordinated debt holders, and shareholders.

Indeed, because banks would be resolved with no or only small negative
net worth, losses to uninsured depositors would be zero or small, and
deposit insurance effectively would be redundant. This is why SEIR
represents deposit insurance reform.

Initial Response to the Proposal

Although Benston and Kaufman were the primary authors of the proposal, it benefitted substantially from the input and comments of the other
members of the American Enterprise Institute (AEI) task force and also
of the members of the associated advisory committee, particularly Thomas
Huertas of Citicorp. The proposal was first presented publicly at an AEI
conference in November 1987 in Washington, D.C., at which the task force
reported its conclusions and recommendations. In early 1988, the proposal
was published in draft form in the Staff Memoranda Series of the Federal
Reserve Bank of Chicago and in final form in the same year in the Monograph Series in Finance and Economics by the Salomon Brothers Center
for the Study of Financial Institutions at New York University and, in a
shorter version, as a chapter in the official report of the project published
by AEI (Benston and Kaufman, 1988a, 1988b, 1988c). In December 1988,
Kaufman (1988) presented the proposal at the annual conference on
savings and loan issues sponsored by the Federal Home Loan Bank of
San Francisco.

The first reactions were mixed. At the American Enterprise Institute
conference, the proposal was supported both by Paul Horvitz, who was a
discussant of the proposal, and by Allan Meltzer, who commented on
the overall task force report. However, the proposal was mildly criticized
by Stanley Silverberg and severely criticized by John Kareken, the other
discussants. Meltzer (1988, p. 443) concluded, "I believe the [AEI] recommendations would be improved if the explicit recommendations of the
Benston and Kaufman study were incorporated, with some amendments

and extensions." Horvitz (1988, p. 102) noted that "there is agreement that optimal closure policy is a crucial element in the supervisory system. This rather obvious point does not appear in the older deposit insurance literature." Silverberg (1988, p. 109) agreed with the general thrust of the proposal and policy recommendations, but believed that "in the real world, some of what Benston and Kaufman advocate would be more difficult to implement than they suggest, and the cost and failure reductions would be less dramatic."

On the other hand, Kareken (1988, pp. 106–108) concluded that "Benston and Kaufman rely on a proposition that in general has been shown to be false: that the probability that a depository institution will fail decreases as equity capital increases." Moreover, "Timely reorganization, arguably a confiscation of private property, could . . . be illegal." As a result, "The policy advocated by Benston and Kaufman is not nearly as practical or workable as they make out."

At the Federal Home Loan Bank of San Francisco conference, the three discussants were also skeptical. William Isaac (1988), former chair of the FDIC, argued that there was nothing new in the proposal: this was the way the FDIC has always operated. Richard Syron (1988), then president of the Federal Home Loan Bank of Boston and currently president of the Federal Reserve Bank of Boston, was unhappy with the provision that institutions with the highest capital would be subject to only "minimum supervision." Lastly, Larry White (1988, p. 224), a member of the Federal Home Loan Bank Board at the time, argued that the proposal should focus on risk-based capital, not on total capital: "The regulators should address risk directly rather than trying to build excessively high capital walls around it."

In December 1988, the SEIR proposal was refined and endorsed by the Shadow Financial Regulatory Committee (1989), (see Benston et al., 1989; Eisenbeis, 1990)[8], of which Benston and Kaufman are members, and, in early 1989, by a task force on Depository Institutions Reform of the Brookings Institution, which included both Benston and Kaufman as members. Members of both groups discussed SEIR at banking and academic meetings, with Congress through testimony at hearings and personal contact with Senators and Representatives and their staffs, and with bank regulators and the Treasury Department through personal contacts. The prompt closing of troubled institutions as soon as their own capital funds were depleted greatly appealed to a Congress under strong political pressure by the public for the extraordinarily large losses in the S&L industry that were perceived to be due to regulatory inaction and political favoritism.

The underlying thrust of SEIR was also supported by the influential U.S. General Accounting Office (1991a, 1991b) and Congressional Budget Office (Bartholomew, 1990). On the other hand, the mandatory and automatic features of the SEIR proposal as well as the emphasis on market values were strongly opposed by some regulators and members of the administration, who had confidence in their ability to choose between troubled institutions that might succeed or fail. In addition, they feared that the reduction in their discretion and flexibility would reduce their own power, influence, and visibility.

Nor was there much support from the majority of the academic community. Their attention was focused primarily on eliminating government deposit insurance altogether or, at minimum, rolling back account coverage to well below $100,000; on introducing risk-based insurance premiums, priced generally on the basis of the output of option-pricing models; and on establishing more restrictive and fail-safe narrow banks. Indeed, through 1991 not a single research article on SEIR appeared in a major academic finance or economic journal by authors not associated with the Shadow or other groups that had endorsed the proposal, nor did such authors present papers on this proposal at academic conferences.[9] In part, this may have reflected the fact that elegant proofs that might justify publication were not required to demonstrate that resolution of institutions before the market value of net worth turned negative would accrue losses only to shareholders and not to depositors or the FDIC. Others questioned why regulators or members of Congress would obey the constraints on their behavior, when both had violated the spirit of the existing regulations so frequently.

Legislative Adoption

Nevertheless, in the fall of 1990, much of the SEIR proposal was incorporated in a bill introduced by Donald Riegle, chair of the Senate Banking Committee (S. 3103 and S. 543). In January 1991, similar provisions were introduced in a bill by Henry Gonzalez, chair of the House Banking Committee (H.R. 6). In February 1991, the general thrust of the proposal was included among the recommendations in the major study *Modernizing the Financial System*, published by the U.S. Treasury Department (1991), and in the legislation that it recommended to Congress the next month (H.R. 1505 and S. 713).

The SEIR proposal of Benston-Kaufman, the Shadow Financial Regulatory Committee, and the Brookings Task Force was modified somewhat in these bills. The number of tranches or categories was increased from four to five, and the mandatory nature of the sanctions in the lower tranches, the emphasis on market values, and the universality of the prompt resolution to all banks regardless of size or importance were weakened, particularly in the Treasury's bill. In addition, one or more of the congressional bills included provisions for risk-based insurance premiums, expanding risk-based capital to account for interest rate and credit concentration risk, and restrictions on Federal Reserve discount window lending to troubled institutions. The bills also included features not directly related to deposit insurance reform, such as permitting banks additional product and geographic powers, provisions intended to increase consumer protection, and recapitalization of the FDIC.

The final FDIC Improvement Act was crafted by a Senate-House Conference Committee in November 1991, as Congress was adjourning for the session, just four years after SEIR's initial unveiling. The act maintained the thrust of the original Benston-Kaufman proposal, but weakened it sufficiently so that deposit insurance is unlikely to be viewed as redundant.[10] Moreover, by not expanding bank powers, the act weakened the potential carrots available to highly capitalized banks and weakened bank profitability in general. Nevertheless, the primary thrust of the act was to reduce the costs of bank insolvencies to near zero.[11] (A summary of differences is shown in table 1–1, and a timetable for implementation of major provisions in table 1–2.) The act delegates to the bank regulators the responsibility both for interpreting many of the provisions and for designing and implementing the rules and regulations. Thus, the regulators have the opportunity to weaken, distort, and even sabotage the intent of the legislation.

Indeed, many of the regulations proposed or adopted to date by the bank and thrift regulatory agencies appear to weaken the effectiveness of the act (Shadow Financial Regulatory Committee, 1992):

1. the highest of the five prompt corrective action tranches or categories, termed "well capitalized," has been defined so as to include more than 90 percent of all banks holding nearly two-thirds of all bank assets in June 1992, and 98 percent of all banks holding 97 percent of all bank assets were classified to be "adequately capitalized", even though 8 percent of all banks holding 14 percent of total assets were on the FDIC's problem bank list at that time;

2. the spread between insurance premiums on the best and worst banks has been set at only eight basis points, a difference much smaller than set by the market on CD rates of banks of differing credit quality; and

Table 1–1. Major Differences Between Benston-Kaufman/Shadow Financial Regulatory Committee Proposal and FDICIA

Item	B-K/SFRC	FDICIA
Number of capital zones	4	5
Top capital zone	>10% MV leverage	>8% BV risk-based >5% BV leverage (tier 1)
Capital ratio for required resolution	3% MV	2% BV tier 1
TBTF exemption to least cost resolution	No	Limited
Expected losses to FDIC	0	Small, except for too-big-to-fail
Final resolution	Immediate	Some delay
Fed discount window loans to undercapitalized banks	With approval of FDIC or uncollateralized	Limited
Deposit insurance premiums	Not required, except for operations cost and fraud	Risk-based in package with "closure" rule
Carrot in carrot-stick incentive structure	More powers, more freedom, less hassle	Not as broad, plus lower insurance premiums
Subordinated debt	Important component of capital	Role delegated to regulators

3. only some 20 percent of all institutions will be required to hold additional capital against their interest rate risk exposure, and those amounts are both substantially inadequate and not sensitive to future unrecognized market-value losses from adverse rate changes.

On the other hand, at least four adopted or proposed regulations strengthen the carrot-stick strategy of the act. Insurance premiums and restrictions on the ability of banks to attract brokered deposits, to attract interbank and correspondent funds and thereby incur credit exposure to other banks, and to offer pass-through insurance coverage on employee-benefit plans are tied to a bank's capital position. The higher a bank's capital, the lower its insurance premiums and the fewer and milder the restrictions on its activities.[12] These regulations should and already are

Table 1–2. Federal Deposit Insurance Corporation Improvement Act of 1991: Implementation Timetable for Deposit Insurance Reform Provisions[a]

December 19, 1991

Least cost resolution (141): resolution at least present value cost to FDIC.

Early resolution (143): encourage early resolution of troubled institutions at least long-term cost to FDIC.

Foreign deposits (312): prohibits protection with exceptions.

June 19, 1992

Brokered deposits (301): restricts and prohibits use by non-well capitalized institutions.

December 19, 1992

Accounting objectives, standards, and requirements (121): requires accurate reports, including market values to extent feasible.

Prompt corrective action (131): establishes five capital categories for regulatory action, including resolution at 2% tangible equity capital, and requires report on "material" losses to FDIC.

Conservatorship and receivership to facilitate prompt regulatory action (133): expands grounds for regulatory resolution.

Interbank liabilities (308): limits interbank risk exposure to reduce systemic risk potential.

June 19, 1993

Improving capital standards (305): regulators to require sufficient capital to prevent loss to FDIC and to facilitate prompt corrective action, including accounting for interest rate risk and concentration of credit risk.

December 1, 1993

Standards for safety and soundness (132): requires regulatory standards for (1) operations and management, (2) asset quality, earnings, and stock valuation, and (3) compensation.

December 19, 1993

Federal Reserve discount window advances (142): restricts loans to undercapitalized and critically undercapitalized institutions.

January 1, 1994

Risk-based assessments (302): FDIC establishes risk-scaled premiums. (Actually imposed on January 1, 1993).

January 1, 1995

Least cost resolution (141): prohibits protecting uninsured depositors with exception for declaration of systemic risk by FDIC with approval of Federal Reserve and the Treasury Department (President). Costs of application of exception paid by special levy on bank assets.

a. Latest permissible date.

encouraging banks to increase their capital positions to qualify for the highest capital tranche. Banks are raising external capital at a record pace and the ratio of book value equity to assets in June 1992 was the highest since the mid-1960s. It should be noted, however, that while the risk-based insurance premiums reinforce SEIR, by themselves without an effective closure rule they would be far less effective.

As noted earlier, FDICIA also contains a number of provisions other than deposit-insurance reform that, for good or bad, impose numerous additional restrictions and reporting burdens on banks. Unfortunately, the response to these provisions by the banks, the regulators, and the administration has been sufficiently negative to have distracted attention away from the more positive and important deposit-insurance reform provisions.[13] This has helped both to make the primary purpose of the act widely misunderstood and to downgrade the perception of its importance, although it promises to shape the efficiency, profitability, and safety of banking for years to come. Indeed, FDICIA promises to permit bankers to reclaim their institutions from excessive government intervention and micromanagement by increasing their capital to levels more consistent with those of their noninsured competitors. If successful, banking may be able to halt its slide toward becoming a public utility. If unsuccessful and banks again encounter solvency problems that threaten taxpayer involvement, more radical congressional surgery that would be far less favorable to banks, such as narrow banking and more government micromanagement, is likely.

Notes

1. Because commercial banks, savings banks, and savings and loan associations are now all insured by the FDIC, FDICIA affects all three types of institutions, and the term *banking* is used generically.

2. The arguments against risk-based premiums are clearly discussed by Paul Horvitz (1983), who argued that such premiums alone would be insufficient to dissuade risk-prone bankers from taking excessive risks, as their expected gains easily could exceed the insurance cost, and that computing premiums that are both economically efficient and operational would be extremely difficult.

3. Edward Kane (1988, p. 380) has stated that "the most stubborn issue in financial reform concerns the need to restructure government regulators' and politicians' incentives."

4. Extensive discussions of the policies of regulators in resolving insolvent institutions in the 1980s appear in Barth (1991), Barth and Brumbaugh (1992), Barth, Brumbaugh, and Litan (1992), and Kane (1989).

5. A review of alternative deposit insurance reform proposals appears in Benston and Kaufman (1988c).

6. Although Benston and Kaufman were unaware of it at the time, the Securities and

Exchange Commission applies a similar early intervention and resolution process to securities and brokerage firms under its supervision (Macchiaroli, 1991; Haberman, 1987).

7. Discussions of the legal aspects of prompt resolution appear in Natter (1991) and Miller (1991).

8. Members of the Shadow Committee at the time included Richard Aspinwall, Lawrence Connell, Franklin Edwards, Robert Eisenbeis, John Hawke, Paul Horvitz, Edward Kane, Roger Mehle, Allan Meltzer, and Kenneth Scott in addition to Benston and Kaufman. It is of interest to note that the SEIR proposal was published by both the American Enterprise Institute and the Brookings Institution, which are generally viewed as being on opposite sides of the political aisle.

9. A few academic papers considering only the prompt closure provision were presented at the 1991 annual Conference on Bank Structure and Competition sponsored by the Federal Reserve Bank of Chicago. In 1989, Herbert Baer (1989) noted the success of a SEIR structure in the securities industry in limiting the number of dealer-broker failures as a consequence of the stock market crash in October 1987 to only two firms, and recommended its application to banks.

10. Two students of regulation have concluded that "the whole approach still relies heavily on the discretion of the banking agencies to take the proper action and make the proper judgments, and the banking agencies will, as before, be operating in a political context and subject to political pressures. For example, the agencies have the authority but are not required to make the calculation of net worth in terms of market rather than historical accounting values" (Scott and Weingast, this book, chapter 2).

11. Because the underlying rationale for SEIR and its intended objective were clearly spelled out in the act as "to resolve the problems of insured depository institutions at the least possible long-term loss to the deposit insurance fund," it is difficult to understand Fed chairman Greenspan's (1992, p. 7) statement that "if prompt regulatory action succeeds both in inducing banks to maintain high capital ratios and in reducing deposit insurance fund losses to acceptable levels, it may well prove to be an *unexpected* benefit of FDICIA" (emphasis added).

A Senate Banking Committee staffer (Carnell, 1992, 1993), who was involved in the drafting of the legislation, has written that "Section 38 [prompt correction action] has a single overriding purpose: to resolve the problems of insured depository institutions at the least-possible long-term cost to the deposit insurance fund. The objective is to avoid or minimize loss to the fund." A careful analysis of many of the provisions of the prompt corrective actions in FDICIA also appears in this paper.

Likewise the director of the General Accounting Office has noted that "it must be kept in mind that one of the goals of the legislation—zero losses to the taxpayers on deposit insurance coverage—reflects a new sense of regulatory accountability to the taxpayers. Not just regulators, but bankers as well, ought to adjust to this new spirit, if for no other reason that to reduce their deposit insurance premiums" (Simmons and Swaim, 1992, p. 6).

12. After proposing regulations that would have permitted only well capitalized banks to incur unlimited exposure to other banks, the Federal Reserve revised the final regulations to broaden this freedom to all adequately or better capitalized banks. As of June 1992, this included all 46 banks with assets in excess of $10 billion, the very banks that attract most of the correspondent banking business and would be most likely to increase their capital ratios to preserve this business. This weakens substantially the intent of the provision in FDICIA to reduce the probability of systemic risk from excessive interbank exposure.

13. Congressional support started to erode shortly after enactment because of loud and continuous negative response by the industry to the additional administrative burden from

the potential significant increase in regulations and rules required by FDICIA, frequently from provisions not associated with SEIR, e.g., truth in savings and executive compensation standards; a perception, particularly by the administration, that the higher capital requirements were the major culprit behind the credit crunch and slow economic recovery; complaints by the regulators about their loss of discretionary powers; and a realization that Congress's own ability to provide favors was restricted. Strong support, however, was maintained by the chairs and staffs of both the Senate and House banking committees.

References

Baer, Herbert, "Expanded Powers After Crash(es)," *American Economic Review*, May 1989, pp. 156–160.

Barth, James R., *The Great Savings and Loan Debacle*, Washington, D.C.: American Enterprise Institute, 1991.

Barth, James R. and R. Dan Brumbaugh, Jr., eds., *The Reform of Deposit Insurance*, New York: HarperBusiness, 1992.

Barth, James R., R. Dan Brumbaugh, Jr. and Robert E. Litan, *The Future of American Banking*, Armonk, N.Y.: M.E. Sharpe, 1992.

Bartholomew, Philip, *Reforming Federal Deposit Insurance*, Washington, D.C.: Congressional Budget Office, September 1990.

Benston, George J., Dan R. Brumbaugh, Jr., Jack M. Guttentag, Richard J. Herring, George G. Kaufman, Robert E. Litan, and Kenneth E. Scott, *Blueprint for Restructuring America's Financial Institutions*, Washington, D.C.: Brookings Institution, 1989.

Benston, George J., Robert A. Eisenbeis, Paul M. Horvitz, Edward J. Kane, and George G. Kaufman; *Perspectives on Safe and Sound Banking*, Cambridge, Mass.: MIT Press, 1986.

Benston, George J. and George G. Kaufman, "Regulating Bank Safety and Performance," in William S. Haraf and Rose Marie Kushmeider, eds., *Restructuring Banking and Financial Services in America*, Washington D.C.: American Enterprise Institute, 1988c, pp. 63–99.

———, "Risk and Solvency Regulation of Depository Institutions: Past Policies and Current Options," *Staff Memoranda* (88–1), Federal Reserve Bank of Chicago, 1988a.

———, *Risk and Solvency Regulation of Depository Institutions*, Monograph Series in Finance and Economics, (88–1), Salomon Brothers Center for the Study of Financial Institutions, New York University, 1988b.

Bierwag, G.O. and George G. Kaufman, "Deposit Insurance with Risk Sensitive Premiums," *Proceedings of a Conference on Bank Structure and Competition*, Chicago: Federal Reserve Bank of Chicago, May 1983a, pp. 223–242.

———, "A Proposal for Federal Deposit Insurance with Risk Sensitive Premiums," *Staff Memoranda* (83–3), Federal Reserve Bank of Chicago, March 1983b.

Carnell, Richard S., "A Partial Antidote to Perverse Incentives: The FDIC Improvement Act of 1991," *Rebuilding Public Confidence through Financial*

Reform, Columbus, Ohio: Ohio State College of Business, June 1993, pp. 31–51.

————, "Prompt Corrective Action Under the FDIC Improvement Act of 1991," paper presented at the Practicing Law Institute, February 3, 1992.

Congressional Budget Office, "The Cost of Forbearance During the Thrift Crisis," *CBO Staff Memorandum*, Washington, D.C., June 1991.

Eisenbeis, Robert A., "Restructuring Banking: The Shadow Financial Regulatory Committee's Program for Banking Reform," in George G. Kaufman, ed., *Restructuring the American Financial System*, Boston: Kluwer Academic, 1990, pp. 23–34.

Federal Deposit Insurance Corporation, *Deposit Insurance in a Changing Environment*, Washington, D.C., 1983.

Federal Home Loan Bank Board, *Agenda for Reform*, Washington, D.C., 1983.

Greenspan, Alan, "Putting FDICIA in Perspective," *Credit Markets in Transition: Summary*, Chicago: Federal Reserve Bank of Chicago, 1992, pp. 3–7.

Haberman, Gary, "Capital Requirements of Commercial and Investment Banks: Contrasts in Regulation," *Quarterly Review*, Federal Reserve Bank of New York, Autumn 1987, pp. 1–10.

Haraf, William S. and Rose Marie Kushmeider, eds., *Restructuring Banking and Financial Services in America*, Washington, D.C.: American Enterprise Institute, 1988.

Horvitz, Paul M., "The Case Against Risk-Related Deposit Insurance Premiums," *Housing Finance Review*, July 1983, pp. 253–263.

————, "Commentary," in William S. Haraf and Rose Marie Kushmeider, eds., *Restructuring Banking and Financial Services in America*, Washington, D.C.: American Enterprise Institute, 1988, pp. 100–104.

————, "A Reconsideration of the Role of Bank Examination," *Journal of Money, Credit and Banking*, November 1980, pp. 654–659.

Isaac, William M., "The Deposit Insurance System: Focusing the Debate," *The Future of the Thrift Industry*, San Francisco: Federal Home Loan Bank of San Francisco, December 8–9, 1988, pp. 209–212.

Kane, Edward J., "How Market Forces Influence the Structure of Financial Regulation," in William S. Haraf and Rose Marie Kushmeider, *Restructuring Financial Services in America*, Washington, D.C.: American Enterprise Institute, 1988, pp. 343–382.

————, *The S&L Insurance Mess: How Did It Happen?*, Washington, D.C.: Urban Institute Press, 1989.

Kareken, John H., "Commentary," in William S. Haraf and Rose Marie Kushmeider, eds., *Restructuring Banking and Financial Services in America*, Washington, D.C.: American Enterprise Institute, 1988, pp. 104–108.

Kaufman, George G., "Bank Capital: Past, Present and Future," *Journal of Financial Services Research*, April 1992, pp. 385–402.

————, "Framework for the Future: Resurrecting and Legitimizing the Thrift Industry," *The Future of the Thrift Industry*, San Francisco: Federal Home Loan Bank of San Francisco, December 8–9, 1988, pp. 191–207.

————, ed., *Restructuring the American Financial System*, Boston: Kluwer Academic, 1990.

Macchiaroli, Michael A., "Early Intervention in the Securities Industry," *Restructuring Banking*, Chicago: Federal Reserve Bank of Chicago, May 1991, pp. 445–450.

Mayer, Thomas, "A Graduated Deposit Insurance Plan," *Review of Economics and Statistics*, February 1965, pp. 114–116.

Mayer, Thomas and Kenneth E. Scott, "Risk and Regulation in Banking," *Stanford Law Review*, May 1971, pp. 857–902.

Meltzer, Allan H., "The Policy Proposals in the AEI Studies," in Williams S. Haraf and Rose Marie Kushmeider, eds., *Restructuring Banking and Financial Services in America*, Washington, D.C.: American Enterprise Institute, 1988, pp. 440–444.

Miller, Geoffrey, Quoted in "Remarks of Senator Riegle," *Congressional Record*, March 5, 1991, p. S2650.

Natter, Raymond, "Current Proposals for Early Intervention," *Rebuilding Banking*, Chicago: Federal Reserve Bank of Chicago, May 1991, pp. 440–444.

Scott, Kenneth E. and Barry R. Weingast, "Banking Reform: Economic Propellants, Political Impediments," *Reforming Financial Institutions and Markets in the United States*, Boston: Kluwer, 1993.

Shadow Financial Regulatory Committee, "An Outline of a Program for Deposit Insurance and Regulatory Reform," Statement No. 41, February 13, 1989 (revision of No. 38), *Journal of Financial Services Research*, August 1992, Supplement, pp. S78–S82.

————, "Rule Proposed by Bank Regulators to Control Interest Rate Risk," Statement No. 87, September 14, 1992, *Journal of Financial Services Research*, January 1993, pp. 101–102.

Silverberg, Stanley C., "Commentary," in William S. Haraf and Rose Marie Kushmeider, eds., *Restructuring Banking and Financial Services in America*, Washington, D.C.: American Enterprise Institute, 1988, pp. 104–108.

Simmons, Craig A. and Stephen C. Swaim, "Girding for Competition," *GAO Journal*, Spring/Summer 1992, pp. 3–9.

Syron, Richard F., "A Framework for the Future," *The Future of the Thrift Industry*, San Francisco: Federal Home Loan Bank of San Francisco, December 8–9, 1988, pp. 215–218.

U.S. General Accounting Office, Bank Supervision: *Prompt and Forceful Regulatory Actions Needed*, Washington, D.C., April 1991a.

————, *Deposit Insurance: A Strategy for Reform*, Washington, D.C., March 1991b.

U.S. Treasury Department, *Modernizing the Financial System: Recommendations for Safer, More Competitive Banks*, Washington, D.C.: Government Printing Office, February 1991.

White, Lawrence J., "A Framework for the Future," *The Future of the Thrift Industry*, San Francisco: Federal Home Loan Bank of San Francisco, December 8–9, 1988, pp. 221–224.

2 BANKING REFORM: ECONOMIC PROPELLANTS, POLITICAL IMPEDIMENTS

Kenneth E. Scott and Barry R. Weingast*

The news out of Washington suggests a series of crises in our financial system: first came Lincoln Savings and Charles Keating; then came Drexel Burnham; and now we have the Bank of Credit and Commerce International (BCCI) and Salomon Brothers. These all qualify as scandals of one sort or another, but although they all point toward problems in the financial sector, they do not have much in common beyond that. Some underlying issues in banking do not command attention on the front page but are costing us all a great deal of money. What went wrong in our financial system, and why is it so hard to fix?

A large number of savings and loan associations and then banks have failed over the past half dozen years. The initial result was a bankrupt Federal Savings and Loan Insurance Corporation (FSLIC), now to be redeemed by a huge taxpayer bailout of more than $200 billion. Moreover,

* The authors gratefully acknowledge the helpful comments of Annelise Anderson. This essay draws substantially on Scott (1990, 1991) and Romer and Weingast (1991) and is an update of a Stanford Centennial seminar given on September 30, 1991. This chapter is a revised version of a paper, reprinted with permission from Stanford University's "Essays in Public Policy" series, published by the Hoover Institution Press, 1993.

a spate of recent reports from the General Accounting Office, the Office of Management and Budget (OMB), and the Congressional Budget Office indicate that the Federal Deposit Insurance Corporation (FDIC), the bank counterpart of the FSLIC, has also become essentially insolvent, with a negative net reserve position estimated by OMB in 1991 to be about $40 billion on an accrual basis. Thus the taxpayers' potential tab is currently more than $240 billion. Because the United States has a population of about 250 million, that amounts to a cost per capita of around $1,000 a person (multiply it across your family). The United States can safely claim to have achieved the worst result in its financial institutions and guarantee system of any major industrialized country in the post–World War II era. How did we accomplish this?

We develop our argument as follows. First, we study the economic propellants of reform—that is, the economic sources of problems under the current regulatory regime that have to be changed if we are to forestall additional banking debacles. Then we turn to the political impediments that hinder reform, making it more likely that the present debacle will continue to deepen. Finally, we examine recent—and failed—attempts to reform the banking system. Our conclusions follow.

Economic Propellants of Reform

Three key hypotheses point toward an explanation of the crises: moral hazard, excessive segmentation of our financial system, and inadequate regulatory supervision. These hypotheses are not mutually exclusive; and all play a role in the story that follows. Thus, we want to ask not only what happened but why. It took a number of factors interacting to produce a debacle of the magnitude we are now experiencing.

The moral-hazard hypothesis tends to be neglected by the public. The concept, which originated in the insurance industry, is that, with insurance, the insured party is relieved of some of the consequences of its behavior and thus may be less concerned about preventing the insured risk from occurring. For example, once a business has obtained fire insurance, it may, quite rationally, be inclined to reduce its expenditures on fire safeguards and fire prevention, thus changing the behavior of the insured in ways that are not easily observed and that are adverse to the insurer. The very presence of insurance increases the level of losses.

Our emphasis on the moral-hazard hypothesis follows the conclusions of most economists who have investigated the thrift debacle (e.g., Barth 1991, Brumbaugh 1988, Kane 1990, Scott 1990).[1] How does moral hazard apply to financial institutions? The risk being covered is the risk of insolvency, with losses to creditors. The depositors are insured explicitly up to $100,000. How does their behavior change? They no longer have any reason to pay attention to, or to be concerned with, the financial condition of the bank. That the insurance eliminates "runs" by depositors is usually presented as a benefit, insofar as runs may spill over onto other banks in a solvent financial condition. But because the threat of bank runs tempers the behavior of banks, deposit insurance removes an important and constructive constraint on the behavior of the firm.

Moral-hazard behavior also implies that, for a slightly higher interest rate on insured deposits, a weak or even insolvent financial institution can obtain almost unlimited funds. That would not be true of any normal form of private firm, but it is true for financial institutions. Insured depositors don't care about the risk of the bank. Why should they?

If depositor indifference were limited to accounts under $100,000, it would affect most strongly only those financial institutions that are financed mainly by such depositors, such as savings and loan associations and small banks. But for accounts or funding sources above $100,000, would there not be creditor concern and therefore creditor discipline? Unfortunately, the answer need not be yes. Deposit insurance is not, in fact, limited to accounts under $100,000. The legal limit is often many times that amount because insured deposits can be held in many different capacities (a family can multiply them to well over $1 million of insurance in a single institution).

More important, the regulators have effectively abolished the legal limit by the way they have chosen to resolve big bank failures. These actions typically give complete protection to large depositors and other uninsured creditors by engaging in a transaction called a "purchase and assumption"—an assisted merger with another financial institution—in which *all* liabilities of the failed bank are assumed by the acquiring bank at the cost, of course, of the insurance corporation. The banking agencies have followed this approach—labeled "too big to fail" (TBTF)—over the last decade for *every bank* with more than $500 million in assets, which is not big for a financial institution. It does, however, leave out a lot of smaller institutions, and although they add up in numbers, in asset terms they don't have nearly the same importance as the larger institutions.

When the banking regulators follow this TBTF policy, there are no debtholders left to act as a constraint on bank managers—that is, to monitor the bank's condition, to charge for risks, to pull out their funds. The only vestige of creditor discipline comes from some lingering doubt as to whether the regulators can be trusted to keep on ignoring the deposit insurance ceiling that is nominally part of the law.

With little or no creditor constraint, what can act as a financial brake on management in making risk-taking decisions? The way banks earn money is to lend capital and take risks, and the way to earn higher expected returns is to take higher expected risks. So what prevents banks from going to extremes? One consideration for management is the possible loss of what economists like to call "human capital." If the bank proves a disaster or even just a routine failure, managers lose their jobs and some of their reputation (their careers are not going to be improved by having presided over a failed institution). This factor can be overborne by other factors, however, particularly if the management has a significant equity stake in the bank, in which case the payoff from successful risk taking may dominate the possible human capital cost.

A second consideration in risk-taking behavior is the possible loss of the stockholders' equity in the bank. The importance of this factor varies in direct proportion to the amount that the stockholders have at stake. If the bank has a high level of capital or net worth, then the possible loss from most investment decisions is going to fall on the stockholders. But if the bank capital is low or negative, then most or all of the risk is going to be borne by the FDIC. Under these circumstances the stockholders do not have to be concerned with losses—only with the positive part of the possible distribution of the returns.

It is at this point that the consequences of moral hazard hit home with full force. Neither the debtholders nor the stockholders are any longer concerned about risk taking. Indeed, the interests of the stockholders are best served if management deliberately adopts a policy of plunging into projects with high expected risk and high expected returns. That behavior is totally rational, noncriminal, and perfectly predictable under those circumstances from the standpoint of the stockholders. From the standpoint of the insurance fund and the taxpayers, however, a disaster may be about to descend.

Deposit insurance has thus to contend with severe moral hazard exposure, which becomes acute when stockholder equity approaches zero or goes negative. In that case, the insurers are the only party with anything left to lose, and the whole burden of trying to counteract and overcome these risk-taking incentives falls on bank supervision, which operates from the outside and largely after the fact.

To this point we have based our argument mainly on logic and theory. The supporting evidence suggests, however, that this hypothesis is consistent with the events of U.S. financial history. Going back to the early 1930s, we start with badly designed systems of financial intermediaries and deposit insurance. Our federal depository institutions, by laws dating from

1927 and 1933, are endowed with high levels of unnecessary risk. Reflecting prohibitions on interstate banking and on engaging in related financial activities, banks in general have poor portfolio diversification and often lack geographic diversification. Both banks and savings and loans have traditionally been narrowly confined in their branching operations—each bank was stuck within its state. Until recently, there were numerous states where banks were stuck within a single community, implying no ability whatever to diversify across regions. This means that banks face a great deal of diversifiable or *nonsystematic risk*—that is, unnecessary risk.

In addition, savings and loans (S&Ls) were worse off than banks because they were largely limited to real estate lending and were saddled with a huge interest-rate risk exposure resulting from a regulation-induced imbalance in the maturity of their assets and liabilities; they combined short-term liabilities with long-term, fixed-rate assets. When interest rates moved up, their assets went down in value, and, at the same time, because they had to pay more for their liabilities (i.e., their deposits), they were caught between the two. Furthermore, it was not hard to drive savings and loans into insolvency because they didn't have much capital to begin with. Most of the industry was mutual in origin; its capital was accumulated out of retained earnings over time and never got very high.

As to our deposit-insurance system, it was designed with a fixed, flat-rate premium structure that paid no attention to an individual institution's risk. Every bank paid at the same rate: about eight cents per hundred dollars of insured deposits. Perhaps the idea was that supervisors would control risk-taking behavior, but experience has proven that there are inherent limits to the effectiveness of bank supervision. Examinations of banks come after the fact. The loans have already been made, and the bets are on the table. Under such circumstances, it's exceedingly difficult—perhaps impossible—for supervisors to thwart management in achieving whatever level of risk they desire in their assets.

Next, to this defective underlying design, add the extraordinary and unanticipated interest and inflation rates of 1979, 1980, 1981—a shock that put tremendous stress on the system's already flawed structure. Interest rates shot up to 15 percent on long-term Treasuries, to 22 percent as the prime rate, and to 18 percent for thirty-year mortgages. But most mortgages on the books of the S&Ls were not paying 18 percent but rather 9, 12, or 14 percent, and they plummeted in value. The savings and loan industry, then, was wiped out by the effects of interest-rate escalation. The S&Ls' assets were worth less than book figures, and, when recalculated in market-value terms, their net worth was negative. According to the chair of the Federal Home Loan Bank Board, by 1982, essentially *every* savings and loan association was economically insolvent. The negative net worth of the industry in market-value terms has been estimated by outsiders to have reached roughly $100 billion. That's no small accomplishment. *An entire industry of more than 4,000 financial intermediaries had all been rendered insolvent.* A lot of commercial banks were in similar trouble, but for that industry as a whole, the situation was less acute; on average, banks were somewhat better diversified and had less maturity imbalance between assets and liabilities than did the S&Ls.

Thus, a badly designed system was hit with a major interest-rate shock, unequalled among Western nations in the postwar period, which wiped out owners' capital and set the stage for moral hazard to take over. Savings and loan managers knew that they would be closed when they became insolvent in book-value terms. But book values are a function of generally accepted accounting principles, made somewhat worse by regulatory accounting principles—both of which were used to prevent or delay the reflection on the books of the decline in the actual value of assets and earnings. Thus, even if an S&L was economically insolvent in terms of the market value of its assets and liabilities, its books did not show it. Indeed, it would not be closed until it became book-value insolvent, which might not occur until months or years after it had become market-value insolvent. Economists have attempted to adjust book values as reported in the 1980s into market-value terms to determine how long the typical S&L remained open after it became insolvent. The median of the estimated distribution is about three years, and some institutions remained open for nine or ten years.

Therefore, there was a substantial time in which these institutions were broke but still in business and they used that time to follow one of two broad approaches. The first, a *passive strategy*, was to try to ride out the interest-rate cycle by carrying on in the usual way—making single-family mortgages, paying a minimum to keep deposits—all the time hoping that interest rates would come down and asset values and operating earnings go back up before the fateful moment when book-value insolvency arrived and they were shut down.

Alternatively, these S&Ls and banks could follow an *active strategy*, attempting to earn their way out of a negative net-worth hole by adopting a high-risk, high-return investment policy. This could take many different forms[2] and may be characterized as self-help or as gambling, as you prefer. It became attractive or possible only because of deposit insurance. The insurance corporation, not the debtholders and not the stockholders, would bear the entire added risk of loss and would not be compensated for it because it would still be charging its same old premium rate of eight cents per hundred dollars. Therefore, all the returns from successful outcomes would go to the owners, not the insurer, creating powerful incentives for managers to take big risks and hope they paid off and for gamblers to buy into the industry at modest cost and make large wagers with federally insured money.

Observing the failures that started to be recognized in large numbers after 1987 and the firms that survived suggests that S&Ls made both choices. Some of each group survived, and some of each group failed. The active strategy encountered bad luck in those regions hit by local economic downturns. A fall in energy prices particularly affected the economies of Texas, Oklahoma, and Louisiana. A drop in agricultural income was particularly concentrated in some of the middle agricultural states. There had been overbuilding and a downturn in commercial real estate values, first in Texas and Florida and later in California and the Northeast. The effects of all these *local* problems were the *locally* concentrated by the lack of nationwide branching and portfolio diversification. In the affected areas, local institutions failed by the score; in other parts of the country, local institutions doing essentially the same thing fared better.

The passive strategy encountered relatively good luck, at least for a while, because interest rates came down sharply after 1981, and, correspondingly, operating margins and the value of fixed assets went back up. Nonetheless, some of those institutions were too far under water to make it all the way back up and were eventually closed. A lot of today's survivors fall in the passive strategy group, however.

In theory, management's choice of strategy might have been constrained by the S&L and bank regulators who could have tried, despite the practical difficulties, to counteract the strong moral hazard that was providing many banks with incentives to go for broke. In practice, the system of regulation and supervision after 1983 proved wholly inadequate, an issue we return to below.

Policy Implications

If the discussion thus far persuades one to take the moral hazard issue seriously, what can be done about it? What kind of responses of public policy ought we to consider? There are two main lessons from the 1980s that ought to guide our choice of response. The first is, do not fully protect all bank creditors, especially large creditors such as corporations, other banks, institutional investors, and so on. The TBTF policy is a prescription for disaster because it takes all the major debtholders out of the game and throws the entire burden of monitoring and action on the banking agencies, whose record to date is truly dismal. In general, by the time they move to resolve a large bank, its net worth is not zero but *hugely* negative. As taxpayer watchdogs, they get an F throughout recent history, down to and including the Bank of New England at the beginning of 1991 and CrossLand Savings in early 1992.

The excuse for having such a policy as TBTF is supposedly the fear of either run contagion or a gridlock shutdown of the whole interconnected payments and banking system. Because it would unduly extend this paper to go into an adequate discussion of *systemic risk*—the term of art for the possibility of some form of systemwide failure[3]—we will note only that the threat is simple to invoke but easy to exaggerate. In effect, the banking authorities predict a chance of Armageddon, without needing any evidence or careful analysis. From their standpoint, even if the risk is vanishingly small—and in many cases where they have used full payouts, the risk was truly insignificant—why should they avoid the cost of invoking "too big to fail"? The cost does not fall on them; it falls on the insurance corporations and the taxpayers. So what if it costs the insurance funds and the taxpayers a few hundred million dollars more or a couple of billion—how does that stack up against avoiding even a trifling chance of being wrong in a particular case, with runs on some banks and careers ended before a congressional committee hearing? Banking regulators have been able to find systemic risks hanging overhead even in the failure of the most implausible banks. The Bank of New England was not a kingpin of national or international finance; CrossLand Savings was not a center of the international payments system.

But even if one shared the banking agencies' intense aversion to imposing any losses on the creditors of any moderately large bank, that would not justify their unwillingness to act until the negative economic net worth of the bank and losses to the insurance fund run into the hundreds of millions or even billions. This leads us to our second response to the moral-hazard problem: never let management operate without substantial net worth or stockholder capital. Even if the debtholders are to be left out of the picture because of the great—if not overblown—concern over systemic risk, substantial stockholder equity still serves as some check on moral hazard behavior (theoretically not enough, but some). Therefore, the problem would be diminished by requiring high levels of operating capital—meaning a required level of capital calculated on the basis of market values that is considerably higher than that currently being talked about by banking authorities in this country or abroad.

Even more crucially, no bank should be permitted to continue under private ownership and management with very low or negative capital. At that point, as we have seen, the moral-hazard hypothesis predicts an explosion of gambling behavior. Thus, a rule of prompt closure or resolution, at a level of market-value net worth that is still somewhat positive, is the real crux of the matter; the key is not to let moral-hazard behavior continue when the stockholders have little left to lose.

Political Impediments to Reform

In this section, we focus on the political logic underlying the events that we just described from an economic point of view. We begin with a general question that focuses on the effects of politics: what happens when a good idea hits the U.S. Congress? Specifically, let us consider a policy problem along with a solution that is designed to mitigate the problem. What do you have to do to get that solution passed as legislation by the Congress? To emphasize the effects of politics, we examine how the solution is transformed from something that solves the problem into something that fits the needs of the politicans in Washington.

Economic analysis, which focuses on the incentives of the banks, has, as discussed above, identified at least three big problems afflicting the U.S. banking system: the problem of moral hazard, the problem of market segmentation induced by the legislation from the 1930s, and the problem of inadequate regulation and supervision of banks. All three played an essential role in the genesis of the crisis. Yet they are not the entire story; one thing is missing—namely, politics.

To see this, let us return to September 1985, when the S&L problem was officially estimated to be $15 billion in magnitude, which forces us to ask, "How did the crisis grow to be $200 or $240 billion? How did that happen?" Clearly, the three problems identified by economists are the mechanisms and the means of this growth. Beyond these mechanisms, however, we had to *let* the problem grow. And as noted above, the median failed thrift was allowed to run for three years with a negative market value. The regulatory system gave banks permission to do this and hence sanctioned excessive risk taking. So there are two questions about politics to ask: (1) Why did regulators fail to stop it? and (2) If regulators failed to stop it, why then did Congress and the president allow the explosive growth to occur? To put it another way, was this growth inevitable? We don't believe so. Indeed, we contend that politics allowed it to grow.

Turning to the two specific questions, there is a simple answer to the first. If we take the situation as of 1985, FSLIC, the federal agency that guarantees savings and loan deposits, had about $6 billion in assets and $15 billion in liabilities, which meant that it did not have enough money to do its job. Insolvency implied that FSLIC could not enforce its safety and soundness regulations because enforcing its regulations requires, as a last resort, that FSLIC take over problem institutions and pay their losses. But if FSLIC didn't have the money, it couldn't take over insolvent institutions, allowing risks to increase and losses to mount. In short, FSLIC's insolvency implied that the problem had already become too big for the regulators to handle.

Knowing this, the regulators went to Congress in September 1985, stating that there were big problems looming in the near future and that they needed more funds. They asked Congress to address this problem, stating that the problem would otherwise get worse.

Thus the answer to the first question is that, in late 1985, the problem was—and had been for some time—too big for the regulatory authorities alone. So then the question becomes, why did Congress and the president fail to respond? It took two years for Congress to react, and then, instead of appropriating the $15 billion that was asked for in 1985, it allowed the FSLIC to borrow $11 billion. Of course, by that time the problem had grown to about $50 billion; thus, the legislation was too little, too late. Meanwhile, insolvent S&Ls remained open; because the regulators were unable to enforce their rules, gambling for resurrection by S&Ls worked every month to make the losses larger and larger.

To understand a little more about the emerging crisis, consider the problem from the standpoint of Congress and the president, again in 1985. First, a lot of agencies in Washington cry "wolf"—that is, they often claim that a particular problem in their bailiwick is so large that "life as we know it" cannot go on unless something is done about it, now. Elected officials in Washington hear it regularly. So here is another agency crying wolf. From the politician's standpoint, can it be true? After all, a problem of this sort has never occurred before and seems incredible. Will a disaster really occur?

Second, 1985 was a time of fiscal austerity in that the Reagan deficits were beginning to mount, which made it difficult for politicians to argue for a massive new expenditure of funds. Democrats in Congress, for example, argued that critical social programs were going by the wayside because of fiscal austerity. In this context, they found it hard to justify a new program that, from the standpoint of their constituents, did not obviously seem needed.

The next piece of the puzzle concerns political constituencies. To focus our attention, we ask, "How do politicians know something?" Members of

Congress react to or know something about a problem not from an objective standpoint but by listening to their constituents. The reason is fairly straightforward. In a sense the objective nature of a problem almost does not matter if the constituency perceives it much differently. After all, if constituents perceive it differently, and if an elected official acts according to objective criteria, his or her actions will appear unresponsive to the constituency. Electoral incentives thus push elected officials away from objectivity toward what constituents believe. When perception and reality differ considerably, a problem emerges.

Turning back to banking and the reaction of politicians, let's examine the political pressures and rewards facing politicians by focusing on the lineup of interest groups in 1985 and early 1986. Four are worth our attention.

The first are the weak thrifts in the industry. Weak thrifts had very clear interests at that time in that they did not want a swift movement of funds to bail out the insurance fund or end the problem because this would close them down. Each wanted to remain open so that it had some chance to regain profitability. For owners and managers of weak thrifts, there was no downside to remaining open, which means that they had an interest in limiting the size of the bailout.

The second are the healthy thrifts. Oddly enough, healthy thrifts at this time had the same preferences as weak thrifts. They wanted to limit the infusion of new funds but for a much different reason. In 1985 and 1986, an infusion of cash would probably not have been provided by taxpayers—either directly through taxes or indirectly through loan guarantees—but by the S&L system itself. That would, in effect, have been a tax on the healthy thrifts to save the weak thrifts. The healthy thrifts had a net worth of approximately $15 billion, about equal to the size of the problem of the weak thrifts. The last thing in the world the healthy thrifts wanted was to take a large part of their capital and tax it away to save *other* institutions. As a consequence, the industry would support added funds for FSLIC of only about a third of what the administration then asked for—about $5 billion, not nearly enough to address the problem—and that in the form of a borrowing by FSLIC against its future premiums.

Depositors are the third important group. As discussed above, deposit insurance and the guarantee system had taken away depositors' incentive to monitor banks. Subject to the proviso that the guarantees would be honored, depositors remained relatively indifferent to what was happening.

The fourth and, in a sense, most important interest group or constituency is the taxpayers. It turns out that the (in)action of this group proved politically pivotal—that is, their inaction determined what was going to happen. At the time, the banking problem was not well known, was not considered a major crisis, and was not obvious to most people. Moreover, taxpayers are too diffused and unorganized to pay careful attention to the large range of issues that affect them. For an issue that is relatively new and not well understood, they are unlikely to act effectively on their own behalf. In particular, they would not provide much support for spending $15 billion unless it appeared absolutely necessary. In 1985, absent awareness of an unfolding crisis, a large infusion of cash would have hardly seemed necessary to the general public.

All this results in a paradox, with taxpayers at the center. It is obvious the taxpayers would be willing to spend $1 billion today to save $10 billion five years from now. The problem is that they have to *know* they will save that amount of money. In 1985, taxpayers had almost no understanding of the problem and hence could not press for attention to their interests. All the pressure from the active voices favored limiting the bailout—that is, to go slow, to foster forbearance, and to allow regulators to avert their eyes from problem banks. Meanwhile, voices of taxpayers—the forces potentially mitigating this reaction—were not sufficiently engaged to counterbalance the active interests.

At the same time, President Reagan wanted to avoid blame for a crisis and did not become active. Members of Congress, even if they were willing to go beyond the interests of their regulated constituents, could not reap much credit for doing something. Thus, in late 1985 and early 1986 there was a striking political impediment to solving the problem when it was relatively small. Because the crisis was not well known, politicians could not take credit for stopping it and so allowed it to grow.

A second piece of the "too little, too late" puzzle occurred in 1986—something that is also directly relevant to the more recent 1991 legislative struggle over banking reform. This concerns the nature of multiple veto groups in Congress, a problem that delayed the legislation from October 1986, when it almost passed, to the summer of 1987.

It is well known that the structure of Congress creates multiple veto groups. For present purposes, we focus on the most obvious, the House versus the Senate. The Constitution requires that they pass exactly the same legislation in order for it to become law; when they pass different versions, these have to be reconciled. If they fail to do so—for whatever reason—the bill fails to become law. In a nutshell, that's what happened in 1986: an additional year's delay occurred because the House and Senate failed to resolve their differences. The interesting question is *why*?

As it turned out, the attempt to add issues unrelated to the banking crisis killed the legislation in 1986. Both the House and the Senate produced bills that would have infused funds for the FSLIC and virtually agreed on

Table 2–1.   Ranking of Various Proposals by Degree of Reform of the Status Quo

Treasury proposal
House Banking Committee bill
Senate Banking Committee bill
Status quo
Dingell bill

how to do it. The problem was that the two chambers added different components to the legislation and then failed to reconcile their differences. The Senate wanted to change aspects of banking regulation while the House wanted to add new housing programs, both of which were peripheral to the S&L crisis. Yet the disagreement over these provisions resulted in a stalemate, delaying the infusion of cash for a year. Meanwhile, the problem continued to grow.

Current Reform Legislation

Banking reform was a high priority of the 102d Congress. A wide range of provisions was proposed, though in the end only limited reform occurred in the enactment of the FDIC Improvement Act of 1991.

The president, through the Department of the Treasury, proposed early in 1991 the most sweeping reforms of the banking industry since World War II. The House then came out with a bill that, though less sweeping, still provided needed cash for the insurance fund and some reform for the banking industry (nationwide branching and entry into securities activities). It also dealt with the moral-hazard issues of deposit insurance by stressing equity capital requirements, prompt closure, and ending the TBTF policy. The bill produced by the Senate committee at the end of the summer was still narrower than the House version. And so we had three different proposals: Treasury's proposal contained the most sweeping reforms, the House produced fewer reforms, and the Senate, even fewer (see table 2–1). They all agreed, however, on the financial aspects—that is, to give an infusion of cash, through borrowing, to the bank insurance fund—though they disagreed on other matters. Also shown in the table is the status quo, reflecting no change in the current system.

As of early September 1991, it appeared that this lineup of legislative positions boded well for reform. Because all agreed on the financial aspects, because there seemed to be some agreement that reform was needed, and because there were no extraneous add-ons on which they disagreed, it appeared to be simply a question of the scope of the reform.

But the world changed during September. The bills that we have discussed thus far were produced by the House and Senate Banking committees. At the behest of Congressman John Dingell, new legislation entered the battle. As the chair of the Energy and Commerce Committee, Dingell asserted jurisdiction over this issue because his committee oversees federal regulation of the securities industry and to some extent the insurance industry. Dingell produced his own legislation, which is represented on the chart below the status quo, because, although it agreed on the portions infusing new funds to FDIC, Dingell wanted to turn back the hands of time insofar as the reform of the banking structure was concerned. He wished to undo the modest reforms that regulators and courts had introduced in the last ten years. Why did he take this stance?

One reason is that Dingell and his committee have close ties with the securities industry, which seems to have led him to forestall legislation that might harm that particular interest, even at the expense of preventing needed reform for banks. By holding up reform, he managed to produce a package suitable to his constituents.

In the end, Dingell prevailed and managed not only to derail reform proposed by the House Banking Committee but to undo in the House bill some of the reforms that have occurred over the past decade. The conflicting bills were reconciled by dropping the bank reform provisions entirely.

So where does all this leave us? First, in contrast to 1986, this time Congress did pass the cash funding and deposit-insurance/moral-hazard portions of the legislation, despite disagreements over other substantive issues. Members of Congress may have learned their lessons about the costs of delaying new funds for addressing problem banks; yet despite the most costly financial debacle of the century, unique among developed countries, Congress has been unable to restructure and reform the banking system. The absence of structural reform leaves us with an unnecessarily weak set of depository institutions, vulnerable to a repeat performance. As long as no one blames Congress for this failure, however, it can avoid facing hard questions, merely providing incremental legislation on a last-minute bailout.

Conclusion

Our analysis unveils a critical paradox. On the one hand, we have a series of critical economic factors—the propellants of reform—pushing us toward reform of the deposit insurance system and the structure of the financial system to avoid further debacles. On the other hand, the political factors—the political impediments to reform—seem sufficient to prevent meaningful reform of the financial intermediary system. Thus one of the worst financial disasters to befall a major nation could well repeat itself.

The economic problems lead to the following broad prescription for reform: (1) remove the needless weakness in our financial intermediaries created by legal barriers to branching and asset diversification, (2) remove the perverse incentives created by moral hazard for bank management, and (3) provide sufficient funds for a policy of mandatory resolution of banks promptly upon economic insolvency.

The 1991 act tried to address the last two elements in its reform and funding provisions for the deposit-insurance system. The banking agencies are to stress soundness regulation and capital levels and to intervene and force capital restoration or closure before net worth becomes negative. To augment its resources, FDIC was authorized to borrow, from the Treasury or through the Federal Financing Bank from the market, as much as $70 billion. Provisions dealing with TBTF endeavor to confine it to rare cases of genuine systemic risk threatening the very economy of a region or the nation.

But the whole approach still relies heavily on the discretion of the banking agencies to take the proper action and make the proper judgments, and the banking agencies will, as before, be operating in a political context and subject to political pressures. For example, the agencies have the authority but are not required to make the calculation of net worth in terms of market rather than historical accounting values. It remains to be seen how much, in actuality, has been accomplished.

As to the first element, however, Congress simply gave up. All aspects of expanded branching or broader product lines were removed from the act. Economists are clear that our system of many small and poorly diversified banks and S&Ls contributed greatly to our ongoing banking crisis and that the legal impediments to diversification need urgently to be removed.

Politics, in contrast, is the art of the possible. Even in the face of these enormous problems, reform seems beyond the grasp of the Congress and the president. To summarize the political impediments to reform, we return to the question asked earlier: What happens when a good idea gets to the U.S. Congress?

We identified two factors that play a systematic role in this particular policy issue and also across many others. The first has to do with the way members of Congress understand and interpret the world, not from an objective stance but through their constitutents' eyes. As a political "decibel meter," an elected official's constituency plays a significant role in determining how that official interprets and evaluates the world. This accounts for the well-known bias of politics toward those interest groups and constituencies that are active and attentive on a given issue. The constituency decibel meter played a big role throughout the financial crisis, especially in allowing it to grow from a $15 billion problem to a $240 billion debacle. The second systematic factor affecting policy choice has to do with the nature of the multiple veto points in the U.S. government and the fact that individual politicians are willing to hold up legislation in order to get something they want.

What is important about both factors is that they influence political choice in the same way: both break the link between the problem and the design of a legislative solution. These political principles pull legislation away from something that is carefully tailored to the problem toward something that meets political needs. For banking, politics has pushed politicians *away* from addressing the regulatory-induced systemic risk. Not only did protection of the major active constituencies prevent the S&L problem from being addressed in the mid-1980s when it was much more manageable, but, just last Fall, it prevented Congress from producing significant industry reform.

Of course, through it all, few people blamed their own representative in Congress, and that's an essential part of why this type of problem persists. The S&L debacle occurred through the conjunction of three separate events, all economic consequences of political choices: first, regulatory-induced market segmentation that exposed the S&L industry to risk from an abrupt rise in interest rates; second, the sudden rise in interest rates in the early 1980s, wiping out the net worth of the industry; and third, the failure of elected officials to deal adequately with the problem in the mid-1980s. Few members of the public, however, perceive this problem to be the result of politics. As a consequence, circumstances similar to the S&L debacle could occur for other financial services—for example, commercial banks, pension funds, or government-sponsored enterprises.

This unfortunate possibility is due to general public ignorance of the political and economic forces bearing on a given industry. That ignorance, in turn, allows elected officials to devise programs that benefit certain constituents while hiding some of the costs in the form of future liabilities. To the extent that the latter are difficult to perceive, officials are better off, as are the favored constituents. Of course, the general taxpayer may well have to pay for the liabilities if they are realized. By that time, however, few taxpayers will associate these liabilities with the structure of the regulatory regime itself, and hence they will not blame the politicians who created the potential for the problem in the first place.

Can anything be done to reduce the chances of repeating a financial debacle? One modest proposal would be to provide a more accurate and informative system of government accounting that would not only report current outlays but keep track of future liabilities as they are incurred.[4] This would help to focus attention on programs with limited current public outlays whose future costs start to increase substantially. Although this proposal is modest, it is unlikely to be appealing to elected officials precisely because it would make it harder to provide benefits to active constituents.

Notes

1. The evidence is not entirely conclusive on this issue. Recently, for example, Benston and Carhill (1992) have provided some evidence inconsistent with this hypothesis. They did not purport to reach definitive conclusions, however, and these remain open issues.

2. The Garn–St Germain Act of 1982 added some additional investment opportunities for S&Ls, and this "deregulation" on the asset side is often pointed to as a cause of the S&L disaster. In our view, the cause is to be found in the moral hazard incentives, which, as we have just indicated, could find their expression in a multitude of ways.

3. For further reading, see Calomiris and Gorton (1991) and Kaufman (1992).

4. See, for example, the recent work of Kane (1991).

References

Barth, James R., *The Great Savings and Loan Debacle*, Washington: AEI Press, 1991.

Benston, George and Mike Carhill, "The Thrift Disaster: Tests of the Moral Hazard, Deregulation, and Other Hypotheses," working paper, Emory University, 1992.

Brumbaugh, R. Dan, Jr., *Thrifts Under Siege: Restoring Order to American Banking*, Cambridge: Ballinger, 1988.

Calomiris, C. and G. Gorton, "The Origins of Banking Panics," in *Financial Markets and Financial Crises*, ed. R. Glenn Hubbard, Chicago: University of Chicago Press, 1991.

Kane, Edward J., *The S&L Insurance Mess*, Washington: Urban Institute Press, 1989.

——, "Taxpayer Losses in Deposit Insurance: The Incentive-Conflict Hypothesis," in R. Herring and A. Shah (eds.), *Reforming the American Banking System*, Philadelphia: Wharton Financial Institutins Center, 1991.

Kaufman, G. June, Bank contagion: Theory and evidence. Working Paper series, Federal Reserve Bank of Chicago, 1992.

Romer, Thomas and Barry R. Weingast, "Political Foundations of the Thrift Debacle." In *Politics and Economics in the 1980s*, ed. Alberto Alesina. Chicago: National Bureau of Economic Research, University of Chicago Press, 1991.

Scott, Kenneth E., *Never Again: The Savings and Loan Bailout Bill*. Essays in Public Policy no. 17. Stanford: Hoover Institution Press, 1990.

——, The Moral hazard hypothesis. In *Reforming the American Banking System*, ed. Herring and Shah, 1991.

3 TAXPAYER LOSS EXPOSURE IN THE BANK INSURANCE FUND

Edward J. Kane*

Accounting Coverups

The root problem in deposit insurance today may be described as a scandal in bank and government accounting. In tough times, the valuation and itemization principles that accountants and regulators use contain reporting options that encourage large opportunity losses to be hidden from public view. They also let discretionary nonrecurring profits be recorded in ways that can overstate current profits and net worths for years on end. The rosy bias in these readings and in projections that are based upon them have much in common with the rigged scales dishonest butchers use to overcharge their clients. With a show of apparent precision, they systematically and repeatedly mismeasure the obligations deposit insurance is putting on to taxpayers' bill.

By feigning ignorance about the extent of these hidden losses and of their long-term economic consequences, Federal Reserve and Treasury

* This chapter is a revised version of a paper published by the Brookings Institution from *Assessing Bank Reform*, edited by Robert Litan, 1993. Reprinted with permission.

officials are mis-serving taxpayers. They are moving the Bank Insurance Fund (BIF) along the same ruts in the same road that led the Federal Savings and Loan Insurance Corporation (FSLIC) to ruin. As thrift regulators did during the 1970s and early 1980s, gambling banking regulators are bifurcating their industry, forcing its healthy members to support a substantial number of hopelessly crippled competitors. They are effectively authorizing a risk-loving herd of living-dead or "zombie" institutions to prey on financial markets.

When past S&L regulators decided to cover up the extent of FSLIC losses in the 1970s and 1980s, and to defer hundreds of needed insolvency resolutions, they could cite four plausible excuses that, by passing the Financial Institutions Reform, Recovery, and Enforcement Act (FIRREA) and the Federal Deposit Insurance Corporation Improvement Act (FDICIA), Congress has made inoperative:

1. Regulators' authority to move against economically insolvent zombie institutions that could show positive accounting net worth depended on examiner writedowns that were difficult to defend both in the courts and in the political arena;
2. Regulators did not have enough borrowing authority to cover the asset writedowns their insurance fund would have to absorb (the Resolution Trust Corporation still faces this problem today);
3. Given the uncertain nature of taxpayer backup, regulators had some reason to fear the admittedly remote possibility that rationally based runs on troubled banks and thrifts by uninsured depositors might degenerate into a costly national crisis;
4. Regulators could not be sure either that Congress would repair deficiencies in insurance-fund reserves with taxpayer funds or that its individual members would not strongly pressure them to go easy on zombie institutions for political reasons;

With these reliable excuses for delay stripped away, faint-hearted banking regulators now have to offer a less convincing excuse for delaying writedowns. They have to claim that it is a good gamble to wait for truly *eager* private buyers to come along to take over each of hundreds of troubled deposit-institution franchises and their weakest assets. To defend this claim, they have to exaggerate the financial and macroeconomic dangers of insisting on prompt recapitalizations. They also have to ignore the interest costs of waiting, ignore the perverse effects on bank investment incentives this strategy introduces, and dismiss or mischaracterize empirical evidence on how much this strategy cost taxpayers in S&L insurance mess.

The fundamental question is, what defects in bureaucratic incentives render regulators deeply reluctant to resolve deposit-institution economic insolvencies when and as they develop? What career or reputational benefits leave them so willing to pretend that plainly nonrecurring and easily reversed accounting profits that can be booked as a result of a nonrepeatable, election-year decline in interest rates have restored hundreds of terminally weak banks and thrifts to long-term health? The economic condition of crippled banks today parallels that of an individual with AIDS who has been lucky enough to get over a bout of pneumonia. Although each crippled bank has received a welcome gift of time, its condition remains seriously distressed.

Leaving a weak bank's insolvency unrepaired is unfair to taxpayers because taxpayers hold the bag for the downside of every interest-rate gamble and other speculative bet economically insolvent zombie institutions manage to put on the table. The rapid expansion of bank positions in government securities and the size of nonrecurring profits reported in securities trading so far in 1992 should have scared regulators into developing truly "effective" rather than sham procedures for disciplining interest-rate risk taking.

Regulator Efforts to Discredit FDICIA

During Bill Clinton's presidential campaign, we heard a great deal about FOBs: Friends of Bill. Job files for FOBs are each said to carry a number that inversely orders the strength of the friendship, so that on the ordering used, Hillary Rodham Clinton would be FOB1. Focusing on enmity rather than friendship, I have been developing a file on FOFs: Foes of FDICIA. So far, the lowest numbers in my file have been won by a few Federal Reserve and Treasury officials, with some miscreant ex-regulators and banking trade-association spokespersons close behind.

In my experience, it is spoiled children who complain the loudest about parental discipline. Taxpayers might be considered "Skeptics of the Bill." Administrators' objections to FDICIA's curtailing of their discretion to forbear are illogical. They ask us to let good possibilities outweigh bad probabilities. They emphasize the good ways agency officials *could* use the lost discretion, while refusing to acknowledge the temptations that have repeatedly led them and their predecessors to abuse this discretion.

At this very moment, officials are pushing the BIF into the same ruts in the same road that FSLIC took in 1983. Their continued willingness to help put off bank asset writedowns and to delay the resolution of economically insolvent deposit institutions places a poor bet for taxpayers, a bet that is nevertheless welcomed by the weakest and loudest segment of the industry. At the same time, it should be recognized that trade-association lobbying positions are apt to be biased in favor of weak institutions. This is because a financial industry's weakest members can and do earn profits from building up a disproportionate and life-sustaining degree of clout in industry trade associations.

Because delay is costly, it breaks faith with other taxpayers and with the spirit of the FDICIA. The central thrust of the 1991 legislation is to insist that, when and as an insured institution's capital position declines, its managers are mandated to recapitalize their firm promptly. The virtue of this exit-policy mandate is that it subjects a weakening firm to the same sort of discipline that its creditors would impose if they weren't insured against loss by the FDIC. It is important to understand that recapitalization does not imply the disappearance of a bank's assets or even of its franchise. What it does imply is a timely repricing of bank assets and a market testing of the value of keeping a troubled institution in play.

Identifying timely demands for recapitalization as regulatory excess that dictates a mindless shrinking of the banking industry is part of a nasty public-relations campaign that bank trade associations and some federal regulators are waging against the FDICIA of 1991. This campaign uses all three of the nonpecuniary tools of the unprincipled special-interest lobbyist: mischaracterization, distortion, and exaggeration. The campaign mischaracterizes transitional costs from changing regulatory patterns as if they were permanent burdens. In addition, it exaggerates FDICIA's curtailment of regulatory discretion as far more restrictive than it truly is. It distorts the extent to which recapitalization pressure is apt to aggravate the nation's financial problems by alleging that it will worsen already-waning shortages of credit and put destructive pressure on weak institutions.

The central purpose of FDICIA is to inhibit the doubling and redoubling of deposit-institution losses that have already occurred. The campaign ignores survey evidence that indicates that a substantial majority of ordinary bankers support this regulatory principle and other regulatory strategies embodied in FDICIA. The FOFs (Foes of FDICIA) characterize the idea of restricting regulators' discretion *not* as a strategy for protecting strong institutions and unwary taxpayers from gambling by weak institutions, but as a recipe for allegedly whipping up actuarially avoidable losses in weak institutions.

Accounting loopholes make the economic value of bank capital hard to observe. As long as lobbyists can hold market-value accounting at bay, the tripwire system of capital discipline needs to be supplemented with secondary triggers able to provide timely signals of a hidden worsening in an insured institution's enterprise-contributed net worth. Parallels exist between the detailed regulatory standards the act requires regulators to develop and covenants in private contracts that convey renegotiation rights in situations where changes in a borrower's condition are hard to observe and can occur suddenly. Recognizing this parallel clarifies that regulators have an *obligation* to waive covenant violations when close investigation shows the violations to be inconsequential. Nevertheless, the call for standards is being depicted as a completely misguided strategy of a regulatory micromanagement. I heard one regulator characterize the FDIC Improvement Act on my campus in October 1992 as an "oxymoron of the first order," full of "asinine provisions" that request regulatory standards that no one needs. One week earlier, Treasury Secretary Brady opined to conferees at the annual meeting of the American Bankers Association that the burden of regulatory compliance "had reached a level that is intolerable" and called for reestablishing "a balanced approach to lending and risk-taking." One wonders whether he meant by a "balanced approach," the approach FSLIC managed to promote.

By and large, federal regulators are carrying out their responsibilities under the act in an unfriendly spirit. I will cite two examples of this.

First, FDICIA requires that regulators incorporate interest-rate risk into the risk-based capital regulatory framework. Interest-rate risk refers to the danger that future movements in market interest rates will induce a net adverse revaluation of the asset and liability positions an institution holds. In response to the FDICIA requirement, federal bank regulators issued in July 1992 a proposed rule that fails to develop either an effective measure of a bank's exposure to interest-rate risk or an effective framework for limiting the extent to which these exposures pass through to the net reserves of the BIF. Although computer software for interest-rate risk analysis is in use at many banks and available from private vendors such as Fiserv, the proposal emphasizes pencil-and-paper simplicity in reporting requirements. It seeks to estimate what would happen to the net value of an institution's on- and off-balance-sheet positions if interest rates moved 100 basis points in either direction. To this end, it assigns each position an "approximate" price-volatility risk weight established by the banking agencies. Finally, the agencies plan to use the resulting measures only to identify and discipline banks that are taking high levels of interest-rate risk relative to their peers.

Given the billions of dollars at stake and the availability of modern information technology, it is outrageous to let simplicity in reporting procedures outweigh the need for banks and regulators to examine how a bank's true exposure to the range of likely interest-rate changes impacts its capital (which occurs by raising the required rate of return on equity) and to calculate the value of the loss exposure interest-rate risk imposes on the BIF. Because interest rates tend to rise and fall in cyclical fashion, potential upward and downward swings in prospective interest rates seldom appear symmetric. Although short-term and long-term rates tend to move in the same direction, swings in these rates do *not* tend to affect asset and liability value equally. Near the start of a recovery, in particular, the speedup range of possible interest-rate increases far exceeds the range of probable decreases and nasty declines in long-term asset values can occur with great suddenness.

Worst of all, the proposal makes no effort to incorporate the cumulative interaction of *past* interest-rate risk taking and actual interest-rate movements into the capital ratio that triggers FDICIA's tripwire system of regulatory discipline. Given the damage interest-rate risk did to FSLIC, it is a disgrace that authorities have not installed an adequate system for measuring interest-rate risk by now. If such a system were in place, it would clarify the urgency of recapitalizing a number of seriously distressed banks as soon as possible. Today, some of these banks are blithely telling us that their bet is okay because long rates are going to fall this year even if short rates rise. (For more analysis, see Shadow Financial Regulatory Committee, Sept. 14, 1992.)

Riddle: *Q*. Which item does not belong on the following list: gonorrhea, AIDS, herpes, interest-rate risk. *A*. Gonorrhea. Why? Because it is the only one that federal authorities are both willing and able to tell taxpayers how to get rid of.

The proposed regulatory structure for measuring and controlling interest-rate risk mandated under FDICIA illustrates the growing conflict developing between the chairs of the congressional banking committees and top federal banking regulators. This tension reinforces the theory that regulatory forbearance exacerbated the FSLIC mess and is underscored by these parties' reluctance to identify the size of the shortage in the BIF's explicit reserves. Consider the contrast between two statements made in March 1991 as comments on the sizable adjustments then being made in FDIC loss estimates for the Bank Insurance Fund. According to chair of the House Banking Committee Henry Gonzalez, "we must avoid a rerun of the shifting numbers, the gimmickry, and the outright deceit that marked so much of the savings and loan crisis," while FDIC public relations officer Alan Whitney stated, "[All estimates] were based on the best information available at those times. It is clear that economic conditions changed over the time."

It is also illustrated by the open ridicule that top Federal Reserve and Treasury officials have heaped on specific elements of FDICIA and their open contempt for the act's attempts to reduce regulatory discretion. They seize virtually every opportunity they can to reinforce industry concerns about excessive regulatory burdens and to communicate their own reluctance to implement various of its provisions (e.g., use of stock market values in assessing soundness and the need to set loan-to-value standards for mortgage loans). Such comments constitute a *second* line of FOF mischaracterizations, exaggerations, and distortions that deserve review.

Several FDICIA initiatives have been unfairly characterized as bank-bashing exercises. One initiative that seems to me to ask authorities to treat divergences between the market value of a bank's stock and the book value of its net worth as a covenant-like signal of hidden problems has been openly mocked by the Federal Reserve. The Fed's request for public comment on this initiative framed the issue as if Congress had asked bank regulators to control bank stock prices. The questions the Fed posed are laden with sarcasm and plainly invite respondents to hold the provision up to ridicule.

Federal banking regulators are so far stubbornly refusing to acknowledge what Congress has clearly grasped: that the lessons of the S&L insurance mess apply to the banking regulators and the BIF. In asking for detailed regulatory norms, Congress is not bashing banks. It is telling regulators to develop enforceable standards of regulatory performance. Such standards would force regulators to leave a clear "audit trail" for regulatory decisions that effectively waive taxpayer covenant rights. Taxpayers and Congress need such standards and audit trails to make top regulators accountable for deposit-insurance losses that accrue *during* their watch (as opposed to losses that are discretionarily realized then).

The False Test of a "December Surprise"

Reluctance to disclose problem situations and to take tough disciplinary actions against an agency's regulatory clientele lies at the heart of the deposit-insurance problem. This is what makes the situation a mess rather than a crisis. The need for regulatory action is hidden, and the cumulative effects of repeatedly deferring needed actions are misrepresented. The result is that public-policy experts end up debating whether action is truly needed rather than focusing on hammering out effective programs of action. Fears of a "December surprise" similarly misframe the central issue in the mess. Treated as a test for industry weakness, this idea focuses on the sideshow of forecasting regulators' highly politicized decisions about whether and when to "fail" or recapitalize economically insolvent banks rather than on measuring and controlling the unbooked losses to which the BIF exposes the federal taxpayer.

I estimated in the summer of 1992 that, as of December 31, 1991, BIF's net loss exposure might amount to $53 billion. Applying the same estimation methods to June 30, 1992, data for banks as computed by the bank-analysis firm Veribanc, Inc., BIF's position improved to between $45 and $50 billion.

However, on the basis of net-worth and earnings data, Veribanc sorts banks into categories patterned after the colors of the standard traffic light. The 1,067 doubtful banks that fall into what Veribanc calls its red, yellow, and very-light green categories correspond roughly to the 1,044 problem banks identified by the FDIC. As table 3–1 shows, the bulk of BIF's unbooked loss exposure lies in two seriously distressed yellow categories. Like a yellow traffic light, their condition should signal a halt to toleration of their weakness. Many of these banks are deeply *economically* insolvent, even though their accounting ratios are not yet desperate enough to force federal regulators either to demand recapitalization or to impose other mandatory disciplines. The danger of their future average deterioration from perverse risk-taking incentives leads me to offer an alternative, larger estimate of BIF's unbooked loss exposure of $54.5 billion.

The electorate must understand that there could have been a surprise in December 1992 only if it came from the policies of the new president and new Congress. It could *not* come from the tangible-capital trigger set by FDICIA. Scheduling a life-and-death exam one year ahead and making the right answer to the test question known in advance gave zombie firms ample opportunity to cram effectively for the test. Those that could not recapitalize themselves straightforwardly have been drawing on whatever accounting options they could find to nudge their capital ratio above the 2 percent threshold. Troubled banks' interest in locating on the edge of the regulatory-tripwire minefield explains why the seriously distressed yellow categories in table 3–1 are so full. Exercising sharp accounting options is, of course, easier when test administrators are anxious not to see too many weak "students" embarrass themselves.

This fall, Veribanc found banks to be rapidly migrating from the list of "critically undercapitalized" institutions it maintains. By late October, a more-aggressive closure policy and regulatory relief had reduced the list to forty-one banks with $10.6 billion in assets. Interestingly, several escapees made it over the wall because of special agreements with the agencies that served to qualify selected categories debt instruments as regulatory capital. By early December, the list had fallen to about twenty banks with only about $6 billion in assets. In October, Veribanc estimated that only another 146 banks with $38 billion in assets were probably in the "undercapitalized" or "significantly undercapitalized" regulatory zones that trigger lesser disciplines.

Table 3–1. Calculating Hypothetical BIF Loss Exposure from Asset Breakdown Given by Veribanc's Partition of FDIC-Insured Commercial and Savings Banks, as of June 30, 1992

Veribanc Category	Number of Banks	Assets (in $ billion)	Hypothetical of Case Resolution	Hypothetical Assets to be Resolved (in $ billion)	Hypothetical Rate of BIF Loss	Hypothetical BIF Loss Exposure (in $ billion)
Red: no stars	143	$34.4	0.9	$31.0	0.3	$9.3
Yellow: no stars	99	28.8	0.9	26.0	0.3	7.8
Yellow: one star	155	225.0	0.6	135.0	0.2	27.0
Yellow: two stars	639	166.8	0.6	100.0	0.2	20.0
Green: no stars	28	8.1	0.4	3.2	0.2	0.6
Green: one star	3	54.4	0.4	21.8	0.2	4.4
All "doubtful" banks	1,067	$517.5		$317.0		$69.1
Green: two star	1,277	$54.4	.005	$0.3	0.2	$.1
Green: three stars	9,801	2,650.7	.001	2.7	0.2	.5
All banks	12,145	$3,222.6		$320.0		$69.7
Less BIF's reserve for its estimated liability for unresolved cases						15.2
BIF's unbooked loss exposure						$54.5

Note: The hypothetical rates of needed case resolution and of BIF loss are offered as indicative guesses. Detailed analysis of past transitions across partitions of bank assets would be needed to establish econometric estimates of these variables.

Not observing a spurt in bank failures or recapitalizations either in the wake of the November 3 election or when FDICIA's 2 percent capital threshold kicked in tells us more about regulatory faintheartedness than about the extent of economic insolvency in the banking industry. In the meantime and probably for months to come, a disturbing number of under-capitalized deposit institutions are free to book short-funded positions in Treasury securities without recapitalizing themselves. Indeed, the weighting pattern used in the risk-based capital system encourages this. These positions are speculative gambles on the course of future interest rates for which taxpayers are unconscionably being made to hold the downside. Even if the managers and stockholder of these institutions end up winning their bets, taxpayers are financing their speculations on an interest-free basis.

Top regulators' penchant for discussing hardheaded insolvency resolutions as a policy that would "close down the industry" disgracefully distorts the recapitalization issue. Just as in a private restructuring, no government supervisor should liquidate an insolvent institution whose franchise can be shown to be valuable enough to continue it in operation. If a troubled but viable firm's stockholders refuse to recapitalize the enterprise, their position should be closed out. While supervisors search for new private investors to take over the bank, the FDIC should routinely seek to offset BIF's loss exposure with a carefully balanced claim on the firm's future cash flows.

The Fraudulent Benefits Claimed for Projected BIF Accounting Profits

Anyone who has helped a loved one face cancer knows that counterproductively denying that a problem exists is prototypically less painful in the short run than confronting that problem head-on. But it is dramatically less beneficial as well. Any thinking person should be disturbed by the economic benefits the FDIC and banking trade-association spokespersons claim for FDIC projections of the net "accounting income" that BIF can generate from future premium receipts. These projections are being used to allege that the BIF can recapitalize *itself* over time by charging relatively safe banks an excessive price for FDIC services. In turn, the allegation that BIF's capital shortage will vanish over time by itself is being used to justify a policy of benignly neglecting the economic insolvency of hundreds of weak banks.

Analyses of BIF loss exposure that forecast large amounts of future net premiums are conceptually flawed. Premiums and additions to reserves should be calculated net of the insurer's loss exposure in each client. Economic theory indicates that setting premiums high above their value to low-risk bank clients is bound to increase BIF's contingent loss exposure. As the Shadow Financial Regulatory Committee has emphasized, burdensome premiums create a virtually irresistible incentive for low-risk institutions to expand their risk-taking to make sure that the value of the insurance services they receive from BIF equal or exceed the charge the FDIC levies on them (Shadow Financial Regulatory Committee, 1992a). This insight clarifies that, in equilibrium, the present value of BIF's future net premiums must be zero. Moreover, it is easy for an institution to expand its risk-taking; e.g., by securitizing or collateralizing strong assets or by mismatching the futurity of an institution's assets and liabilities. This means that any transitional benefits to BIF reserves from raising premiums are bound to dissipate quickly.

Putting off the insolvency resolution of crippled banks and using accounting games to suggest the possibility of a painless recapitalization for BIF are faithless actions that strongly capitalized institutions and other informed parties ought to protest. For BIF to become truly self-financing, it is not enough to rebuild its reserves in an accounting sense. Although it can price and police its services to avoid future losses, outside resources must be tapped to overcome the imbedded losses that represent the effects of past forbearance policies. Resources to cover past losses can only be collected through taxes of some kind. If temporarily very-profitable survivor banks are truly going to be asked to share the recapitalization burden with the general taxpayer, Congress had best plan to enact a one-time special tax assessment against bank income or assets.

References

Federal Deposit Insurance Corporation, Department of the Treasury, and Federal Reserve System, "Risk-Based Capital Standards: Joint Advance Notice of Proposed Rule Making," 12 C.F.R. pt. 325, 12 C.F.R. pt. 3, and 12 C.F.R. pts. 208 and 225, Washington, D.C., 1992.

McTague, Jim, "2,000 Failures? Much Media Ado Over Very Little," *The American Banker*, vol. 157, October 13, 1992.

Shadow Financial Regulatory Committee, "The FDIC's Proposed Schedule of Risk Sensitive Premiums," Statement no. 83, June 1, 1992a.

———, "Rule Proposed by Bank Regulators to Control Interest Rate Risk," Statement no. 87, September 14, 1992b.

4 THE ROLE OF FORBEARANCE AND ITS COSTS IN HANDLING TROUBLED AND FAILED DEPOSITORY INSTITUTIONS

Robert A. Eisenbeis and Paul M. Horvitz

Introduction

The banking regulatory agencies have had, up to now, very wide discretion in the handling of troubled banks and thrifts. This could range from increased examination frequency to informal supervisory agreements to formal cease-and-desist actions to declarations of insolvency. The latter step would be followed by liquidation of the bank or sale to a buyer willing to recapitalize it. In some cases the FDIC has assisted in the recapitalization of the bank without a declaration of insolvency (open-bank assistance).

In most situations, *insolvency* has a precise meaning: it is the inability to meet obligations as they come due. (The term *technical insolvency* is reserved for those situations when the firm is meeting current obligations but has negative net worth.) Meeting current obligations is never a problem for an insured bank because even a severely troubled bank can always attract insured deposits if it is willing to pay the price. Technical insolvency is also a somewhat fuzzy concept because of the peculiarities of the bank accounting and supervisory systems. Under normal circumstances, most bank assets are carried on the books at historical cost. Market values are appropriate under GAAP when there is doubt as to the bank's ability to continue in operation. Further, the supervisors have authority to require additional reserves or to write down the value of assets when there is doubt as to their collectibility, and they have broad discretion as to when or under what conditions they will take such action. As a result, it is unclear whether insolvency should be defined in terms of zero-book-value net worth, zero-market-value net worth, or something else. In recognition of this problem, the finance literature has shifted attention from insolvency to closure rules, or the policy the agencies follow in determining when to take action against a troubled bank.

Several studies aimed at estimating fair deposit insurance premiums, or estimating the subsidy involved in the flat-rate deposit-insurance premium structure, have assumed a particular closure rule. The FDIC does not appear to have a firm closure rule, and regardless of any general policy (such as closure at zero book value net worth), the FDIC reserves the right to "forbear" from exercising the rule. Recent studies have demonstrated that a varying closure rule, can, under certain circumstances, either increase or decrease the deposit insurance subsidy (Davies and McMannus, 1991).

The FDICIA of 1991 substantially reduces FDIC discretion in the handling of troubled banks. It also limits the FDIC's ability to exercise forbearance for banks that fail to meet rather precisely defined capital requirements. The Shadow Financial Regulatory Committee has been in the forefront of those who have been critical of agency forbearance and have urged that restrictions be placed on agency discretion. It is important to recognize, however, that the agencies still retain a significant amount of discretion both with respect to forbearance and to handling failures (Carnell, 1992).

Forbearance has been widely blamed for increasing the cost of the saving and loan debacle. Some of the attacks on forbearance represent a broad policy preference for "rules" over "authority" and are reminiscent of the similar debate on monetary policy. Other critics (particularly Kane, 1989) have rather carefully spelled out the agency or incentive problems that make forbearance a bad bet for the taxpayer (though the taxpayer may win some of these bets). There has been, however, recent reevaluation of forbearance, with several studies attempting to determine the circumstances in which forbearance may be an appropriate policy. This revisionism comes from economists: the supervisors have never doubted the benefits of forbearance (their objection has been only to congressionally mandated forbearance, as in the Competitive Equality Banking Act, which limits their discretion).

This chapter, reviews the recent theoretical literature on the conditions under which regulatory forbearance would be rational. We consider the empirical evidence on the success or failure of forbearance policies. A considerable amount of such evidence now exists, though some of it is anecdotal. Finally, we consider whether the discretion-limiting rules resulting from FDICIA have gone too far to allow an optimal forbearance policy.

The Arguments Concerning Forbearance

We view forbearance as a conscious decision to delay enforcing a regulation or supervisory policy. In the context of a closure rule, "forbearance is the policy of granting the institution time to return to solvency before the closure rule is enforced" (Allen and Saunders, 1991, p. 2). There are some implications of this definition for this discussion. First, forbearance is not the same as having a weak closure rule. That is, a policy of not closing banks until book net worth is –5 percent of assets is not forbearance, but given such a policy, deciding to allow a bank to operate with –6 percent net worth *is* forbearance. Second, forbearance is not the same as inaction. If the FDIC lacks good information (because of a poor accounting or monitoring system), a bank that might otherwise fail the closure rule may continue in operation. That is not forbearance.[1] Similarly, if the FDIC fails to act because of some failure of the bureaucratic decision-making system, that is not forbearance. We stress this point because we accept Kane's analysis of the agency problems that encourage inaction, but that is not necessarily an argument against a reasoned, conscious decision that in a particular case, forbearance might be the optimal policy.

The traditional argument against forbearance is the simple one of moral hazard. In a world of deposit insurance and limited liability, the owners and managers of a bank with negative net worth, if allowed to continue in operation, have an incentive to take high risks. If they are successful, they receive all the gains. If they are unsuccessful, they will suffer no additional losses. In Brumbaugh's phrase, they will be inclined to "gamble for resurrection." In search of the high variance investment, they will even be willing to undertake negative expected return projects. While some may be successful in some states of the world, on average, there will be losses. Further, even if the payoffs are positive on average, the FDIC suffers net losses, since it generally does not share in the positive returns. This situation is worse than the frequently cited analogy of the "Hail Mary" pass by the losing team at the end of a football game: the pass has low odds of success, but it cannot worsen the result. Even apart from high-risk gambles, the insolvent bank is likely to be riskier than the solvent bank because it must earn a higher return on assets to cover interest costs on its liabilities, which, by definition, are larger than assets.[2]

The argument for forbearance turns, as most such arguments in finance do, on questions of market imperfections. One such imperfection is bankruptcy costs. Former FDIC chairman William Seidman has claimed that bank assets decline in value by about 25 percent once the bank is taken over by the FDIC. This is almost certainly wrong, but James (1991) found that the direct costs associated with bank closures averaged 10 percent of the bank's assets. Bovenzi and Murton (1990) and Brown and Epstein (1992) also suggest that bankruptcy costs may be significant. If a weak bank can return to solvency without the need for explicit FDIC action, these deadweight bankruptcy costs can be saved. Another imperfection may be that assets are not efficiently priced or that asset markets are imperfect. In addition, there may be information asymmetries that may lead the FDIC to believe that some assets may be better managed by the institution that originated them than by the FDIC liquidators. If those assets have greater value under control of the ongoing bank, then forbearance may result in lower costs to the FDIC. Also, if the troubled bank is to be sold, its true franchise value may not be realized in a distressed sale because of the limited number of potential buyers.

Of course, if assets are efficiently priced, and the market for bank capital is perfect, then a troubled but salvageable bank would be able to attract investors and be recapitalized without need for forbearance. Given the imperfections that may exist, in some cases it might be argued that the solution with the least cost would be forbearance to allow the bank time to return to solvency and capital compliance.

A major basis for forbearance by the regulators is fear of macroeconomic effects of enforcement of closure rules. One type of macroeconomic concern is the risk of systemic collapse that might follow the closing of a very large bank. This is the traditional "too big to fail" argument, invoked in the case of Continental-Illinois and some other smaller cases. The other situation is the reluctance to close a large number of institutions in a market. Applying traditional closure policy would have resulted in closing many hundreds of agricultural banks in the Midwest in the 1980s.

Review of Theoretical Literature on Forbearance

The finance literature on forbearance focuses on four distinct issues. The first, and most recent, issue is how different closure rules affect the value of deposit insurance. These rules can be used to infer the conditions under which the government has incentives to postpone closing troubled institutions, thus engaging in forbearance. This literature helps to clarify, the conditions under which forbearance may be optimal and the informational or other advantages regulators must have to assess those conditions. The second issue is the incentive effect of imposing an early closure rule on institutions as compared with potentially engaging in forbearance. The third category of literature seeks to document the extent to which institutions with low net worth engage in moral hazard behavior, thereby imposing costs on the taxpayer. Finally, some researchers look at how the consequences of forbearance affect costs to the taxpayer. We consider each of these issues in turn.

Optimal Closure Policies

The now traditional models of risk-based deposit insurance pricing employing Black-Scholes options pricing methodology assume that an institution would be closed when an insolvency state is detected at the time of examination (see Merton, 1977, 1978; Pennacchi, 1987; Ronn and Verma, 1986; Marcus and Shaked, 1984). Ronn and Verma (1986) recognized that the insurer did not always close a bank when insolvency was discovered. They modified the options pricing model to allow for forbearance and as a consequence obtain higher estimated fair deposit insurance premiums than previous researchers, especially Marcus and Shaked (1984).[3] O'Brien (1992) and others (Kuester-King and O'Brien, 1990, 1991) have pointed out specification problems with Ronn and Verma's approach concerning their implicit assumption that both solvent and insolvent institutions receive capital injections from the insurer, the treatment of dividends, and their handling of insurance premiums in insolvent institutions. After correcting for the deficiencies, O'Brien finds that forbearance proves to be more costly than closing institutions when insolvency is discovered. These higher costs are reflected in higher premiums and direct taxpayer subsidies, depending on how the costs of a forbearance policy are divided. While allowing for forbearance, neither Ronn and Verma nor their commentators address the issue of when it might be optimal for the insurer to engage in forbearance.

Allen and Saunders (1990) suggest a way both to model forbearance and to price it. They model insurance values with a closure rule in an options pricing framework as a callable put. When Merton (1977) originally modeled insurance, he structured it as a put option that gave equity holders the right to walk away if the bank was insolvent, leaving the insurance agency to pay off insured claims. Allen and Saunders, however, argue that equity holders may not always choose to exercise the put, even when it is in the money, because it would mean liquidation of the bank and loss of future revenues. Here, limited liability plays an important role as an incentive for this shareholder decision. On the other hand, the insurer would clearly exercise its right to exercise its call on the bank's assets to limit its losses. Hence, the callable put model. The insurance agency closure rule will be less strict than that of the owners' when one of four conditions exists: (1) the FDIC has special information leading it to believe the volatility of the bank's assets are less than what the bank's owners believe; (2) deposit insurance has been mispriced, as is the present case with the current flat rate system; (3) there are diversification possibilities in insurance; or (4) social or systemic risk considerations lead the insurer to want to subsidize the banking system.[4] Their analysis allows one expressly to value the cost of forbearance to the insurance fund/taxpayer as the "foregone value of the insurer's call provision."

Acharya and Dreyfus (1989) use a dynamic programming model to extend the idea of forbearance to analyze cases when it might be optimal for the insurer to keep an institution open. Their approach assumes the insurer's objective is to charge an actuarially fair premium for each bank and to balance the costs of closing an insolvent bank now, against future insurance liabilities and audit costs that might accrue if it forbore.[5] Using a non–options-based model, they show that forbearance will be optimal only in a noncompetitive banking world where the spread between the bank's return on assets and its deposit costs exceeds the premium the insurer must charge to cover its expected liability plus its auditing costs. In such a monopolistically competitive world, forbearance is paid for by effectively taxing bank customers (in those markets where the bank has monopolistic profits through higher prices) and transferring wealth to shareholders. Such a policy is hard to justify from a social welfare perspective. In a competitive banking world, Acharya and Dreyfus find it is optimal to close the bank whenever it can't earn sufficient income to cover its insurance premiums and before net worth goes to zero.[6] Interestingly, they also show that the closure rule is bank specific and depends on the net return on the bank's assets, the growth in deposits and the insurer's audit and administration costs.

Dreyfus, Saunders, and Allen (1992) examine the case of a fixed deposit insurance premium (that may be mispriced) and an insurance agency that attempts to control its risk exposure by imposing or relaxing caps on the amount of insured deposits that may be raised. While this may appear at first to be an artificial situation, since the banking agencies have not traditionally had this power, FDICIA now grants the banking authorities authority to limit inadequately capitalized banks from raising brokered deposits. Relevant to the forbearance issue is Dreyfus, Saunders, and Allen's conclusion that when liquidation costs exist, then the insurance agency may find it advantageous to subsidize a bank by permitting it to raise additional insured deposits—which is the same as engaging in forbearance.[7] When there are no liquidation costs, then early closure is optimal. They argue that early liquidation costs may result when one or more of three circumstances occur: (1) the insurance agency is unable to realize the "true market value of assets" because they have to be liquidated at "fire sale" values; (2) transfer of assets results in deadweight liquidation costs due to loss of specialized information or to incurring transactions and/or reorganization costs; or (3) the insurance agency faces a budget constraint.

Kumar and Morgan (1993) extend the options-type models in both a two- and three-period setting, which allows the regulatory agencies to engage in forbearance when insolvency occurs. In their writer-extendible call option model, they find that optimal closure policies require early intervention and underpricing of the premium. However, if an institution's net worth suddenly becomes deeply negative, then the FDIC should engage in forbearance, both because moral hazard incentives are small by comparison with what they are when an institution is only slightly insolvent and because improvement is more likely than further deterioration.

Finally, Nagarajan and Sealey (1993) indicate that forbearance has no role in regulatory policy when asset values are measured without error and when all project risk is project specific. If, however, project risk cannot be perfectly assessed or if market risk is present, then forbearance may be justified, but only in conjunction with a minimum capital requirement.

Rather than justifying forbearance, however, a careful examination of the models provides a glimpse of the incentives that bias regulators' decisions on forbearance and how to eliminate these incentives. First, if, for political or budget constraint reasons, regulators' incentives are not aligned with those of the taxpayer, then the insurance agency will have the incentive to engage in forbearance. These incentives have been well documented and discussed by Kane (1986, 1989) and are consistent with the predictions of the theoretical models. The budget and political considerations become irrelevant as a justification for forbearance if the insurer is charged, as it now is under FDICIA, to minimize losses to the taxpayer, rather than minimize loss to the insurance fund. In other words, forbearance results in this case from misdesign of the insurance system rather than from the inherent desirability of forbearance.

Second, if closure rules are based on book rather than market values, then the value of specialized information or other franchise value will not be appropriately reflected on the bank's books. If they were, then the institution would not have violated the closure rule. This rationale for forbearance rests on misdesign of the asset-measurement system and the closure rule. If a market-value closure rule were used, then the franchise value would have been considered when the closure rule was invoked, rather than introduced as a factor after closure. This suggests that Dreyfus, Saunders, and Allen really have in mind a situation where all a bank's assets aren't considered when the closure rule is set. Similarly, the monopoly power assumed in the Acharya and Dreyfus model could be viewed as part of franchise value.

Finally, if assets would have to be liquidated at less than their true market values because of the "fire sale" nature of a resolution transaction, then a loss-minimizing insurer might engage in forbearance. To avoid this problem, the insurance agency must explore alternative ways of disposing of institutions besides fire sales of assets and/or balance the interest costs of temporarily carrying these assets until they can be sold against the fire sale losses that might otherwise be incurred. This requires the agency to have reliable estimates of the true market value of the bank and of the costs of disposal.[8] Mullins and Pyle (1992) devote particular attention to the interaction among liquidation costs, fairly priced insurance premiums, capital adequacy requirements, and portfolio diversification. They show that failure to consider deadweight bankruptcy costs in setting fair premiums, capital requirements, or closure rules may lead to underpriced insurance or too low capital requirements and closure rules for the risks borne by the insurance fund.

The Incentive Effects of an Early Closure Rule

The theoretical work on the incentives to engage in risk-taking behavior due to the existence of limited liability and mispriced deposit insurance has evolved. Merton's first paper, because it assumed a one-time premium, came up with the unusual result that the incentive to engage in risk-taking behavior increased as net worth increased. This result was reversed when audit costs were recognized. With a one-time premium and audit costs paid by the insurer, the value of insurance first declined and then increased as net worth increased. The most intuitive result followed from Pyle (1983, 1986), who argued that with renewable insurance, if a bank were assessed audit costs, then ultimately the costs of insurance were borne by depositors and the audit costs were borne by equity holders, which involved the tradeoff between the cost of raising new equity as compared with costs of monitoring.

Theory indicates that in the presence of mispriced deposit insurance and moral hazard, banks will exploit the insurance mispricing by restructuring their balance sheets to take on more risk or will increase their leverage. Kim and Santomero (1988) and Koehn and Santomero (1980) suggest that banks will trade off risk against return and increase their risk taking as required capital is increased. Keeley and Furlong (1990), however, point out that this inference rests on their not considering the change in the option value of insurance as leverage increases. When this correction is made, an increase in the required capital ratio—and by inference an increase in the closure threshold—will reduce risk-taking incentives. Keeton (1988) finds that when desired capital levels are determined endogenously, then increasing capital requirements may either increase or decrease the incentives to take risk, depending upon the correlation among asset returns.

Using a model similar to Keeton's, Davies and McManus (1991) investigate the effect on risk taking when institutions are operating under closure rules similar to those in FDICIA. They look at risk-taking incentives when closure rules are increased and obtain results similar to Keeton, in that the effects can vary depending on the institution's utility function and coefficient of risk aversion. This leads them to suggest that implementation of an effective closure rule may also require increased monitoring and other restrictions, such as limits on growth or on taking brokered deposits.

More recently, Lai and Sinkey (1992) extend the Ronn and Verma model to consider situations where the insurance agency's closure rule is uncertain in a world with a flat premium and the agency has the discretion to intervene. They conclude that an uncertain closure rule—discretionary intervention—increases the value of the deposit insurance subsidy. By inference, given flat-rate premiums, forbearance that permits agency discretion increases the expected costs to taxpayers.

Finally, Hendershott (1992) examines the situation where forbearance is predictable. In addition to incentives for individual institutions to take advantage of that forbearance by taking on more risks, he finds that these risks are highly correlated across institutions. These incentives greatly expand the taxpayer's risk exposure, especially as the financial condition of insured institutions declines.

Implications of the Theoretical Work

This theoretical work has several implications for policy formation. First, it implies that errors in measurement of asset values and reliance on book- rather than market-value closure rules means that forbearance and hence costly closures are more likely. Second, if closure rules are not enforced on a timely basis—are not credible—then forbearance and increased costs of failure to taxpayers may result (see Lai and Sinkey, 1992). Third, in the absence of market imperfections, forbearance cannot exist as an optimal policy in the case where insurance is properly priced. Fourth, costly forbearance may result if the incentives of the insurer are not aligned with the interests of the taxpayers. Fifth, forbearance may be optimal when the insurer has information on the true market value of assets superior to that of management. Finally, temporary forbearance may be justified if closure would mean incurring "fire sale" losses or large deadweight bankruptcy costs.

Evidence on Forbearance and Risk-Taking Behavior

The theoretical literature suggests that with mispriced insurance, institutions will take on risk as equity declines.[9] If this is true, why have more banks not attempted to exploit mispriced instance and take on more risk? Several explanations have been offered. Keeley and Furlong (1990) suggest that although taking the money and running (betting the bank) and putting it back to the insurer may be rational stockholder behavior in a single-period model, if there is value to having a bank charter, then this may offset the incentive. They have demonstrated empirically, as has Kwan (1991) that banks do appear to have charter value and that this value has decreased dramatically over the 1980s. This then might explain why banks seem to have more incentives to take on more risk now as their value declines than they did in the past. This empirical observation is also consistent with the work of Benston and Carhill (1992), who suggest that S&Ls did not engage in moral hazard behavior after they became insolvent.

Managers' incentives to keep their jobs to maintain their income or preserve their employability may also act in a multiperiod model to restrict undue risk taking by management, even with mispriced insurance. Finally, there is the possibility that banking regulators have in fact intervened to prevent banks from taking undue risk. This possibility is explored in some detail by Gilbert (1992), who concludes that early intervention will not prevent bank failures because regulators already have followed such procedures with little success. Ultimately, however, it is an empirical question whether insured institutions have engaged in moral hazard and undue risk-taking behavior.

Consequences of Forbearance

Much of our experience with forbearance results from a failure of the agencies to take action, rather than a rational decision that forbearance is the optimal means of handling a particular problem. The Federal Home Loan Bank Board (FHLBB) never considered closing all economically insolvent thrifts in 1981–1982. It didn't have the funds to do that, and it may not have had the legal authority, since most of the institutions were solvent on a book-value basis. Much of the criticism of forbearance tends to be directed at the regulators, but Congress has entered the scene on more than one occasion to extend forbearance to institutions. As a result, we have had substantial experience with two situations in which closure rules were not enforced—industrywide problems and forbearance granted on a discretionary basis to individual institutions. Most of these cases represent opportunistic forbearance rather than a rationally calculated forbearance decision.

On an industrywide basis, the situation of the thrift industry in the high-rate period of 1981–1982 is an example of widespread agency-sanctioned forbearance. The systematic policy of the Federal Home Loan Bank Board was to avoid closing institutions that were market-value insolvent during this period. In fact, most of the industry was economically insolvent on a market basis. Closing such insolvent institutions, it has been estimated by Kane (1985, table 4.6), would have involved potential costs of about $150 billion in 1981 or $109 billion in 1982. Although most of these institutions were technically book-value solvent, they clearly posed a great risk to the taxpayer, whose realization depended on what happened to interest rates. When interest rates fell after 1982, many of these insolvent institutions returned to solvency. It is unclear whether closing insolvent institutions in 1982 would have saved money compared with alternative actions. Comparing Kane's estimated present-value loss of $109 billion in 1982 with current estimates that cleaning up the S&L mess will cost about $140 billion suggests that the taxpayer may have been better off if the banks had been closed in 1982 (Barth and Brumbaugh, 1992, table 2.3). On the other hand, many banks moved into riskier assets that resulted in larger losses when the economy became unfavorable to real estate.

Instead of acting promptly to resolve these problem institutions, the FSLIC, both because of financial constraints and political considerations, engaged in a series of accounting and related gimmicks to give the illusion that these GAAP insolvent institutions were in fact solvent. Actually, systematic forbearance activities by the FHLBB began even as the increase in rates began in 1979, as accounting rules employed by the FHLBB began to deviate significantly from GAAP. In that year, S&Ls were allowed to book 250 basis points of loan origination fees directly into income, which then was flowed directly to net worth. In 1981, the FHLBB initiated several other accounting changes that had similar effects. Regulatory accounting procedures (or RAP accounting) were introduced that avoided recognition of declines in asset values. Losses on assets sold at below-market rates were permitted to be amortized over the life of the loan rather than booked immediately. FSLIC also purchased capital certificates and income capital certificates to inject funds directly into capital deficient institutions. In 1982, certain short-term liability accounts (such as loans in process) were reclassified as contra asset accounts, which reduced thrift liabilities and hence improved capital ratios. In the case of acquisitions, institutions were permitted to amortize good will over a 40-year period and to write up income from asset revaluations over a shorter period of time, thereby improving the earnings stream and enabling some reported earnings to flow into capital.

It is easy to find other examples of situations in which inaction worked out for the best, at least for some banks. For example, the banking agencies have engaged in institution-by-institution forbearance for several money-center and regional banks that experienced problems with their holdings of third world debt during the 1980s. Had these institutions been required to mark their sometimes substantial holdings of underwater debt to market or to increase loan loss reserves to levels close to the expected losses on this debt (as measured by secondary market prices), then institutions such as Manufacturers Hanover, Bank of America, and perhaps Citicorp would have been insolvent. Bank of America, in particular, is often cited as a success story of discretionary forbearance.

The FDIC has noted that "the simple fact is that most FDIC-insured depository institutions identified as posing a definite threat of loss to the insurance fund are successfully restored to a safe-and-sound operating condition and do *not* ultimately fail. Effective supervision, including the use of discretionary supervisory forbearance, has proven to be a very cost-effective loss prevention mechanism for the deposit insurance fund" (FDIC, 1989, p. 162). Unfortunately, the FDIC does not provide that proof, though Cobos (1989) presents data on the movement of banks from the FDIC's problem list: of the 1,624 banks on the problem list as of July 1, 1987, 422 were removed from the list by June 30, 1988 because of significant improvement in their condition, and another 87 were acquired in nonassisted mergers.

The thrift regulators have held a similar position with respect to forbearance. The FHLBB (1983) argued that "many S&Ls with negative net worth can be expected to be profitable in the future, on the basis of yields and costs currently prevailing in the market, given their existing location, organization, and management." The FHLBB does not cite evidence of its ability to distinguish between those which will become profitable (and solvent) and those whose losses will increase. A recent study by DeGennaro and Thomson (1993) tests this hypothesis directly. They compared the present value of the costs of closure for 996 FSLIC-insured savings and loans that did not meet the regulatory minimum capital standards as of December 31, 1979 with an estimate of the embedded market-to-market losses in these institutions.[10] They concluded, on the basis of this experiment, that the taxpayer lost on this regulatory forbearance by a two-to-one margin: that is, the present value of the resolution costs was twice the embedded market-to-market losses that would have been incurred if the savings and loans had been closed in 1979.

The Shadow Financial Regulatory Committee evaluated the evidence—empirical and anecdotal—in preparing its Program for Deposit Insurance and Regulatory Reform in February 1989 and concluded that "policies of regulatory forbearance . . . permitted economically insolvent institutions to keep operating. This has substantially increased the eventual costs of solving the problems which ultimately will be paid by taxpayers" (Shadow Financial Regulatory Committee, statement 41).

Since that time, and perhaps as a result of the renewed interest in an analytical approach to forbearance as discussed in this chapter, several empirical studies have appeared that shed some light on the issue.

Rudolph (1989) reported on the 1987 status of the 237 thrifts that were GAAP insolvent in 1982. During that time, 92 were merged or closed, and 77 remained insolvent. However, 68 (29 percent) became GAAP solvent, with an average capital to asset ratio of 5.6 percent. Again, these results do not tell us whether the ultimate losses were greater or less than they would have been if all 237 had been closed in 1982 (or before). However, the study does show that prediction of which institutions would remain solvent was difficult and that important variables and their coefficients changed yearly. This suggests that it would have been difficult to forecast with any degree of accuracy which institutions would or would not have recovered.

Benston and Carhill (1992) attempt to provide a direct answer to the question of whether early closure would have reduced costs. They estimate that the cost of closing market-value insolvent thrifts in 1988 would have been $21 billion higher than if the FHLBB had adopted such a closure rule in 1985. Over some periods of time, however, broad nondiscretionary forbearance would have lower costs as compared with a market-value insolvency rule. During 1985, for example, 651 thrifts that were insolvent at year-end 1984 became solvent again. The Benston-Carhill paper is a careful estimate of market values, but the forbearance policy it evaluates is one of more or less inaction rather than a selection of institutions that were expected to benefit from forbearance.

There have been at least two programs that offered opportunity to assess the agencies' ability to discriminate in making such selections. The Competitive Equity in Banking Act of 1987 (CEBA) provides an example of congressionally sanctioned forbearance. Under title 7 of the act, banks with heavy concentrations of underwater agricultural loans were allowed to defer loss recognition in their portfolio by amortizing losses over several years. Implementing regulations permitted qualifying institutions to apply for inclusion in the deferred loss recognition program. According to Cobos (1989), between 1987–1988, 35 of 62 applying institutions in southern, midwestern, and southwestern states in agricultural areas were approved for participation. The intent of the legislation was to allow time for fundamentally viable but temporarily inadequately capitalized institutions to improve their capital position. There was no indication in the legislative to permit insolvent or unviable institutions the right to participate in the program (see *Cong. Rec.,* March 26, 1987, p. S.3941). Regulatory discretion was to determine eligibility and whether an institution was viable.

The FDIC had initiated its own capital forbearance plan in March 1986 and revised it in July 1987 for institutions with capital deficiencies due to agricultural and energy lending.[11] The FDIC and CEBA mandated forbearance programs allowed 326 banks—all book solvent—to operate with less than the required amounts of capital. These banks were granted forbearance on the basis of an FDIC finding that they had competent management and that their problems were due to the troubles of the local economy. In a recently completed dissertation, Huang (1993) examined the performance of 263 of these banks. One year after admission into the program, 93 had capital-to-assets ratios that had increased during that period, while 170 experienced declines during that period. Less than one-half of those that improved during the first year had a further improvement during the second year.

Huang's dissertation was not aimed at evaluating the success of the program but rather was an attempt to detect differences in starting conditions or strategies followed by those banks that improved while enjoying forbearance and those that did not. It was, in a sense, an application of the early-warning-system methodology to the recovery of failed banks. Huang did find variables that are, in a statistical sense, significant in classifying banks into those likely to recover and not likely to do so. At best, however, he is able to classify banks with results that are only moderately better than chance. This evidence is discouraging to forbearance success in that the banks in the FDIC forbearance program were hand-picked as good prospects for success.

Data compiled by Barth and Brumbaugh (1992) and in a related series of studies provide one of the strongest indictments of forbearance. In examining the consequences of the FSLIC's efforts to delay closing institutions, they looked at the 205 institutions that were closed in 1988. They found that these institutions were resolved at a present-value cost of $31.8 billion and had been permitted to operate with negative tangible net worth for an average of 3.5 years.[12] Moreover, they conclude that there was a positive relationship between the length of time these insolvent institutions had been left open and their resolution costs. They also find evidence of moral hazard behavior in their data. This pattern continued into 1989. Barth (1991) reports that of the 37 S&Ls that were resolved in 1989, the average cost was 58 percent of assets, and the average time they were allowed to remain open was 40 months.

Similar patterns also appear when banks and credit unions are permitted to remain open after net worth approaches zero. Barth (1991) reports that of the 896 banks closed from 1985 through 1989, the average resolution cost (loss to the insurance fund) was 18 percent of assets. The average length of time that a bank with a seriously deficient CAMEL rating of 4 or 5 was permitted to continue operating was 28 months, and the maximum was 88 months.[13] Resolution of problem credit union cases between 1985 and 1989 was more costly, 26 percent of assets, than for commercial banks, but less than for S&Ls. Barth (1991) provides a table for the most costly credit union resolutions between 1983 and 1989 that shows that these too were sometimes permitted to operate for many months after having been given a CAMEL rating of 4 or 5. The average length of time was 24 months (with a high of 231 months), which is actually down from the average of 70 months in 1980.

As noted earlier, the moral hazard problem is a serious one for advocates of fobearance. Since the evidence does indicate that *some* banks will improve if granted forbearance, while others will not, a crucial consideration is whether the supervisors can deal successfully with the moral hazard problem and control risk-taking by weak institutions operating with forbearance. Barrow and Horvitz (1992) investigated this question in connection with the FHLBB's Management Consignment Program (MCP). Under this program, book-insolvent thrifts continued to operate under management selected by and controlled by FSLIC. These institutions could not be expected to return to solvency under normal conditions and might be expected to engage in high-risk activities. In fact, however, the MCP thrifts became less risky as compared with similar institutions not in the MCP. MCP managements were paid on a flat-rate basis that provided no incentive to operate in a risky fashion (or to operate efficiently, for that matter), and FSLIC monitoring costs were high. None of these institutions returned to solvency, but the ultimate losses to the FSLIC from the failure of these thrifts were less than for the comparable non-MCP institutions. This provides some evidence that although controlling risk-taking by banks receiving forbearance is possible, it may not be efficient to do so.

Concluding Observations

In reviewing the theoretical literature on forbearance, the key justifications found for engaging in forbearance rest on some form of market imperfections. For example, the existence of monopoly power in the banking market permits the institution to cover any increase in actual or implied actuarially fair premiums that result through forbearance. This shifts the cost of forbearance to those taxpayers who are the customers of the bank, essentially transferring wealth from these customers to bank shareholders. From a public policy perspective, this hardly seems to be a justification for engaging in forbearance.

The other rationale hinges on the existence of asymmetric information in which the regulators have superior knowledge from that of the market, shareholders, or bank customers about the values of assets and future prospects for the bank. The inferential evidence on whether this knowledge exists is questionable. While some forbearance decisions have worked out, recent research suggests that when forbearance is granted, the agencies' ability to predict is limited at best. Moreover, decisions to delay closing institutions have been shown to result in large losses to taxpayers.

One of the main reasons used to justify congressionally mandated forbearance is the desire to insulate geographically undiversified institutions (such as institutions located in depressed agricultural areas) or institutions with undiversified asset portfolios (such as thrifts, money-center institutions with from less developed countries (LDCs), or banks located in New England or other depressed economic areas). The need for this action results from regulatory restrictions on geographic expansion or restrictions that result in forced specialization in certain asset-liability categories, which prove vulnerable when exogenous macroeconomic shocks occur. The theoretical literature has not addressed this issue directly. Experience suggests, again, that policies to implement this forbearance situation have met with mixed results. Clearly, the taxpayer has suffered great loss in the case of the thrift mess. Losses in the agricultural area have been minimal (and those included in the program have been limited). Some believe that is also true of the costs of the LDC debt situation. The analysis suggests that the need for such forbearance might be ameliorated with certain regulatory changes to relax restrictions on bank asset powers and limits on interstate banking.

In addition, appropriate implementation of prompt corrective action and early intervention, as now required by FDICIA of 1991, should introduce market incentives that would induce institutions to take advantage of geographic and asset diversification, thereby reducing the need for industrywide forbearance. A more direct result of FDICIA may be the effect on bank behavior when early intervention is prescribed by law and forbearance is restricted. Under these conditions, there may be a significant shift in bank asset choice to minimize the risk of becoming "critically undercapitalized." This may be much more important than any possible gains from forbearance once a bank becomes insolvent.[14]

Notes

1. The consequences of this inaction may be the same as certain types of "forbearance," however.

2. Let A = total assets, L = total liabilities, r = average yield on assets, c = average cost of liabilities, H = total overhead costs. To earn a profit, $(rA - cL - H)$ must exceed zero. If $(rA - cL - H > 0)$, then $rA > cL + H$ or $r > c\,(L/A) + H/A$. For an insolvent bank, $L > A$. Since c is determined by the market, and an insolvent bank is unlikely to have lower overhead costs than a solvent bank, the minimum yield on assets required for an insolvent bank to be profitable must exceed the required yield for a solvent bank. Since higher yields are associated with greater risk, the insolvent bank is likely to hold higher-risk assets than a solvent bank.

3. Osterberg and Thomson (1992) extend the analysis to include subordinated debt. They find that forbearance reduces the effectiveness of subordinated debt (and, by analogy, uninsured deposits) as a source of market discipline when the insuring agency engages in forbearance. The required returns on both are reduced for given levels of risk.

4. If the bank is valued at current market values and insurance is correctly priced, then it is not clear how the scenario Allen and Saunders set up, where equity holders would fail to exercise their put, would hold up.

5. It is important to point out that systemic risks are neither considered nor are their costs considered by O'Brien (1992) or Ronn and Verma (1986) or any other deposit insurance model. No attempt is made to interject systemic risk considerations or other reasons why the insurer might not close an institution. Acharya and Dreyfus recognize this limitation and leave the problem for future research. Moreover, the zero profit insurance premium abstracts from any diversification benefits that might accrue from insuring many banks.

6. Mallath and Mester (1991) claim to show that there are circumstances where it is

optimal for the regulator to forbear, but do so in the unusual world where the expected return on a risky asset is less than the expected return on the safe asset.

7. This incentive is reduced when moral hazard is present. One problem with their analysis is that the model ignores the incentives imposed on a bank to raise capital as the level of uninsured deposits increases the risk premium on uninsured deposits.

8. Again, the analysis does not include consideration of systemic risk.

9. Kumar and Morgan (1993) argue that these incentives decline as net worth declines.

10. They stopped their calculations as of year end 1992 and thus, did not include the present value of the resolution costs of over 70 institutions that were likely to be closed in 1993.

11. It was extended for FDIC insured institutions until 1995 to deal with capital problems resulting from economic problems beyond the institutions' control.

12. The maximum time one of the S&Ls was permitted to remain open was 90 months.

13. Several of these institutions imposed costs on the insurance fund of as much as 56 to as high as 104 percent of assets.

14. We are indebted to David Pyle for this point.

References

Acharya, Sankarsahan and Jean-Francois Dreyfus, "Optimal Bank Reorganization Policies and the Pricing of Federal Deposit Insurance," *Journal of Finance*, December 1990.

Allen, Linda and Anthony Saunders, "Forbearance and Valuation of Deposit Insurance as a Callable Put," working paper, Baruch College, December 1990.

Barrow, Janice M. and Paul M. Horvitz, "Management Incentives and Solvency Effects of Financially Distressed Government Controlled Institutions," *Financial Management*, 1992.

Barth, James R., "Statement on the Subject of Deposit Insurance Reform Before the Committee on Banking, Housing, and Urban Affairs," U.S. Senate, March 12, 1991.

Barth, James R., and R. Dan Brumbaugh Jr., *Reform of Federal Deposit Insurance*, New York: HarperBusiness, 1992.

Barth, James R., R. Dan Brumbaugh, Jr., and Robert E. Litan, *The Future of American Banking*, Armonk, N.Y.: M.E. Sharpe, 1992.

Benston, George J. and Mike Carhill, "The Thrift Disaster: Tests of the Moral-Hazard, Deregulation, and Other Hypotheses," unpublished paper, Emory University, 1992.

Bovenzi, John F. and A.J. Murton, "Resolution Costs of Bank Failures," *FDIC Banking Review*, vol. 3, 1990.

Brown, R.A. and S. Epstein, "Resolution Costs of Bank Failures: An Update of the FDIC Historical Loss Model," *FDIC Banking Review*, vol. 5, 1992.

Carnell, Richard S., "Prompt Corrective Action Under the FDIC Improvement Act of 1991," paper presented at the Practicing Law Institute, February 3, 1992, revised September 8, 1992.

Cobos, Dean Forrester, "Forbearance: Practices and Proposed Standards," *FDIC Banking Review*, 1989.

Davies, Sally M. and Douglas A. McManus, "The Effects of Closure Policies on Bank Risk-Taking," *Journal of Banking and Finance*, vol. 15, 1991.

DeGennaro, Ramon P. and James B. Thomson, "Capital Forbearance and Thrifts: An Ex Post Examination of Regulatory Gambling," paper presented at a Conference on Bank Structure and Competition, Federal Reserve Bank of Chicago, May 1993.

Dreyfus, Jean-Francois, Anthony Saunders, and Linda Allen, "Deposit Insurance and Regulatory Forbearance: Are Caps on Insured Deposits Optimal?," *Journal of Money, Credit and Banking*, June 1992.

Federal Deposit Insurance Corporation, *Deposit Insurance for the Nineties*, 1989.

Federal Home Loan Bank Board, *Agenda for Reform*, 1983.

Gilbert, R. Alton, "The Effects of Legislating Prompt Corrective Action on the Bank Insurance Fund," *Economic Review*, Federal Reserve Board of St. Louis, July-August, 1992.

Hendershott, Robert J., "Forbearance, Financial Stability, and the Social Cost of Deposit Insurance," mimeo, August 1992.

Huang, Ying-Lin, "Supervisory Capital Forbearance: An Empirical Investigation of Policy and Practices," Ph.D. dissertation, University of Houston, 1993.

James, Christopher, "The Losses Realized in Bank Failures," *Journal of Finance*, September 1991.

Kane, Edward J., "Appearance and Reality in Deposit Insurance Reform: The Case for Reform," *Journal of Banking and Finance*, vol. 10, 1986, pp. 175–188.

———, *The S&L Insurance Mess: How Did It Happen?*, Washington, D.C.: Urban Institute, 1989.

Keeley, M.C., "Deposit Insurance, Risk, and Market Power in Banking," *American Economic Review*, 1990.

Keeton, W.R., "Substitutes and Compliments in Bank Risk-Taking and the Effectiveness of Regulation," unpublished paper, 1988.

Kim, D. and Anthony M. Santomero, "Risk in Banking and Capital Regulation," *Journal of Finance*, vol. 43, 1988, pp. 1219–1233.

Koehn, M. and Anthony M. Santomero, "Regulation of Bank Capital and Portfolio Risk," *Journal of Finance*, vol. 35, 1980, pp. 1235–1250.

Kuester-King, Kathleen A. and James M. O'Brien, "Market-Based Deposit Insurance Premiums," paper presented at the Conference on Bank Structure and Competition, Federal Reserve Bank of Chicago, May 1990.

Kuester-King, Kathleen A. and James M. O'Brien, "Market-Based, Risk-Adjusted Examination Schedules for Depository Institutions," *Journal of Banking and Finance*, September 1991.

Kumar, Raman and George Emir Morgan, "Bank Regulatory Triage: Optimal Closure Rules, Forbearance, and Early Closure," paper presented at a Conference on Bank Structure and Competition, Federal Reserve Bank of Chicago, May 5–7, 1993.

Kwan, Simon, "Re-examination of Interest Rate Sensitivity of Commercial Bank

Stock Returns Using a Random Coefficient Model," *Journal of Financial Services Research*, vol. 5, no. 1, March 1991.

Lai, Van Son and Joseph F. Sinkey, Jr., "The Effects of Variation in Strictness (or Laxity) of Closure Rules on the Valuation of Deposit Insurance," University of Georgia, mimeo, November 1992.

Lang, William W. and Leonard I. Nakamura, "Optimal Bank Closure for Deposit Insurers," Working Paper No. 90–12, Federal Reserve Bank of Philadelphia, January 1990.

Mallath, George J. and Loretta J. Mester, "When Do Regulators Close Banks? When Should They?," working paper no. 91–24, May 1991, revised November 1991.

Marcus, Alan J. and Israel Shaked, "The Valuation of FDIC Deposit Insurance Using Option Pricing Estimates," *Journal of Money, Credit and Banking*, November 1984.

Merton, Robert C., "An Analytic Derivation of the Cost of Deposit Insurance and Loan Guarantees: An Application of Modern Option Pricing Theory," *Journal of Banking and Finance*, June 1977.

———, "On the Cost of Deposit Insurance When There Are Surveillance Costs," *Journal of Business*, December 1978.

Mullins, Helena M. and David H. Pyle, "Liquidation Costs and Risk-Based Bank Capital," mimeo, November 1992.

Nagarajan, S. and C.W. Sealey, "Forbearance, Prompt Closure, and Incentive Compatible Bank Regulation," paper presented at a Conference on Bank Structure and Competition, Federal Reserve Bank of Chicago, May 5–7, 1993.

O'Brien, James M., "Deposit Insurance and Equity Values with Direct Assistance in Ronn and Verma," Board of Governors of the Federal Reserve System, November 1992.

Osterberg, William P. and James B. Thomson, "Forbearance, Subordinated Debt, and the Cost of Capital for Insured Depository Institutions," *Economic Review*, Federal Review Board of Cleveland, vol. 28, no. 3, 1992.

Pennacchi, George C., "A Reexamination of the Over- (or Under-) Pricing of Deposit Insurance," *Journal of Money, Credit and Banking*, August 1987.

Pyle, David, "Capital Regulation and Deposit Insurance," *Journal of Banking and Finance*, vol. 10, 1986.

———, "Pricing Deposit Insurance: The Effects of Mismeasurement," October 1983.

Ronn, Ehud and Avinash K. Verma, "Pricing Risk-Adjusted Deposit Insurance: An Options Based Model," *Journal of Finance*, September 1986.

Rudolph, Patricia M., "Insolvent Thrifts of 1982: Where Are They Now?," *AREUEA Journal*, vol. 17, no. 4, 1989.

Stanton, Thomas H., *A State of Risk*, New York: Harper Business, 1992.

Thompson, James B., "FSLIC Forbearances to Stockholders and the Value of Savings and Loan Shares," *Economic Review*, Federal Reserve Board of Cleveland, November 1987.

5 LONG-RUN BENEFITS IN FINANCIAL REGULATION FROM INCREASED ACCOUNTABILITY AND PRIVATIZATION

Edward J. Kane*

As have numerous government enterprises around the world, federal deposit insurance came into being as an emergency program for rescuing a deeply troubled economic sector. President Franklin Roosevelt predicted that the immediate benefits of such a rescue would come at the expense of longer-run inefficiencies that would "make the U.S. government liable for the mistakes and errors of individual banks and put a premium on unsound banking in the future" (quoted by Adams, 1990, pp. 11–12).

This projected evolution from boon to bane casts the deposit insurance problem as a progressive disease that society needs to arrest or cure. According to this model, federal regulators (including elected politicians) become doctors who have lapsed into regulatory malpractice. Regulators who fail to follow up on important symptoms of institutional weakness and content themselves with far from definitive tests of their clients' condition

* The author is James F. Cleary, professor in finance at Boston College. For helpful comments on an earlier draft of this chapter, he wishes to thank Richard Aspinwall, Al Burger, Andrew Chen, Paul Chiu, George Kaufman, Marvin Phaup, Joseph Sinkey, and Larry Wall.

are like doctors who satisfy themselves with superficial tests and treatments. Doctors should find out precisely what's wrong with their patients and treat diseased parties in the best way possible.

In the same vein, the range of actual and proposed regulatory and supervisory reforms can be thought of as prescriptions that have been based on inadequate diagnoses (i.e., superficial theories) of what fundamentally ails taxpayers and insured institutions. Reforms enacted so far fall far short of the therapies that promise to be most effective in the long run. Far from mixing the medicines the financial system needs, authorities have dosed us with palliatives (substances that only treat symptoms) and placebos (substances known to have no pharmacological effect but given to placate a patient who feels a need for medicine). The danger of turning to counterfeit and incomplete programs of therapy is that inadequate treatments may allow irreversible deterioration to develop and even engender irreversible resistance to genuine healing agents.

Incentive conflict inherent in political and bureaucratic environments disposes government-managed deposit-insurance systems toward inefficient monitoring and loss-control policies. In government enterprises, incentive conflict is reinforced by U.S. labor and financial markets' limited capacity to monitor and discipline the actions of elected and appointed officials.

These problems suggest the value of jettisoning government deposit insurance. However, analyses of political and bureaucratic incentives suggest that elimination is not truly a feasible course of action. Even in the absence of an explicit system of guarantees, incumbent politicians and top government regulators would continue to find it in their career and reputational interests to forbear from distributing losses promptly when important deposit institutions or deposit-institution sectors fall into trouble.

To improve the economic efficiency of decision making in deposit insurance or indeed any government enterprise, society can take either or both of two complementary approaches. On the one hand, managers of government firms can be made subject to statutory restraints that oblige them to calculate market signals and respond to them appropriately. On the other hand, the enterprise itself can be privatized to some degree. In this context, privatization can mean "any loosening of government controls, including the sale of a minority interest in a state-owned enterprise to private buyers, the delegation of management responsibility for a state-owned enterprise to private managers, and even the relaxation of a state monopoly to allow private entry into the market" (Vernon, 1988, p. 2).

Lessening incentive conflicts that foster inefficiencies entails making government decision-makers more accountable for measuring, pricing, and managing the value of implicit and explicit federal guarantees. This chapter seeks to explain the types of ethical constraints and patterns of privatization that might best increase the efficiency and fairness of federal deposit insurance.

It is easy to show that the statutory restraints and penalties needed to establish accountability directly are much more extensive than authorities have so far proved willing to contemplate (Kane, 1991b). The reluctance of managers to expose themselves to tough ethical reforms suggests that reformers would do well to focus on possibilities for privatizing loss-control decisions.

Privatization can serve both as a check on the quality of official supervision and as a source of complementary loss control. Obtaining these effects does not require that the private guarantor or "surety" accept the same loss exposures as the government enterprise (Kane, 1992). This is because anytime that poor or self-interested loss management allows a *private* guarantor's particular loss exposure to overrun its gross reserves, corrective forces come into play. First, returns exist that can be realized by private parties who ferret out and act upon information showing that the surety's guarantees have become less credible. The decline in credibility decreases the demand for the surety's services and increases the regulatory scrutiny it must face. Second, the increase in expected losses and fall in demand reduce the surety's current and projected earnings and depress the market value of the surety's stock and outstanding guarantees. This creates pressure for stockholders and creditors to press for better management and for outside firms to see the surety as an attractive takeover target.

The chapter concludes by summarizing from Kane (1992) a discussion of what classes of private risk-takers and risk-sharing provisions might be able to transmit appropriate market discipline at minimum cost. A tiered system of explicit private and government guarantees and loss control is recommended both to accomplish this task and as a way to depoliticize decisions about whether or not to extend expanded powers to federally insured institutions.

Decomposing Deposit Insurance into Six Component Subsystems[1]

Portraying the deposit-insurance problem as a disease suggests viewing a deposit-insurance fund as an organism whose overall health net value depends on the functioning of a series of interacting subsystems. Each subsystem is dedicated to organizing a set of activities vital to the fund's health. Regarding deposit insurance as a diseased entity implies the need to identify the most troubled subsystems and to treat them in an effective way.

In deposit insurance, six vital subsystems may be distinguished: the information, monitoring, enforcement, pricing, funding, and incentive subsystems. Political debate has focused predominantly on making technical adjustments in the monitoring, pricing, and enforcement subsystems. It has done this even though the system's long-run weaknesses trace predominantly to problems in the information, funding, and incentive subsystems (Kane, 1991a).

The information subsystem establishes methods of defining and measuring the fund's loss exposure in client institutions. The methods used are (1) itemization principles that differ in their inclusiveness, (2) valuation principles that are divorced to some extent from the economic realities of the marketplace, and (3) features that require or encourage the *nondisclosure* of information on an institution's supervisory rating and the date of the examination in which that rating was assessed. Accountability for deposit-insurance losses would be improved greatly if a market-value accounting of all sources of client value were required and if examination ratings were recorded in large characters on the FDIC-insured decals that deposit institutions display.

The funding subsystem includes provisions that seek to measure and reserve only partially for the risk that insured institutions pass through to the taxpayer. In evaluating the funding subsystem, the major issues are the ultimate source of the funds whose use is being transferred to the fund and how much net worth (if any) these transfers truly inject into the fund's balance sheet. Every banker knows that no amount of borrowings can raise the net worth of a troubled entity. Borrowing merely raises assets and liabilities in equal degrees.

The incentive subsystem comprises the structure of net rewards that decision makers reap from adopting alternative courses of action. The fundamental source of taxpayer losses in deposit insurance is not any defect in the structure of the risk-management controls that have been written into deposit-insurance contracts. The critical defects lie instead in incentive conflicts that—in tough times and tough cases—lead government officials *not to enforce* the underwriting standards, coverage limitations, and takeover rights that are already included in existing contracts.

The Source of the Deposit-Insurance Mess

In November 1991, the Federal Deposit Insurance Corporation Improvement Act (FDICIA) introduced some notable changes in the structure of the regulatory bureaucracy and in the powers the restructured bureaucracy can wield. In the main, these and similar changes in structural details enacted in the Financial Institutions Reform Recovery and Enforcement Act of 1989 (FIRREA) serve to distract the press and the public from the need to strengthen officials' will to regulate.

Persistent weaknesses in a policymaking environment constitute evidence that elected politicians receive payoffs from assigning to government regulatory enterprises a combination of inadequate financial resources and policy weapons. The roots of the still-spreading deposit-insurance mess lie in longstanding defects in political and bureaucratic accountability. The overriding problem is that the short horizons and narrow career and reputational interests of responsible politicians and bureaucrats makes denying or covering up evidence of insurance-fund weakness and engaging in regulatory forbearance a rational response to the emergence of widespread industry insolvency. It pays politicians to work behind the scenes for lenient treatment of their troubled constituents. It pays regulators to use their discretion to conceal emerging problems (e.g., in the Bank Insurance Fund) and to postpone what look to be painful adjustments until a successor's watch. This strategy of concealment and deferral is attractive because broadcast journalists and the press routinely mismonitor the performance of federal regulators. As a result, the public fails to grasp the tradeoffs between short-run and long-run costs and benefits inherent in the decisions regulators make. Voters blame officials disproportionately for the particular problems that happen to surface while they are in office and tend not to penalize authorities for the anticipatable future damage that they create when they adopt short-sighted policies.

The resulting incentive subsystem confronts authorities with a painful tradeoff—between scrupulously protecting the economic interests of general taxpayers and avoiding the reputational and career damage apt to follow from incurring the displeasure of politically strong regulatory clients and their political allies. For this tradeoff to be made more favorable to general taxpayers, political-bureaucratic incentives must be totally reworked. Markets must be made to reward rather than punish whistleblowers, and taxpayers must require politicians and deposit-insurance officials to surrender the discretion they now enjoy with respect to the information they choose to report and the forbearances they choose to give.

Popular debate on the deposit-insurance mess concerns itself more with shifting blame to designated scapegoats than it does with designing a better financial system. It is no accident that blame for the debacle is hard to pin down. Deposit-institution regulatory officials have been allowed to fashion and publicize misleading indices of the quality of their own performance. The fundamental weakness in deposit insurance and banking regulation is the absence of timely accountability for losses that accrue to taxpayers from governmental acts of financial misregulation.

For two and a half decades, top regulatory officials, deposit-institution trade associations, and selected politicians have cooperated in denying and covering up the size of the industry's and insurers' growing capital shortage. They have done this primarily in two ways. First, they have used or authorized accounting options that conceal weaknesses by delaying the accounting realization of developing losses. Second, they have labored to mischaracterize and discredit the honest efforts of outside critics to measure realistically the net reserve position of the federal deposit-insurance funds.

The same mistakes that ruined FSLIC are being repeated today by FDIC officials who run the bank insurance fund (BIF). The FDIC leadership has adopted the same costly strategy of officially understating the extent of their fund's growing financial weakness by routinely suppressing unfavorable information on the BIF's loss exposure, granting accounting and regulatory forbearances to decapitalized client firms, throwing its weight behind counterfeit schemes for "recapitalizing" the fund with borrowed money, and supporting the extension of inadequately supervised new powers to members of its client base.

This cosmetic strategy protects the reputations of sitting politicians and regulators from immediate criticism. However, because it breaks faith with taxpayers, in the long run it exposes successor officials to considerable taxpayer anger—particularly members of Congress and especially the members of its banking committees.

Among the strongest examples of faith-breaking behavior to come out of the FSLIC debacle are House Speaker James Wright's publicly documented efforts to prevent the closure of a series of deeply insolvent Texas thrifts and the success that the owner of Lincoln Savings and Loan met in persuading five senators to lobby the Federal Home Loan Bank Board (FHLBB) to shift it off the Federal Home Loan Bank of San Francisco's case load when it was moving to close it down. It is disheartening that allegedly corrective post-1989 legislation, which increased penalties for fraud and fiduciary violations for managers of federally insured entities, include no penalties for fiduciary violations by federal regulators or elected officials. Legislation is needed to designate it a crime for a regulator to choose not to reserve for readily appraisable losses, to use smoke-and-mirrors accounting to cover up inadequacies in its own bureaucratic performance, and to sell out broad taxpayer interests in response to narrow political pressure.

Most politicians and regulators claim to have been blindsided by the expanding costs of deposit-insurance subsidies to risk-taking. If their claim is true, officials' repeated propensity to overlook developing evidence testifies to an insensitivity to their duty to analyze and clarify the long-run consequences of the policies they accept. What is most disturbing about this insensitivity is that it suggests the exists a systematic anesthetization of official consciences to the moral dimensions of the tradeoffs that political pressure leads them to foist on underinformed taxpayers. In choosing not to reserve fully for appraisable or de facto losses that were plainly developing in decapitalized clients, FSLIC and BIF officials strengthened the deposit-institution industry's capacity to lobby against more-effective premium structures and regulatory frameworks. Underreporting loss exposures has meant that options for delaying the recording of client losses in official accounting records have had to be played out before regulators could move to bring troubled institutions under control.

Ethical Incentive Reform as Accountability Reform

During a 1991 police sting operation using a hidden camera, an Arizona legislator was taped making the following statement to a lobbyist seeking to purchase his vote: "There isn't an issue in the world I give a shit about. I do deals." Just in case the lobbyist might miss what he was driving at, this same legislator went on to clarify that the most important feature of a deal was "what's in it for me."

Such amoral influence-peddling is disturbing, but the work of even the most conscientious legislator involves cutting deals with interested parties. By understanding the desires of the various bargainers, they can negotiate a middleground position that all parties can live with.

FDICIA puts the onus for avoiding future acts of misregulation squarely on the regulators. Its weakness is that it fails to constrain important conflicts of interest: keeping open options for regulators to misinform the public about the quality of their current and cumulative performances and for Congress and the president to mediate perversely between bankers and regulators. While formally espousing mandatory early intervention, FDICIA effectively preserves officials' dangerous discretion to misdesign regulatory triggers and responses.

FDICIA does enhance the position of the taxpayer in three ways: by improving the information subsystem by pushing regulators toward using market valuations and tangible itemization standards; by monitoring and enforcing through annual exams, early intervention and limitations on paying off uninsured depositors in insolvency resolutions; and by making deposit-insurance pricing risk-sensitive and improving fund capitalization by strengthening coverage limitations and risk-based capital requirements.

While each of these actions promotes greater long-run efficiency, FDICIA fails to address a stressed regulator's incentive to misregulate. Full accountability requires additional accounting, funding, ethical, and campaign-financing reforms. Missing are arrangements for quickly and reliably repairing future deficiencies in deposit-insurance reserves as they rise and for establishing timely budgetary responsibility for the implicit and explicit financial implications of subsystem adjustments as they are made. FDICIA imposes a formal obligation on the FDIC to intervene strongly and predictably into the affairs of every capital-deficient firm before exhaustion of the market value of its capital becomes a serious threat. But the act leaves it to conflicted regulators to develop specific intervention criteria. Without incentive reform, it is unlikely that these criteria will evolve into reproducible and nondiscretionary tests. To an important extent, authorities remain free to tailor specific regulatory penalties to individual situations. As the February 1992 CrossLand Savings Bank nationalization attests, the FDIC's right to extend unlimited insurance coverage after the fact to the formally uninsured obligations of a failing client has been abridged but not eliminated. The specific limits imposed on covering insured balances are based on flexible least-cost calculations that appear not have to pass a publicly reproducible "smell" test. Although the U.S. General Accounting Office (1992) has criticized the incompleteness of the particular calculations documented in the CrossLand case, the dispute indicates that FDIC analysis of whatever calculations are made by its staff can be manipulated adversely to taxpayers' economic interests when political or career pressures make this desirable.

Deposit insurance losses cannot be traced to technical ignorance about how to design a workable insurance contract. The problem lies in the selective and repeated nonenforcement of key contract provisions that a private surety would want to enforce. Taxpayer losses are rooted in unresolved and intolerable conflicts of interest between government officials and taxpayers that support inefficient regulatory forbearances. These conflicts are the source of the structural weaknesses that have transformed federal deposit insurance into a disaster area.

To establish genuine accountability for deposit-insurance loss exposures, the first step is to improve insurers' cost efficiency by perfecting the timeliness of the way that outside monitoring and budget discipline impact on the enterprise. To align regulatory incentives more closely with the interests of taxpayers, the key step is to improve the monitoring capability of the press by developing workable measures of the implicit and explicit budgetary implications of deposit-insurance decisions at the time they are being made.

BIF is traveling the same ruts in the road to financial disaster the FSLIC traveled earlier. FSLIC was allowed to understate the value of contingent assistance to acquirers of failing thrifts and to neglect the value of tax forgivenesses and regulatory forbearances in its purchase-and-assumption transactions. Today, the Congressional Budget Office, Office of Management and Budget, and the General Accounting Office are challenging the FDIC to report its loss exposures more accurately. Nevertheless, BIF is being valued by costing out selected near-term "failures" rather than by costing out what taxpayers would have to pay an efficient private entity to take its net loss exposure from current and anticipated insolvencies off taxpayer hands.

The FDIC and its top officials have been set up to serve as scapegoats for the next disaster. In 1989, the president and Congress underfunded the Resolution Trust Corporation and loaded it and other enormous administrative burdens onto an already overstretched FDIC. In 1991, Congress and the president increased the FDIC's borrowing authority. But they are still not giving the agency the funds it needs to clean up the RTC's problems or to restore BIF's net worth on a fully reserved basis. As long as the extent of the FDIC's capital shortage remains understated, federal officials' fundamental incentive conflicts are severe.

These incentive conflicts tempt politicians and regulators to cover up and to defer accounting recognition of deposit-insurance losses. This is done with contorted refinancing schemes, lenient supervision, and de facto nationalizations of troubled banks and assets. To establish incentives for regulators and politicians to function more steadfastly in the taxpayer's interest requires a new incentive subsystem for banking regulators and politicians.

Accountability for regulatory performance must begin with accurate information. Throughout the mess, authorities have shown a propensity for blocking the flow of unfavorable information. Legislation is needed to assure the timeliness and accuracy of information supplied by managers of insured institutions, managers of deposit insurance funds, and incumbent politicians. Reform must reduce the scope for coverups. The most straightforward path for removing potential blockages from the information flow is to impose self-reporting obligations and comprehensive market-value accounting principles on regulators and insured institutions to force them to measure their performance and loss exposure as accurately as they can. This entails penalizing parties who can be shown even after they leave office to have willfully provided less than their best estimate of their enterprise's market value.

These accounting reforms have two advantages: (1) they would help to clarify the capitalized cost to taxpayers of politicians' choosing to pressure regulators to allow insolvent deposit institutions to stay in operation; and (2) they would assist the press to help voters to assign blame for future messes by limiting incumbent politicians' opportunities to claim ignorance of the long-term consequences of ruinous policies.

However, merely developing better information is not enough. To reduce the scope for official procrastination, we must also introduce a series of "action-forcing rules." These new rules must redefine and penalize *dereliction of duty* at all levels. It is necessary to specify the ethical duties of federal officials far more completely. At a minimum, we must

1. require FDIC managers to recapitalize their insurance funds promptly (i.e., according to a prespecified timetable) whenever the market value of their loss exposure increases;
2. require deposit-insurance losses to be passed through the federal budget as they accrue:
3. lessen the advantages of incumbency to strengthen electoral challenges of unsatisfactory congressional performers. My specific plan requires all incumbent members of Congress to transfer half of the campaign contributions they receive to their party to be used in other electoral districts to fund campaigns by challengers of incumbents of the opposite party. Besides making elections more competitive, the plan provides prosecutable temptations to cheat that will selectively establish term limits for the most venal members of Congress.
4. require members of Congress and the administration
   (a) to set explicit limits on their ability to intervene ethically into the process of closing individual institutions;
   (b) to report all interventions to congressional banking and ethics committees for explicit review;
   (c) to subject committee reviews (such as the Senate ethics committee's cynical whitewash of all but one of the Keating Five) to regular evaluation by "disinterested" outside experts.

The Alternative of Privatization

The political difficulty of enacting these direct incentive reforms is as obvious as it is disheartening. The unlikelihood of enacting these reforms testifies to the depth and stubbornness of the accountability problem in U.S. public life. Whether adequate ethical reform will ever seem desirable to officials depends on the electorate's willingness to face the country's deepseated governmental failures and during next few elections to penalize appropriate incumbents for deferring treatment of urgent problems such as the S&L and BIF messes.

An alternative approach is to develop loss-sharing arrangements that reassign responsibility for making the monitoring and proactive decisions necessary to control deposit-insurance losses to the private sector. The idea is to create loss-sharing private parties who will have both reason and opportunity to ensure that government officials do not let deposit-institution managers expose them to unreasonable risks. This chapter argues that the most effective private parties would be institutional "sureties" that would agree to coinsure in every institutional failure the first X dollars of loss that federal deposit insurance underwrites. These sureties would overcome political and bureaucratic blockages in critical information flows and loss-control actions by developing their own examination and police forces.

For government managers, existing opportunities to defer the treatment of emerging risks are reinforced by their access to hidden (i.e., "implicit") sources of financing that allow an agency to produce credible financial guarantees at virtually zero cost to itself. On the funding side, conjectural or actual taxpayer backup gives a governmental deposit insurer implicit resources that far exceed its accumulated fund of explicit reserves. The value of taxpayer backup is confirmed by the vast amount of unfunded guarantees that an explicitly insolvent FSLIC was able to issue before its demise. As long as market participants trust in the breadth and depth of this backup, inadequacies either in a federal insurer's loss-control system or in the explicit value of its net reserves need not lessen the market value of the bonding services it supplies.

In contrast, private sureties have limited opportunities to defer the treatment of emerging problems. As recent experience in Ohio, Maryland, and Rhode Island shows, whenever poor or self-interested management allows a private surety's loss exposure to begin to overwhelm its gross reserves, two corrective forces come into play. First, the surety's guarantees become increasingly less credible. This causes the demand for its services to fall. It also increases the intensity of the regulatory scrutiny it receives from private rating agencies and state insurance commissioners. Second, since a fall in demand makes the surety's earnings decline, the market values of the surety's stock and outstanding guarantees decrease also. The decline in stock price creates pressure for the corporation's stockholders and creditors to press for better management and for outside parties to take over the firm either to liquidate it or to manage its affairs more effectively. It is important to see that, in informationally efficient financial markets, these forces would exert themselves irrespective of accounting tricks that permit the managers of a private surety to keep their firm's financial weakness from being formally reported in its balance sheets and income statements.

Under current arrangements, government and industry disinformation about the extent of a federal deposit insurer's loss exposure is not directly and routinely tested by the marketplace. Authorities have lessened their exposure to customer, creditor, and taxpayer discipline by leaving incomplete the linkage between the market for their credit-enhancement services and markets for financing their liabilities. When managers of a troubled government deposit insurer decide not to acknowledge developing financial weakness in their public reports, taxpayers-creditors fail to receive a clear signal that a managerial breakdown is under way. Even though sophisticated investors could discern an opportunity for profitably installing a better risk-management system, the absence of a stock market for federal deposit-insurance enterprises prevents them from mounting a takeover bid.

Choosing Efficiently Among Alternative Loss-Sharing Private Parties

There are five proximate targets for risk-sharing provisions:

1. *Depositors and other creditors:* As underscored by authorities' use of too-big-to-fail and systemic-risk loopholes, this form of risk sharing requires effective limitations on the extent to which nominally uninsured and subordinated debt or deposit contracts are themselves informally guaranteed against loss;
2. *Stockholders (or mutual stakeholders) of individual depositories:* This form of risk sharing focuses on providing extended liability for deposit-institution stockholders or assuring that authorities administer genuinely risk-based capital requirements;
3. *Outside consultants and members of each institution's board of directors:* This form of risk sharing seeks to extend the civil liability of advisors and individual directors for losses suffered by federal insurers;
4. *Stockholders (or mutual stakeholders) in the industry as a whole:* This form of risk sharing involves the use of prepaid or contingent cross-guarantees of insolvency losses by members of the industry

being insured. As illustrated by programs for guaranteeing insurance liabilities both in Canada and in individual U.S. states, cross-
guarantees ordinarily set strict limits on each participant's maximum
liability;
5. *Private sureties:* This form of risk sharing functions through coinsurance and reinsurance contracts that assign responsibility for specific
   coverages to nongovernmental insurers.

To choose an optimal combination of risk bearers, the relative economic
efficiency of alternative ways to shift federal risks to these private parties
must be evaluated. A risk-shifting provision may be deemed maximally
efficient if it promises to transmit appropriate market discipline at minimum cost. To judge efficiency, two questions must be addressed: (1) the
timeliness and reliability of the discipline generated and (2) the political
obstacles and economic costs apt to be encountered in enforcing and
negotiating the contractual arrangement.

Differences in the Timeliness and Reliability of Discipline from Alternative Parties

An outside party's ability to provide appropriate discipline is a function
of its ability to identify, measure, and control deposit-institution risk taking.
Monitoring is difficult because individual deposit institutions are "informationally opaque" entities. To identify and measure changes in risk exposure caused by managerial decisions, an outside party must be able to
persuade institutional managers to open their books in ever-changing and
nonstandard ways. To avoid unnecessary disruption, the party must also
possess the expertise and contractual power to control at low cost any
inappropriate risk taking it happens to observe. In what follows, we discuss differences in how well alternative parties might perform these
functions.

Depositors and Other Creditors.   Small depositors (those whose account
holdings aggregate less than $10,000) score poorly on all counts. Provid-
ing them timely access to relevant information is costly, and they lack the
expertise and range of contractual controls to respond efficiently in any
case. Their principal loss-control tool is to move withdrawable deposits
to a safer haven. A widely used loss-control technique is to use political
pressure in the event of loss to entice regulators or elected politicians to

release them from the contractual obligations they had previously assumed. These loss-control responses impose substantial costs on taxpayers, depositors, and institutions alike. To avoid these costs, it is reasonable to promise full coverage for small account holders and to allocate residual risk to parties that can monitor, absorb, and discipline risks more efficiently.

More attractive risk-bearing candidates are larger depositors and nondeposit creditors whose claims can be formally subordinated to those of depositors. From a contract-enforcement perspective, these parties may be presumed to be more sophisticated and better motivated to negotiate information flows and risk-control safeguards with depository firms. This makes it reasonable for insurers to promote the use of subordinated debt (Benston et al., 1986; Wall, 1989) and to graduate or eliminate coverage once a depositor's balance rises above a critical level. However, uninsured depositors can limit their losses by borrowing against their deposits or by shifting their funds out of a troubled institution before regulators act to close it. In similar fashion, subordinated debtholders can seek to exploit a troubled institution's inevitable violations of the debt's package of protective covenants either to accelerate their repayment schedule or to develop a more fully collateralized position. These avoidance opportunities complicate the task of enforcing the formal schedule of participation, particularly when political realities make it hard for insurers to assert their loss-sharing rights promptly or fully.

The stronger the opportunities by which a loss-sharing creditor can tempt government officials not to enforce loss-participation provisions, the less reliably contractual provisions actually shift risk to that party. Wall's ingenious proposal (1989) to require banks to issue "puttable" (i.e., instantly redeemable) subordinated debt confronts this problem squarely. It requires that federally insured institutions maintain a minimum amount of redeemable subordinated debt and that redemptions of its debt be suspended whenever the resulting outflow of funds would put an institution in violation of regulatory standards. After 90 days in suspension, any institution that did not succeed in strengthening itself sufficiently to comply with regulatory standards would be deemed insolvent and closed.

What I see as the weakness in this scheme is that government officials would retain responsibility for monitoring the condition of individual banks and for blowing the whistle on violations of regulatory standards. As under current arrangements, influence peddling or threats of highly visible runs by subordinated debt holders that might engender multiple suspensions could tempt officials to delay the release of unfavorable information to holders of subordinated debt or in other ways to monitor and enforce regulatory standards too loosely. This temptation would allow subordinated debt holders to anticipate laying a claim to implicit federal guarantees in at least some states of the world.

Whenever forbearance or administrative lags delay a bank's closure long enough for subordinated debtholders to face net losses, we must expect debtholders to play upon public sympathies. In the past, government officials have often decided to back off from fully enforcing the loss-participation provisions applicable to uninsured creditors. They defend this option as a way to control systemic risk (Corrigan, 1991), but it is clearly also a way of reducing the exposure to outside criticism that they and their bureaucratic enterprise face.

It is hard to enforce loss sharing if it can be established that federal regulators negligently failed to prevent the risk-sharing party from being misled about its true exposure to loss. The more credibly a case for regulatory negligence can be built after the fact, the weaker the incentive for any class of uninsured creditor to act as a source of effective market discipline.

Stockholders, Directors, and Other Institution-Affiliated Parties. Because an institution's stockholders, directors, attorneys, and consultants may be construed to be insiders that have "volunteered" for their risk-bearing responsibilities, in the event of a failure it is hard for them to marshal much public sympathy for their cause. Their principal loss-control tools consist of behind-the-scenes activity: (1) taking advantage of the dictates of limited liability and protections provided by bankruptcy law to insulate their wealth from being taken from them if their institution fails and (2) wielding political and clientele pressure to soften the nature of the loss-control measures that regulators choose to direct against a firm when it is struggling to survive. As illustrated in the pattern of charges filed against the infamous thrift mogul, Charles Keating, these activities are mutually reinforcing in that using pressure to buy time supports the use of the time gained to transform corporate funds into assets that pass into the putative risk-bearer's direct control.

For directors and consultants, liability for deposit-institution losses cannot fairly be expanded without first carefully defining each party's specific fiduciary duties to federal deposit insurers. Then, to ensure collectability, reliable methods are needed for bonding the obligations being nominally imposed. These difficulties underscore that efforts to use supervisory enforcement powers to impose loss participation on institutional insiders transform themselves into a need to clarify covered responsibilities and to establish a system of monitoring and loss management by institutions that underwrite the various bonds.

Intraindustry and Other Private Reinsurers. Efficiently extending the scope of private deposit-insurance activity is not as easy a task as proponents of privatization such as Ely (1986) and Wallison (1990) suggest. Attempts to allocate specific tiers of residual risk in deposit-institution insolvencies to creditors, stockholders, directors, or other insiders transform the discipline problem without truly resolving it. These potential risk bearers have hard-to-control opportunities to engage in countervailing action specifically designed to render, in the event of loss, much of their risk-sharing obligations costly (if not impossible) for government officials to collect.

To shift completely a tier of insolvency risk to the private sector, the would-be risk-bearing party must pass two tests. First, it must be well-positioned to engage in proactive risk-assessment and loss-control activities. Second, it must be poorly positioned to use political pressure to shift developing losses to federal taxpayers.

The near-absence of private underwriters from deposit insurance today should not be interpreted as evidence of an unconditional disinterest in underwriting deposit-institution risk. Over the years, below-cost pricing of federal deposit insurers has limited private entry by preventing private capital from being able to project coinsurance and reinsurance profits. Deposit institutions and insurance companies will participate in these markets if and only if they can confidently project a fair market return on their investment in associated facilities. This cannot be done as long as critical monitoring, pricing and loss-management decisions are assigned to conflicted government managers. Profitable operation requires politicians and federal deposit insurers to delegate substantial pricing, monitoring, and loss-control powers to private sureties.

In turn, to make this delegation reasonable to authorities, each surety will have to open its books and loss-control programs to close and continual monitoring by the federal insurer. Nevertheless, federal oversight need not place much additional burden on private sureties. Much of the information federal regulators require is already being produced by private rating agencies and state insurance commissioners, whose task has always been to ensure the ongoing credibility of individual companies' insurance and bonding services.

In any case, loss sharing cannot succeed if federal regulation of sureties becomes onerous enough to eliminate bonding profits. The cost of fully collateralizing an insurer's maximum loss exposure threatens, for example, to scuttle the otherwise exemplary plan proposed by Baer (1985). Projectable future coinsurance or bonding profits—and not accounting measures of accumulated deposit-institution and insurance-company net worth—are the proper measure of the private financial industry's capacity for coinsuring deposit-insurance losses. In the absence of bonding profits, how large a financial industry's accumulated capital happens to be becomes irrelevant. Any industry will resist attempts to expropriate its capital to underwrite an unprofitable program.

Federal politicians and regulators must be able to perceive net benefits for themselves and taxpayers as well. Understandably, they are not going to cede turf to private decision makers until they can be made confident that the concessions made will not return to damage their careers and reputations.

A Six-Part Plan for Tiering Government and Private Bonding Activity

Capital markets impose on private sureties incentives to optimize their loss-control systems and bonding prices. But formally privatizing deposit insurance is not enough to restore societywide compatibility among the incentives of depositors, financial institutions, sureties, and taxpayers.

First, market participants may reasonably expect the government to bail out private sureties after the fact if and when they become insolvent. Second, to the extent that market participants expect the government to bail out uninsured financial intermediaries in the event of widespread weakness, the rigor of private surety operations would tend to encourage an inefficient expansion of uninsured financial-services firms. Third, society might worry that lack of competition in the private market for loss-sharing services could lead to collusion and cartel pricing that would dictate a socially suboptimal use of bonding services.

A straightforward way to control the costs of residual government bailouts and to guard against collusive pricing is to set up an explicit system of tiered private and government guarantees. With minimal disruption to depositors, federal deposit-insurance coverages could be rewritten to make private companies responsible for bonding the first dollars of specific tiers or categories of depositor losses in any deposit-institution insolvency (Scott and Mayer, 1971, p. 575). The plan could allow depositors to be covered de jure as fully as they wish but would require private corporations to underwrite a scheduled percentage of all bonding losses incurred.

An important consequence of the reform would be to work out in private markets economically rational patterns of monitoring, deductibles, and coverage limits and to fashion a workable definition of a deposit-insurance "catastrophe" as the possibility that private sureties could not cover their obligations. The formal and informal federal coverages in place now have little to recommend them. Nevertheless, the current de jure coverage pattern could be preserved by dictating that private coverage rise to 100 percent for account-holder balances up to $100,000. Current de facto patterns of too-big-to-fail coverage could be reproduced by letting the schedule of private participation vary with indices of an institution's asset size and political importance.

The primary goal is to make the loss control system respond more efficiently to changes in the financial environment. This can be done by transferring out of government hands day-to-day responsibility both for pricing guarantee services and for enforcing the spirit of ethical, capital, range-of activity, and competency restraints that constitute bonding safeguards.

Here are the broad outlines of a plan that could accomplish this task:

1. Every federally insured deposit institution would be required by law to carry private insurance with an authorized private carrier that would be free to set their own premiums. For each class of deposit institution, prudential requirements for capital and management necessary to qualify as an authorized carrier would be established, supervised, and enforced by the secondary federal insurer designated for institutions of that class. Federally *un*insured institutions could exist as state-chartered institutions, but once insured an institution could not convert to uninsured status without paying off all outstanding depositors and funding itself afresh.

2. Insured deposit institutions would be free to strengthen themselves by offering any innovative service or product that their authorized carrier proved willing to underwrite.

3. In the event that no authorized carrier is willing to renew an institution's insurance coverage, the institution would either have to adjust its risk exposure to regain insurability, to convert itself to uninsured status, or to permit itself to be declared insolvent by its chartering authority (Baer, 1985).

4. To simplify the tasks of federal screening and oversight, authorized carriers would have to be organized as a single-line surety, managed and capitalized separately from any affiliated firm. Whether organized as mutual or stock companies or even as spread-loss pools,[2] private sureties would be free to enter this line if and only if they met the prudential requirements established by the appropriate federal insurers.

5. Subsequent to entry, each secondary federal insurer would be

responsible for monitoring and policing the financial condition and loss-control policies of all authorized private insurers that fall in its purview. In effect, monitoring and loss-control services currently produced within the federal insurance bureaucracy would be *outsourced* to private supervisors. As under current arrangements, top managers of each federal insurer would be responsible for pricing and managing the catastrophic risk this scheme assigns to them. But public accountability for these responsibilities would be easier to establish. It would be enough for each insurer to face two specific requirements: to prepare and to publicize reproducible estimates of the evolving loss exposure of its own insurance fund and to recapitalize this fund promptly whenever its estimated net reserves slipped below an adequate level.

6. This plan envisages the discipline of potential entry into the surety industry as establishing a useful supplement to policyholder and stockholder pressure. Still, because of the fixed cost of training a loss-control police force and the advantages of spreading a surety's risk across a large segment of the industry, it is likely that only a small number of private sureties would actively offer deposit insurance at any time. To provide additional short-run flexibility, any surety that is organized as a mutual would have to be accountable democratically to client policyholders for its coverage strategies and loss-control decisions. For both mutual and stock sureties, policyholder committees ought to be empowered to review and to challenge management decisions about what potential product-line expansions should and should not be underwritten by the industry's private sureties.

This six-part scheme would expand the market for private bonding services and push the monitoring and rulemaking responsibilities of federal sureties back a step. It would shift government attention away from examining and supervising deposit institutions and refocus it onto appraising the consequences for taxpayers of the risk-management safeguards and funding activities that are undertaken by the private sureties responsible for absorbing the private tier of bonding losses. Although subject to government review and oversight, private risk-management rules and procedures aimed at controlling deposit-institution losses could not be quietly and selectively forced into suspension by hidden political pressure. Applicable safeguards would be renegotiated adaptively in a less politicized forum and would be subjected to the discipline of both the market for guarantee services and markets for the securities of surety firms.

From the taxpayer's point of view, requiring federal insurers to coinsure their loss exposures with private sureties is a way simultaneously to generate efficient limits on accountholder coverages and to make these limits more enforceable. Transferring responsibility for absorbing federally uninsured losses to specialized firms would let federal coverage limits exert improved market discipline and would render these limits harder to challenge politically. Market discipline would be improved because private sureties would be better-equipped and better-motivated than individual depositors, government supervisors, and competing institutions to monitor and discipline institutional and governmental risk-taking. Potential disciplinary actions include price and coverage adjustments, contractually established penalties, activity adjustments, and cancellation privileges. By item 3 of the tiering plan, cancellation would require a recalcitrant firm to qualify itself for coverage with another surety or be declared insolvent.

Coverage limits would be more enforceable in the event of a client institution's insolvency because the financial sophistication of private sureties would make it hard to build a politically persuasive case for bailing them out of losses to which they had deliberately contracted to expose themselves. Assigning a federally uninsured portion of depositor losses to private bonding companies would recruit a tiered risk-management and problem-resolution "police force" from the private and government sectors. Lack of timely and accurate accountability for losses has been a major problem with government deposit-insurance schemes. In turn, weaknesses in enforcement powers and in reserve availability have plagued private schemes (Calomiris, 1992; Kane, 1991). The aim of adopting a hybrid system of tiered regulation is to overcome authorities' demonstrated unwillingness to make themselves truly accountable for the forbearances they provide troubled financial firms. While a number of details remain to be worked out, the broad promise of the scheme is clear: to combine efficiently the greater accountability and timeliness that are characteristic of private responses with the deep pockets and strong legal empowerments possessed by a government agency.

What Are We Waiting For?

The strongest evidence for the incentive-conflict theory of deposit-insurance losses comes from the repetitive and secularly escalating nature of the mess. Like dirty laundry moldering under a teenager's bed, regulatory malpractice has produced a growing stink.

Regulatory forbearance constitutes an anti-exit policy that in preserving preexisting bureaucratic empires severely distorts the equilibrium market structure of financial-services competition. What ought to be a pattern of small and frequent losses for private stakeholders in deposit institutions is transformed into an exposure of federal taxpayers to infrequent but catastrophic losses.

To cure taxpayer loss exposure in the long run requires a major reworking of the incentives deposit-insurance officials face. Whether this is to be accomplished through ethical reform or privatization, it is past time to start the process.

Notes

1. The next three sections adapt analysis previously presented in Kane (1991b).
2. Spread-loss pools are modeled on the self-insurance schemes adopted in early Italian maritime insurance. Members contribute a pool of reserves in advance and face no obligation to cover losses that exceed this pool. Pool administrators are responsible to members for policing risks and for risk-rating member contributions.

References

Adams, James Ring, *The Big Fix: Inside the S&L Scandal*, New York: John Wiley & Sons, 1990.

Baer, Herbert, "Private Prices, Public Insurance: The Pricing of Federal Deposit Insurance," *Economic Perspectives*, Federal Reserve Bank of Chicago (September-October), 1990, pp. 45–57.

Benston, George, Robert Eisenbeis, Paul Horvitz, Edward Kane, and George Kaufman, *Perspectives on Safe and Sound Banking: Past, Present, and Future*, Cambridge, Mass.: American Bankers Association and MIT Press, 1986.

Calomiris, Charles W., "Getting the Incentives Right in the Current Deposit Insurance System: Successes from the Pre-FDIC Era," in James R. Barth and R. Dan Brumbaugh, Jr. (eds.), *The Reform of Federal Deposit Insurance: Disciplining Government and Protecting Taxpayers*, New York: HarperCollins, 1992.

Corrigan, E. Gerald, "Statement," prepared as testimony before the U.S. Senate Committee on Banking, Housing and Urban Affairs, May 15, 1991.

Ely, Bert, "Private Sector Depositor Protection Is Still a Viable Alternative to Federal Deposit Insurance," *Issues in Bank Regulation*, Winter 1986, pp. 40–47.

Kane, Edward J., *Econometric Estimates of the 1986–1989 Time Profile of Taxpayer Losses in the S&L Insurance Mess*, with an Appendix prepared by Min-Teh Yu, Final project report, Congressional Budget Office, Washington, D.C., February 18, 1991a.

———, "Dissecting Current Legislative Proposals for Deposit Insurance Reform," in *Proceedings of the 27th Annual Conference on Bank Structure and Competition*, Chicago: Federal Reserve Bank, 1991b, pp. 126–135.

————, "Privatizing Proactive Loss-Control Decisions: Lessons from the Credit Union Movement," Published as *Deposit Insurance Reform: A Plan for the Credit Union Movement*, Madison: Center for Credit Union Research, Univ. of Wisconsin and Filene Research Institute, September, 1992.

Scott, Kenneth and Thomas Mayer, "Risk and Regulation in Banking: Some Proposals for Deposit Insurance," *Stanford Law Review*, vol. 23, May 1971, pp. 537–582.

United States General Accounting Office, *Failed Bank: FDIC Documentation of CrossLand Savings FSB, Decision Was Inadequate*, GAO/GGD-92-92, Washington, July 1992.

Vernon, Raymond (ed.), *The Promise of Privatization: A Challenge for American Foreign Policy*, New York: Council on Foreign Relations, 1988.

Wall, Larry D., "A Plan for Reducing Future Deposit Insurance Losses: Puttable Subordinated Debt," *Economic Review*, Federal Reserve Bank of Atlanta, July-August, 1989, pp. 2–17.

Wallison, Peter J., *Back from the Brink: A Practical Plan for Privatizing Deposit Insurance and Strengthening Our Banks and Thrifts*, Washington: American Enterprise Institute for Public Policy Research, 1990.

6 THE APPLICATION OF PRIVATE INSURANCE TO BANKING OVERSIGHT

Richard C. Aspinwall*

Introduction

The problems underlying deposit insurance as administered over the past 60 years are well known. First, federal deposit insurance was neither designed nor administered as insurance in the formal sense of that term. No effort has been made by the Federal Deposit Insurance Corporation (FDIC) to diversify risks. In fact, no effort has been made to ascertain what diversification would entail.

Second, until changes mandated by the Federal Deposit Insurance Corporation Improvement Act of 1991 (FDICIA), coverage was offered at uniform prices to all banks, regardless of their capital positions and regardless of the riskiness of businesses in which they are engaged. Indeed,

* An earlier version of this paper was presented at a conference on "Rebuilding Public Confidence Through Financial Reform," The Ohio State University, June 25, 1992. Comments on that version from Edward Kane and Robert Eisenbeis are gratefully acknowledged. Subsequent advice from Mary Messner also is acknowledged with thanks.

even the structure of rate premiums instituted by FDIC for 1993 reflects little evidence of risk sensitivity.

Third, FDIC has covered losses not stipulated in the insurance contract. That is, deposits above the $100,000 ceiling as well as nondeposit liabilities were made good in the past resolutions of failures. These actions were defended on the grounds that they were the "least cost" procedures, although evidence for such conclusions has never been made publicly available. In this process the Federal Reserve also played a role in encouraging the extension of assurance coverage—in particular, to the uninsured liabilities of large institutions (the "too-big-to-fail" doctrine).

Fourth, capital-impaired institutions have not been identified and action has not been taken soon enough to avoid massive losses to the insuring agency and ultimately to the public. Regulatory resistance to the discipline of market valuations in assessing capital adequacy has reflected forbearance preferences. The combination of virtually inclusive coverage and resolution delay has encouraged the weak and the risk seekers to increase risky positions (see Barth, Bartholomew, and Bradley, 1991; Congressional Budget Office, 1990).

Fifth, large amounts of recognized and potential losses to the insuring agency have caused deposit insurance premiums to be raised and a sizable coinsurance cost—also not specified in the deposit insurance contract—has been inflicted on institutions not guilty of abusing the tenets of their coverage. The issue of how to distribute the costs of cleaning up old problems is not yet resolved. Nor, for that matter, is a rational cost structure dealing with the future administration of a deposit insurance program yet in place.

Role of Private Insurance

The major shortcoming in the administration of deposit insurance in recent years has been the selective unenforcement of key insurance contract provisions. That is, conflicts of interest between government officials and ultimately taxpayers that perpetuate costly forms of regulatory forbearance have gone unresolved.

Action-forcing rules are needed to reduce the scope for official procrastination. This need was not met by FDICIA, although somewhat greater discipline was contained in that act (see Kane, June 25, 1992). Briefly, FDICIA requires that regulatory agencies (1) define capital positions in five categories, or tranches: well capitalized, adequately capitalized, undercapitalized, significantly undercapitalized, and critically undercapitalized; (2) apply more restrictive operating constraints on banks having lower capital positions in this hierarchy and also require the formulation of programs to raise new capital; and (3) take prompt corrective action—including appointment of a receiver or conservator—for those institutions falling into the critically undercapitalized category. So far, measures of capital are based on generally accepted accounting principles, not market valuations.

The primary role of private deposit insurance should be regarded as the application of market forces so as to impose credible pressures on regulatory agencies to perform promptly *their* duties. The basic objective would be to create a reputable base of sureties—that is, loss-sharing private parties. Sureties would add value to oversight of entities eligible for insurance by acting in ways necessary to ensure that government officials did not expose them to unreasonable risks. The private sureties would do this by coinsuring a portion of the first X dollars of loss underwritten by federal deposit insurance. Initially, X would be large enough to be a material exposure for participating sureties but not so large that sufficiency of reserves to be maintained against these risks would be open to question. That is, if private assets at risk are not credible—given the magnitude of the risks— privatization will not have been achieved. True risk shifting will be maximally efficient if it transmits appropriate market discipline at minimum cost. In other words, this process should be viewed as a signaling mechanism that produces timely and reliable action by regulatory authorities in the cases of capital deficiencies.

In this context, a useful distinction may be made between two-party insurance (e.g., protection against losses from casualty risks) and performance bonding. Bonding is a trilateral contract where a surety guarantees a beneficiary against loss experienced by the failure to perform on the part of a third party. Fidelity and construction-performance bonds are examples. In applications to deposit insurance, the protection would go to the depositor against nonperformance by the third-party issuer of insured deposits. Performance would take the form of maintaining not less than a stipulated minimum economic capital position (see Kane, June 27, 1992).

The conditions needed to establish private emulation of market discipline are also required for effective regulatory oversight. These include evaluation of bank assets and liabilities in economic terms, the establishment of capital-based operating ground rules based on market valuations, the implementation of an early resolution policy for failure to meet minimum market-based capital requirements, and accountability for regulatory performance.[1] In addition, effective emulation requires that surety condition be fully disclosed, the terms of surety coverage publicized, and cancellations or failures to renew disclosed.

A private insurance program would not be free of conflicts of interest.

Three are worth identifying at the outset. First, federal regulators impose at least three classes of constraints on the activities of depository institutions. These may impair profit maximizing behavior by such institutions and thus could be contrary to the interests of sureties. These constraints consist of government preferences for credit allocation (e.g., encouragements, formal and informal, in support of borrowing sectors); restraints or influences on the pricing of loans, deposits, and other services; and market protection. Examples of market protection include branching restrictions and limits on the range of permitted securities activities.

Second, conflicts of interest would exist between banks and sureties as well. Affiliates of sureties and insured banks are likely to be competitors in some, if not many, markets. Banks may be unwilling to divulge operating information sought by private sureties regarding strategies, line-of-business profitability, asset quality, and market positioning.

Third, private sureties will have incentives to defer bank-problem recognition if there are potentially adverse consequences for their own positions. In this they are not unlike some banks in their treatment of loan problems.

Private Insurance Proposals

A wide variety of proposals have been made for private deposit insurance. Three examples are reviewed here. The one that comes closest to embodying the principles of market discipline identified above is that advanced by Edward Kane (June 25, 1992). His privatization plan contains five elements:

1. Federally insured deposit institutions would be required to carry private insurance;
2. Insured institutions would be free to offer any services for which an authorized carrier was willing to accept risk;
3. If at the expiration of a contract of insurance a carrier was unwilling to renew coverage, a deposit institution would have to improve its risk profile so as to qualify for reinstated coverage from the previous surety, find another carrier, or be declared insolvent by its chartering agent;
4. Authorized carriers would have to be organized as single-line entities; the description does not prohibit affiliate linkages (including those with banks themselves), nor is risk pooling addressed;
5. Each private surety itself would be subject to federal oversight;

estimates of the loss exposure of a surety's operations would have to be made to an overseer, and if reserves fell to inadequate levels recapitalization would be required in order to remain eligible to continue operation as a deposit surety.

This approach would require more in structural separation than the two others to be reviewed. It is not evident, given the cross-subsidization characteristic of insurance functions today, that even high-volume deposit insurance would generate requisite resource commitment for a network of single-purpose sureties. This is an instance where relaxation of the separateness stipulation would undoubtedly expand the population of prospective suppliers. The cost would be risk of competitive conflicts of interest. That being the case, a more realistic trial or pilot could entail separately incorporated affiliates of any organization possessing the requisite dedicated capital.

A second proposal stems from a requirement under FDICIA that FDIC, in consultation with others, conduct a study of the feasibility of establishing a private reinsurance system. While FDICIA did not state precisely what liabilities of what size and for what holders were to be reinsured, replication in the private sector of functions performed by FDIC itself appears to have been the congressional objective. The most important of these functions, of course, are the pricing and underwriting of risk.

As a first step FDIC has sought response to a pilot project to ascertain whether premiums that would be charged by private reinsurers should be taken into account in establishing assessment insurance premium classifications. Specifically, in January 1993 FDIC announced the initiation of a pilot reinsurance program, as authorized by FDICIA, intended as a component of a broader examination of the feasibility of private deposit reinsurance (FDIC, 1993). Pilot reinsurance, according to FDIC, would cover not more than 10 percent of any loss incurred by FDIC with respect to an insured depository institution. That institution's semiannual deposit insurance assessment would be based, wholly or partially, on the cost of the private reinsurance. Private reinsurers would be invited to participate for the purpose of deriving market-based deposit-reinsurance prices for eligible (not defined by FDIC) insured depository institutions. Reinsurers would be required to enter into contracts with the FDIC containing terms and conditions of participation. The reinsurer would be liable for some portion of the loss or cost of assistance incurred by FDIC (apparently not to exceed 10 percent) in connection with an insured institution that fails or is provided assistance. A reinsurer would assume liability for specific institutions. Interested reinsurers would be required to demonstrate that they meet eligibility criteria established by the FDIC (not specified). The FDIC intends to set a maximum acceptable reinsurance price for all institutions designated as being eligible by FDIC for the reinsurance pilot program. According to FDIC, most data necessary for determining reinsurance premiums would be generated based on the quarterly consolidated reports of condition and income and other publicly available information. The FDIC also raised the possibility of access to reports of examination.

The FDIC proposal is deficient in at least four respects. First, there is no indication of accountability by FDIC itself for the prompt resolution of bank problems. That is, despite the stipulations of FDICIA, FDIC has sufficient latitude that it could compromise the interests of a reinsurer by not undertaking prompt remedial action. Failure to implement market valuations in capital discipline is the foremost of these. Under current operating procedures a reinsurer would have little basis for assessing its exposure to prospects that FDIC will incur loss. Second, the proposal denies to reinsurers any right to cancel coverage prior to the expiration of the reinsurance contract for reasons of adverse disclosure, adverse developments, or (perhaps especially) actions or delays of actions by regulatory authorities contrary to the interests of sureties. Such right of cancellation constitutes an important form of discipline on FDIC. Third, FDIC requires consent from a surety's primary supervisory agency as to the surety's fitness to participate in the pilot. Since FDIC is a party to the reinsurance process, however, *its* financial standards, rather than those of the primary supervisor of the reinsurer, should govern the acceptability of a reinsurance company. Such responsibility requires the development of condition measurement criteria beyond those that may be imposed on many prospective reinsurers by their own supervisors. Fourth, while FDICIA does not require regulatory authorities to use market valuations in analyzing capital sufficiency, it is unlikely private insurers would fail to do so. Current reports of condition and examination reports are highly deficient in providing these evaluation data.

Shortcomings of the FDIC proposal are avoided but new ones are added in a proposal by Peter Wallison (1990). In effect, Wallison's program provides excess coverage, i.e., applies to deposits in accounts greater than $100,000, as well as some unspecified nondeposit liabilities. It would use market-value accounting, regarding that process as the starting point in determining a bank's probability of failure. Consortia of banks and other interested participants would form syndicates that would guarantee the covered liabilities of other depository institutions not members of the syndicate. Each syndicate would use designated agents assigned to oversee specific banks. These would be employees of the syndicate itself, not of individual members. In effect, insuring entities would base their judgments of insurability on the analyses of designated agents. Their own ability to perform insurability "due diligence" apparently would be highly restricted. As with the FDIC proposal of 1993, under this program the duty of the FDIC to resolve a problem bank before the bank's equity is exhausted is ambiguous. Unlike the FDIC proposal, however, there is potential for conflicts of interest in cases where criticism by syndicate agents of a given bank's practices or valuations could reflect on assessments or valuations of the position of syndicate members themselves in dealings with other syndicates insuring them. Moreover, no provision is made for marking to market the risk exposure of individual syndicate members engaged in reinsurance, nor are standards for syndicate eligibility established. In short, the Wallison plan appears to be doubling up on bank capital—leveraging a private insurance program with a capital source that itself is insufficient to support existing programs of many banks.[2]

Conclusion

A privatization process in the case of deposit insurance should seek to provide financial-market replication of values attaching to a form of performance guarantee. The central elements of this guarantee are the pricing of the surety service and early resolution of risks that are unacceptable to a surety. Although private pricing practices will guide regulators in pricing federal deposit insurance on a risk-adjusted basis, the chief contribution of private insurance will be to signal the need for prompt resolution by regulators of threatened insolvencies.

Embodied in all private surety structures is the risk that while private deposit insurance initially may shift conflict resolution to the private sector, it will not keep it there, Successful privatization requires resolution of major problems now afflicting the conduct of federal deposit insurance. Foremost of needed reforms are the valuation in economic terms of entities offering insured deposits, predictable discipline for resolution action, and accountability for results. Private insurance also requires new elements of oversight cost. Those include oversight of the condition of the surety itself and monitoring the prompt performance of the surety's function. While some of these new costs could be offset by less direct FDIC costs, since FDIC will remain insurer of final resort, this partial outsourcing seems unlikely to reduce net deposit-insurance costs. In addition, in order to be credible, private resources must be mobilized in volume sufficient to meet potential problems that are sizable in aggregate amount.

The starting point for incentive conflict is the delegation of authority to regulators. Regulatory discretion inevitably entails tradeoffs that take account of the preferences (often contrary to regulatory objectives) of numerous constituents. Better information on institution condition—notably market valuations—offers the single most promising source of public leverage on regulatory conduct. Without such improved information, privatization of deposit insurance would change superficially the form but not the substance of conflict resolution. With such information, privatization would provide a mechanism to signal responses of holders of private capital to changes in the condition of entities issuing insured deposits.

Notes

1. In such an environment a deposit-insurance fund per se is needed chiefly for the funding of "old" problems. The service needed from regulatory oversight is prompt resolution enforcement. New messes (net) under a regime of binding capital rules should be minimal and could be charged directly to the federal budget. Instead of insurance premiums, costs of administering oversight could be imposed directly on regulated institutions with charges to institutions geared to reflect the scope and complexity of the activities subject to oversight.

2. FDICIA provides some precedent for this kind of perversity by requiring (section 141) that all banks are subject to special assessment to cover FDIC losses if they are incurred in covering obligations where loss threatened (in the eyes of authorities) serious adverse effects on economic conditions or financial stability. Such effects would most probably be associated with relatively large institutions.

References

Barth, James R., Philip F. Bartholomew, and Michael G. Bradley, "Reforming Federal Deposit Insurance: What Can Be Learned from Private Insurance Practices?," Consumer Finance Law *Quarterly Report*, vol. 45, no. 2, Spring 1991.

Congressional Budget Office, *Reforming Federal Deposit Insurance,* September 1990.

Federal Deposit Insurance Corporation, *Pilot Reinsurance Program*, Request for comment, January 22, 1993 (draft).

Kane, Edward J., "Long-Run Benefits in Financial Regulation from Increased Accountability and Privatization," paper presented at a conference on "Rebuilding Public Confidence Through Financial Reform," The Ohio State University, June 25, 1992.

——, "Taxpayer Losses in the Deposit-Insurance Mess: An Agency-Cost and Bonding Perspective," unpublished paper, June 27, 1992.

Wallison, Peter, *Back from the Brink*, Washington, D.C.: AEI Press, 1990.

7 IMPROVING THE FDIC IMPROVEMENT ACT: WHAT WAS DONE AND WHAT STILL NEEDS TO BE DONE TO FIX THE DEPOSIT INSURANCE PROBLEM

George J. Benston and George G. Kaufman*

The Federal Deposit Insurance Corporation Improvement Act (FDICIA) of 1991 is perhaps both the most important banking legislation since the Banking (Glass-Steagall) Act of 1933 and the most misunderstood. It represents the first attempt to reform the federal deposit-insurance system since the system's inception almost 60 years ago. This chapter reviews the theory underlying how the act attempts to cure the adverse side effects of the current structure of deposit insurance, the major provisions of the act, and the barriers to its success.

The Theory of Structured Early Intervention and Resolution (SEIR)

The Basic Concept

Structured early intervention and resolution (SEIR) calls for prespecified rules that govern when and how the bank supervisory authority in a world

* An earlier draft was presented at the American Finance Association Annual Meeting in Anaheim, California on January 6, 1993. We are indebted to the participants at the session for their suggestions and comments.

with federal deposit insurance first may and then must impose sanctions, including ultimate resolution, should a bank's capital decline below pre-specified percentages of total assets. Benston and Kaufman (1988a, 1988b) proposed this system in 1988 (see Benston and Kaufman, this book, for the history of this proposal). Since then, it has been refined and endorsed by a Brookings Institution Task Force (Benston et al., 1989) and by the Shadow Financial Regulatory Committee (1989). A modified version is included in the Federal Deposit Insurance Corporation Improvement Act of 1991.

SEIR is based on the belief that, if both the capital ratios and the sanctions imposed were consistent with those that would exist in the absence of federal deposit insurance, banks would voluntarily maintain their capital or go out of business when faced with prespecified costly sanctions. Should capital-short banks not take advantage of these options, the deposit insurance fund would incur only small losses if the banks were resolved before their capital declined to zero. Deposit insurance would effectively become redundant, and insurance premiums would be reduced to cover mostly the costs of monitoring, supervision, and fraud, which would remain as the major source of loss to the FDIC. Because bank owners would have sufficient capital to absorb all or almost all of the losses that might result, banks can and should be permitted to provide any product or service that the FDIC could monitor adequately.

Indeed, SEIR employs a carrot and stick approach. Not only would poor performance be punished by restrictions on activities, but good performance and high capital would be rewarded by permission to engage in a broader range of activities with less government regulation and intervention. Because, as long as federal deposit insurance exists, the government has a financial stake in the health of the banking industry and will protect its interests through regulation, SEIR is the most market compatible and least intrusive structure that can be designed. It is incentive compatible and corrects the incentive incompatibility of the previous deposit-insurance structure. As a result, it reduces the moral hazard both of banks to take excessive risk and of regulators to forbear from resolving economically insolvent institutions promptly.

The Benston-Kaufman Proposal

In the Benston-Kaufman proposal, bank capital is defined to include equity and all debt that is explicitly not guaranteed by the deposit-insurance agency or government and that cannot be redeemed by the bank before the supervisory authority can act. Subordinated debentures with present maturities of at least one year fit this requirement. Capital should be measured in terms of the economic market values of a bank's assets and liabilities. However, the proposed scheme also can be effective when capital is measured according to traditional accounting values.

Four explicit, predetermined ranges or tranches of capital-to-asset ratios are specified. Assets include off–balance-sheet accounts. Assets are not classified according to risk because of the difficulties in measuring risk accurately and the dangers inherent in measuring it incorrectly.

1. Banks are considered to have *adequate capital* when capital is, say, 10 percent or more of their total assets, measured in terms of market or current values. Banks falling into this first tranche would be subject to minimal regulation and supervision and be permitted a broad range of services.

2. Banks with capital-to-asset ratios of, say, 6 to 9.9 percent are at the *first level of supervisory concern.* A bank in this second tranche is subject to increased regulatory supervision and more frequent monitoring of its activities. It is required to submit a business plan to raise more capital. At its discretion, the bank supervisory authority could require the bank to suspend dividend payments and obtain approval before transferring funds within a holding-company system and could restrict the bank's asset growth.

3. The third tranche is the *second level of supervisory concern;* it is reached when a bank's capital ratio falls below 6 percent and is at least 3 percent. Banks in this range are subject to intense regulatory supervision and monitoring. The supervisory authority is required to suspend dividends, interest payments on subordinated debt, and unapproved outflows of funds to the bank's parent or affiliates. The institution must submit an emergency plan for its immediate recapitalization to the tranche one level.

4. Finally, when a bank's capital falls below 3 percent of its assets, it is in tranche four—*mandatory recapitalization and reorganization.* The supervisory authority is required to quickly recapitalize the bank, merge it, or liquidate it in an orderly fashion by the sale of individual assets. The present owners and subordinated debt holders (who might, by then, be the owners) have the option either of implementing quickly the plan submitted when the institution moved into tranche three or of electing not to inject additional funds into the bank. If the owners and debt holders elected not to recapitalize the bank, any residual value from its sale or liquidation of its assets would be returned to them, after allowing for costs incurred.

The Advantages of SEIR

SEIR offers several advantages. These include increased substitution of market forces for supervisory judgment and actions; low cost to the deposit-insurance fund and, consequently, low premiums; avoidance of the deadweight cost of closure and the moral-hazard costs of forbearance; greater efficiency in bank regulation and supervision; and operational and political feasibility.

Substitution of Market Forces for Supervisory Judgment and Actions. Market forces should operate to give incentives to bankers to operate their banks so as not to inflict losses on their depositors or creditors, including the deposit-insurance fund. SEIR calls for a maintained level of capital that is sufficient to absorb most losses that banks might incur. Hence, even though depositors whose accounts are fully insured (de jure or de facto) have little reason to monitor their banks' activities, the owners of the capital do have this incentive. Because capital owners' incentives to organize banks' portfolios and activities to constrain risk decline as their capital investments decline (and the limited-liability put option's value increases), SEIR prescribes penalties that increase in magnitude as capital declines. Bankers can and should avoid these penalties by maintaining capital or by replacing depleted capital promptly.

Subordinated debentures offer an additional market-derived constraint on bank risk taking. Debenture holders bear the cost of bank losses once equity capital is depleted but do not share in gains that exceed coupon payments. Hence, they increase the interest rate demanded when equity holders are expected to take risks or do not provide sufficient assurances that excessive risks will not be taken. As agency theory demonstrates, the cost of risk taking thus is shifted to equity holders, who have incentives to assure uninsured debt holders that their promises are credible. Consequently, the market's judgment on optimal risk can be substituted for the regulator's judgment. The regulator's task is to determine that banks report correctly and maintain required capital.

The interest rates paid on publicly traded subordinated debentures offer the supervisory authority an early warning that a bank may be in financial trouble. A similar warning may be obtained from the difficulties a bank might experience in rolling over maturing subordinated debt. These warnings, coming from people whose funds are at risk, should usefully be supplementary to the reports of bank examiners and supervisors, if not superior to them. Thus, the market can aid regulators to determine when and the extent to which banks should be closely examined and supervised.

Low Cost to the Deposit-Insurance Fund. If banks are taken over by the FDIC and restructured or dissolved before their capital declines to zero, the deposit-insurance fund would suffer little in the way of losses. Losses could result when conditions deteriorate before the authority could act, capital is overstated, and government agents manage taken-over banks' assets incompetently. The first situation can be reduced, if not eliminated, by the required structured early intervention process and relatively high capital levels. The second can be reduced by market-value (or current-value) accounting in place of historical-cost (traditional) accounting, which often yields significantly overstated capital. The third cost, government agents' mismanagement of banks assets, is likely, as government agents' incentives tend to make them poor managers of private assets. SEIR works to avoid this cost both by making government takeover of banks unlikely and by remitting to the shareholders of the seized institutions only the remaining net value at final resolution. This should serve to encourage shareholders to increase their capital contribution or voluntarily sell or liquidate their banks to avoid being taken over.

Hence, with SEIR, deposit-insurance premiums would be required primarily to pay only administrative and monitoring costs and to compensate depositors in banks that failed because of fraud, gross mismanagement, or particularly adverse endogenous conditions. The premiums, therefore, should be low.

Avoidance of the Deadweight Costs of Closure and the Moral-Hazard Costs of Forbearance. Deadweight closure costs include losses on assets disposed of at "fire sale" prices; mismanagement of assets and liabilities by government agents after closure; loss of goodwill, employee training, and other intangible assets; and legal and administrative costs. Because application of SEIR should generally result in banks being recapitalized or voluntarily disposed rather than taken over and involuntarily resolved, these deadweight costs generally will be avoided.

The alternative of forbearance may save deadweight closure costs but at the expense of moral-hazard costs (see Eisenbeis and Horvitz, this book). Given deposit insurance, depositors have little reason for concern about losses their banks might incur. If bankers believe that they will not be forced to raise additional capital if they take losses, they are more likely to be imprudent by maintaining higher ratios of debt (deposits) to capital and by gambling. Indeed, this is what appears to have happened since federal deposit insurance was enacted and accepted as credible. Banks' capital has declined to the point where losses, that are relatively small by pre–deposit-insurance experience, have been sufficient to render many banks economically insolvent. Another, more active, aspect of moral hazard is the possibility that banker owners will deliberately assume higher risks when their bank's capital is depleted—that is, that they gamble for resurrection, realizing that they will get all of the gains but take only some of the losses. The cost of both kinds of moral hazard can be avoided by SEIR, under which banks have incentives to maintain adequate capital and to replenish it before it becomes severely depleted.

Greater Bank Efficiency.   Banks' efficiency would be increased by not having them follow the dictates of regulators and by not restraining the products and services they can offer and assets they can hold. The present constraints are frequently justified as necessary to protect the deposit-insurance fund from excessive risk-taking by bankers who are not monitored by insured depositors. Because SEIR provides adequate protection to the deposit-insurance fund, the constraints generally would be superfluous. Consequently, banks would be freer to change their products and operations to meet changing market conditions and operations costs. The result would be a more efficient allocation of resources and greater consumer welfare.

In fact, continued constraints on banks would be based principally on only two factors: politically determined restrictions on competition, and the inability of bank supervisors to assess the value of certain assets or the risk inherent in certain activities. Adoption of current-value accounting and SEIR would remove most bank-safety concerns about asset valuations and excessively risky activities. As is discussed above, banks with relatively high levels of capital would have incentives to control risk and, in any event, would bear the cost of risks that turned out badly. As is discussed below, current-value accounting with statements attested to by certified public accountants, would obviate the need for bank supervisors to value unusual, not readily marketed assets. However, although government restrictions on competition are economically undesirable for consumers, they may be continued because those who benefit have sufficient political power to maintain their rents.

Greater Regulatory Efficiency.   SEIR reduces the need for regulatory control and supervision of banks that are well capitalized. For most banks, regulators would not have to pass on applications for branches, mergers, product offerings, and the like. Instead, supervisors can concentrate on banks with lesser levels of capital and on assets that are difficult to value. These banks would be closely monitored, and their activities would be constrained, as outlined above. Thus, most regulations would be restricted to those dealing with less than adequately capitalized banks. Furthermore, as noted above, the banking authority could get early warnings of problems with individual banks if banks' capital included subordinated debentures.

Operational and Political Feasibility. Unlike schemes such as the "narrow" fail-safe bank, almost no operational change in the existing banking, regulatory, and safety-net structures would be required to implement SEIR. Banks would not have to give up some or all of their lending activities and would not lose the economies of scope in information and administration that they now enjoy. Customers would not have to give up relationship banking.

Capital-deficient banks would not have to sell additional equity. Rather, they could convert some of their partially insured greater than $100,000 certificates of deposit with maturities of at least one year into similar but completely and explicitly uninsured debentures. Alternatively, banks could increase their capital by issuing additional equity shares or subordinated debentures. Small banks, particularly those controlled by a few shareholders, probably would find floating debentures more desirable than raising equity capital. Such shareholders might object to increasing their equity because they do not have the personal resources, are loath to give up control to new investors, or expect that new investors would demand a relatively large discount to accept a minority position. Furthermore, research evidence supports the expectation that the issuance of new equity tends to reduce the market value of corporations, apparently because risk is shifted from debt to equity holders or because of information asymmetry between inside shareholders and managers and new investors. These concerns should not affect the sale of subordinated debentures.

Nor need there be a long transition period. Banks that cannot sell debentures or equity to investors are thereby indicating that they cannot continue operations without government-subsidized deposit insurance. These banks should not be permitted to continue operations. They should merge with other banks or go out of business by selling off their assets and paying off their liabilities. If they do not choose or are unable to follow this course, they are admitting that they are economically insolvent. Nevertheless, it might be less expensive to give them support to dissolve or merge rather than be taken over by government agents. Or they might he permitted to continue operations under strict controls. But the sooner these banks leave the scene, the better.

SEIR is politically feasible because well-run, strong banks would benefit from the weaker banks' demise. As noted, the strong banks would not have to change their operations, except to take advantage of their new powers. These bankers, then, would have incentives to operate their banks effectively. Hence, strong banks should support the change.

Regulators who want to protect the deposit insurance fund and reduce other costs imposed on the economy should welcome SEIR, as it is compatible with these related goals. Banks that meet the first capital tranche would require little supervision. Regulators could exercise discretion in dealing with banks in the second tranche. The mandatory actions that must be imposed when banks decline into the third tranche would free regulators from political pressures. As noted, few banks would fall into the last tranche and have to be taken over. Moreover, except for fraud and inadequate regulatory monitoring and intervention, losses would be limited to shareholders, who would not be expected to lobby for protection.

Politicians benefit from SEIR because it will reduce losses to the insurance fund that may have to be funded by taxpayers, as was the case in the savings and loan debacle. No or small losses to the FDIC protects legislators from angry constituents.

Weak banks and regulators who enjoy discretionary power, though, would tend to lose, as is discussed below. Hence, as is discussed later, they would tend to oppose SEIR.

Possible Shortcomings of SEIR

Some critics have claimed that SEIR has five important shortcomings that limit its usefulness. One is the claim that higher capital requirements would impose costs on banks that would prevent them from competing successfully with alternative, nondepository suppliers of financial services. The second is that a rule requiring the taking over of banks with positive capital is or should be seen as an illegal taking of private property. Third, early intervention would result in banks taking even greater risks prior to intervention. Fourth, market-value accounting is not feasible, and without market-value accounting, SEIR would not work. Fifth, SEIR does not take account of differences in risk among banks or even measure the potential cost of risk (Many of these criticisms are discussed in Kaufman and Litan, 1993). We consider each of the possible shortcomings. Our analysis leads us to conclude that the concerns are not valid, with the partial exception of the fifth objection.

Higher Bank Capital Costs and Competitive Equality. Equity capital generally is costly for several reasons. First, factor payments to shareholders are not a deductible expense for corporate income tax, unlike interest on debt. Second, higher levels of equity reduce the value of the limited-liability put option. In private capital markets, this later situation is dealt with by equity holders offering debt holders assurances that the option will not be used, by such means as covenants and collateral and levels of equity sufficient to absorb most losses. Alternatively, debt holders charge higher interest payments in exchange for the option.

The deposit insurance agency can similarly be protected by requiring banks to hold higher levels of capital. Since subordinated debt both protects the deposit-insurance fund and permits banks to deduct interest payments as an expense, bank capital costs would increase only to the extent that banks lose the subsidy from underpriced deposit insurance. Loss of this subsidy should not keep them from competing successfully with alternative suppliers of financial services, particularly if the banks are simultaneously freed from regulatory constraints and supervisory costs.

Government Takeover of Solvent Banks May Be Expropriation of Private Capital. An FDIC takeover of a book-value solvent bank should not be considered to be an illegal or improper taking of private capital. The current shareholders could avoid the situation by recapitalizing the bank to bring it into conformance with the capital requirements, merging it with another institution, or selling the assets and paying off the liabilities. By allowing the FDIC to exercise its option to take over the bank, the shareholders are indicating that they believe the bank is economically insolvent. In any event, the shareholders would be paid the net value the FDIC received for the institution from a sale, merger, or liquidation. Expert legal opinion supports this argument (Miller, 1991). Moreover, to the extent that SEIR was effective, few banks would deteriorate through all the tranches, so there would be few failures and takeovers.

Early Intervention Would Result in Banks Taking Greater Risks. It has been well documented that in a world of limited shareholder liability and flat-rate deposit insurance, shareholders have an incentive to assume progressively greater risk as a bank's net worth approaches zero. This reflects the fact that the shareholders will bear little or any of the cost of higher rates on deposits or further losses should their bank fail but will realize all of the gains, and that the FDIC appears to have been less effective in preventing such risk-taking behavior than private creditors have been. As a result, the lower a bank's capital, the greater is the value of the put option bought by the bank from the FDIC at a fixed price. More recently, a number of studies have shown that such moral hazard behavior is not reduced by "early" resolution of banks at positive levels of capital (Levonian, 1991, 1992; Davies and McManus, 1991).

It is for that very reason that SEIR supplements prompt resolution before a bank's capital is fully depleted with a series of capital tranches that impose prespecified progressively increasing and more mandatory penalties on banks for poor performance. No longer is the game a zero-one (solvent or insolvent) game, which encourages moral hazard risk-taking behavior. Rather, consistent with theory, the series of tranches with gradual increasing penalties serve to reduce the incentive for risk taking and increase the incentive for corrective action. Such a structure proxies the operation of the market in dealing with troubled firms in unregulated industries. Moreover, SEIR also serves to slow the deterioration of banks, thus providing time for the authority to take effective corrective action as well as to develop a paper trail of regulatory initiatives in case banks later challenge the actions on the basis of arbitrariness or insufficient warning. Indeed, a leading critic (Levonian, 1992, p. 3; see also McManus and Rosen, 1991) of early resolution has concluded that

> a policy that imposes appropriately gradual pressure on troubled banks would avoid most of the undesirable moral hazard effects of early intervention. . . . Early closure flips a switch, plunging abruptly to black, whereas the ideal policy for reducing moral hazard would turn a knob to dim the lights gradually.

The initial Benston-Kaufman/Shadow Financial Regulatory Committee/Brookings SEIR proposal recommended four tranches. FDICIA expanded the number to five. Thus, it appears that FDICIA deals appropriately with the moral hazard problem.

Moreover, SEIR reduces the potential for moral hazard even further by increasing both the quantity and quality of monitoring and examination. In FDICIA, full-scope on-site examinations are required at least annually, and more frequent examinations are required for banks in the lower capital tranches. The quality of monitoring is improved by encouraging the regulators to employ market or current-value reporting to the extent feasible and by requiring annual audits by independent auditing firms.

Market-Value Accounting Is Not Feasible But Is Required for SEIR. SEIR would work better if capital were stated in terms of economic market values rather than traditional historical-cost values. Generally accepted accounting principles were not designed to and often do not reflect economic values. Hence, a bank may be economically insolvent and yet have positive book-value equity.

The original cost of assets, adjusted by predetermined rules established when the assets were recorded on a bank's books (e.g., depreciation), often provide poor measures of the assets' current economic value. Among other shortcomings, changes in the purchasing power of the dollar and changes in demand and supply conditions are not generally accounted for. Liabilities also may not be stated at their economic market values. Intangible assets usually are not recorded as assets but are written off as expenses, and contingent assets and liabilities often are not included in the balance sheet.

Market-value accounting for bank capital clearly would be an improvement—some might say, a necessity. Nevertheless, SEIR can be effective under present, traditional accounting. One can require a sufficiently high level of capital to overcome most accounting understatements. Indeed, in conditions when interest rates are stable or asset and liabilities have short or equal durations, and when market values are not rapidly changing, book values tend to understate market equity values, as intangible assets usually are not recorded. Under many (perhaps most) conditions, then, a somewhat higher level of capital would be more than adequate when traditional accounting is used to measure equity.

Alternatively, some relatively simple changes in GAAP could bring accounting values for banks into reasonably close conformance with the desired economic values and permit lower required capital levels. Banks could be required, at least for regulatory reports, to record all marketable securities at market value. This is already required for securities in trading accounts. Securities designated as "held for sale" are accounted for at the lower of cost or market, which tends to understate bank capital. The market value of these securities, now given in footnotes, could be incorporated easily into the capital reported to the supervisory authorities.

More generally, banks could be required to account for changes in market rates of interest. All that would be required would be for them to discount the expected cash flows from individual or portfolios of loans and other nontraded assets and liabilities at the interest rate currently applied to these obligations. They also could take account of the full distribution of the probability of nonrepayment, not only in the most probable outcome. The result would be current values, or value in use, which is more relevant to a going concern and to the bank supervisory authority than market values, or value in exchange.

Intangible assets and liabilities as well as those that are difficult to value by discounting cash flows could be recorded at their estimated values, with CPAs attesting to these values. Because CPAs tend toward conservatism, assets that cannot be readily valued would tend to be understated and liabilities, overstated. Thus, banks would be required to hold more capital when they invest in hard-to-value assets and liabilities.

Finally, intangible asset values (such as the core-deposit intangible) and asset values based on appraisals (such as buildings) could be changed no more often than annually with increases delayed a year to give the authorities an opportunity to examine and challenge (if they wish) the basis for the estimates.

Thus, the more relevant current values could readily and inexpensively replace traditional historical-cost numbers. For purposes of SEIR, it would not be necessary to include changes in these valuations in banks' statements of income and expense.

SEIR Does Not Account for Risk Differences.   SEIR does not explicitly include adjusting capital to account for differences in risk among banks. Consequently, banks with poorly diversified portfolios and banks investing in assets subject to widely varying cash flows would have the same capital requirement as banks investing in, say, short-term government securities. Furthermore, current-value accounting does not include measurement of risk. A junk bond bearing a 20 percent rate of interest and limited marketability may have the same market or current value as a lower coupon U.S. Treasury bond with the same duration because the interest rates reflect the differences in expected cash flows and transactions costs.

Diversification rules might be constructed to reduce the cost of adverse endogenous or exogenous events. However, these rules might penalize banks that can achieve economies of specialization and those of a size that can serve only limited markets. Structuring capital requirements that differ according to the asset risk of various groupings of assets, such as is specified in the Basle risk-based capital requirements, would not be a desirable change. These risk categories are arbitrary and not based on market information (e.g., all commercial loans are considered to be equally risky, and all residential mortgages are considered to be half as risky as all commercial loans). Furthermore, covariances of cash flows are not taken into account. These and similar problems probably would plague any system of risk categorization.

Consequently, we believe that risk considerations can best be dealt with by requiring all banks to hold higher levels of capital. Such higher levels do not impose costs on banks as long as they are no higher than those on their noninsured competitors, they can include subordinated debentures fully in capital, and the banks are not otherwise constrained. In addition, banks that are poorly diversified or that specialize in risky assets can be more closely monitored by the supervisory authority.

However, it should be noted that fully implemented SEIR does indeed impose risk-based capital requirements and market-determined risk-adjusted costs on banks. For example, banks with unmarketable (i.e., risky) assets would be required to hold additional capital when their CPAs wrote down these assets. Also, banks with subordinated debentures would be required by holders of this debt to pay interest rates that reflect the risk; in effect, subordinated debentures offer a market-based risk-adjusted deposit-insurance premium. What is important under SEIR is that capital be sufficient to absorb most if not all unrecorded losses if and when an institution pierces the last capital tranche and is required to be resolved.

The Deposit-Insurance Provisions of FDICIA

Outline of the Act

FDICIA is a broad and complex act that deals with many areas and concerns other than deposit insurance. It may be divided into five major areas: (1) deposit-insurance reform to correct the perverse incentives in the current insurance structure, (2) recapitalization of the FDIC, (3) supervision of U.S. offices of foreign banks, (4) consumer and related regulations, and (5) "bank bashing." In this chapter we consider only the provisions that relate to deposit-insurance reform, even though much of the ongoing criticism of the act concerns excessive regulatory burdens imposed on the banks from implementation of the other parts, e.g., truth in savings and executive compensation standards. FDICIA has become a lightening rod for bankers' frustrations with increasingly costly regulation and increasingly declining market shares. The criticism has been fanned both by regulators, who are dissatisfied with the reduction in their discretionary "flexibility" by the act, which they believe reduces their power and visibility, and by regulatory lawyers and consultants, who expect to increase their influence and business by painting as destructive a picture of the act as possible, and then representing themselves as "knights on white horses."

A modified version of SEIR is the centerpiece of the deposit-insurance reform provisions of FDICIA under the titles of "Prompt Corrective Action" (PCA) and "Least-Cost Resolution" (LCR). The act also includes provisions for risk-based deposit-insurance premiums, limiting the use of Federal Reserve discount window loans to seriously troubled institutions, encouraging the regulatory agencies move to market-value accounting "to the extent feasible and practicable," annual examinations of all banks, annual independent audits of all banks, inclusion of interest-rate and

asset-concentration risks in the determination of risk-based capital requirements, and prohibiting deposit insurance for deposits at overseas offices
of U.S. banks. Some major differences between SEIR as proposed by
Benston-Kaufman/Shadow Financial Regulatory Committee/Brookings are
highlighted in table 1–1 in chapter 1 of this book (p. 11).

Except for the failure-resolution level, specification of the precise values of the capital ranges for each of the act's five capital tranches is del-
egated to the regulatory agencies. Final resolution is required when tangible
equity capital declines to no less than 2 percent of total assets. The major
sanctions specified in each zone are summarized in table 7–1. The regulators also have the authority to downgrade an institution or impose one
or more sanctions from a lower capital tranche if it finds the institution
engaging in unsafe and unsound activities. These provisions, including the
resolution of institutions with less than 2 percent tangible equity capital,
went into effect on December 19, 1992, the first anniversary of the signing
of the act by President George Bush. A listing of the major provisions
related to deposit-insurance reform and their scheduled dates of implementation appears in table 1–2 in chapter 1 (p. 11).

Also effective December 19, 1992 is a provision giving the regulators
expanded powers to resolve financially troubled institutions for a number
of reasons in addition to being undercapitalized. These include operating
in an unsafe and unsound manner, willful violations of prior regulatory
orders, inability to meet depositor obligations, pending large losses that
will deplete its capital, and unlawful behavior. These provisions correct the
previous situation wherein regulators could not resolve banks when their
book-value capital was greater than zero without almost certain legal challenges, which contributed to the costly forbearance policies of the 1980s.
The act also requires the FDIC to resolve institutions so that

> the total amount of expenditures by the Corporation and the obligations in-
> curred by the Corporation (including any immediate and long-term obligation
> of the corporation and any direct or contingent liability for future payment by
> the Corporation) . . . is the least costly to the deposit insurance fund of all possible
> methods for meeting the Corporation's obligations under this section.

Least cost is defined as present value costs, using a realistic discount rate;
its computation must be documented. This provision became effective with
enactment. Beginning January 1, 1995, the FDIC will not be permitted to
make domestic depositors at resolved institutions whole if that would increase its losses, except if it is determined that not making all depositors
whole "would have serious adverse effects on economic conditions or
financial stability." But such determination must be made by the secretary

Zone	Mandatory Provisions	Discretionary Provisions
1. Well capitalized		
2. Adequately capitalized	No brokered deposits, except with FDIC approval	
3. Undercapitalized	Suspend dividends and management fees Require capital restoration plan Restrict asset growth Approval required for acquisitions, branching, and new activities No brokered deposits	Order recapitalization Restrict interaffiliate transactions Restrict deposit interest rates Restrict certain other activities Any other action that would better carry out prompt corrective action
4. Significantly undercapitalized	Same as for zone 3 Order recapitalization[a] Restrict interaffiliate transactions[a] Restrict deposit interest rates[a] Pay of officers restricted	Any zone 3 discretionary actions Conservatorship or receivership if falls to submit or implement plan or recapitalize pursuant to order Any other zone 5 provision, if such action is necessary to carry out prompt corrective action
5. Critically undercapitalized	Same as for zone 4 Receiver/conservator within 90 days[a] Receiver if still in zone 5 four quarters after becoming critically undercapitalized Suspend payments on subordinated debt[a] Restrict certain other activities	

Source: Myron L. Kwast, Board of Governors of the Federal Reserve System, 1992.
a. Not required if primary supervisor determines action would not serve purpose of prompt corrective action or if certain other conditions are met.

of the treasury in consultation with the president and upon written recommendation of two-thirds of both the board of governors of the Federal Reserve system and the board of directors of the FDIC.

If the FDIC incurs a "material" loss in resolving any institution after June 1, 1993, the inspector general of the bank's responsible supervising agency must prepare a written report on why this occurred and how such losses can be prevented in the future. The report must be provided to the comptroller general, the FDIC, and any congressperson who requests it. The definition of "material" is the greater of $25 million or 7 percent of a bank's assets. This percentage decreases annually to a final level of 2 percent of assets, effective July 1, 1997.

Shortcomings of the Act and Its Implementation

In terms of deposit-insurance reform, the SEIR provisions in FDICIA represent a major potential step forward. It is only a potential step because the act contains many exemptions and opportunities for delay in the application of the sanctions, including exemptions for making uninsured depositors whole in banks considered "too big to fail" and delays in resolving banks whose capital drops below 2 percent of assets; encouraging rather than requiring the use of market values to measure capital; not giving full value to subordinated debt as capital; and, most importantly, delegating substantial authority to the regulatory agencies both to interpret the provisions and to write and implement the required regulations. This gives the regulators the opportunity either to weaken the act or even to sabotage its intent. We discuss below three of a larger number of ways wherein the regulators have taken the opportunity to weaken the effectiveness of the act significantly.

Capital Ratios Are Too Low.   Capital is the key element in SEIR. If it is misspecified, SEIR will not achieve its maximum potential. FDICIA does not require final resolution until an institution's tangible equity declines to 2 percent of its assets. But this value is probably too low to absorb all unrecognized losses at the time of resolution because of inadequate monitoring, abrupt decline in asset values or increase in liability values, or fraud. Thus, losses may accrue to the FDIC. Moreover, this ratio is measured not in market values but in book-value terms, which generally underestimates market values at low levels of capital because institutions increasingly tend to delay and understate their loss reserves at these levels but to recognize capital gains by selling appreciated assets.

The effectiveness of the capital tranches were weakened by the regulators when they defined the boundaries. *Well capitalized* was defined to include banks that had minimum book-value total capital ratios of 10 percent on a risk-based basis, 6 percent on a tier one (primarily equity) risk-based basis, and 5 percent on a tier one not risk-adjusted (leverage) ratio. As of June 30, 1992, this definition included some 92 percent of all commercial banks, holding some 65 percent of total assets. *Adequately capitalized* institutions were defined as those with minimum values for these ratios of 8, 4, and 4 percent, respectively. Some 98 percent of all banks holding 97 percent of total assets, including all 46 banks with assets in excess of $10 billion, qualified for this designation. Thus, only some 250 banks, or 2 percent of all banks with only 3 percent of total assets, were classified as undercapitalized and subject to strong sanctions. As 956 commercial banks, or 8 percent of all banks, with assets of nearly $500 billion, or 14 percent of total assets, were on the FDIC's problem bank list on that date, the small number of banks classified as undercapitalized shows that the ratios specified are severely underestimated.

This action by the regulators clearly weakens the intent of the act to slow the deterioration of troubled banks and require the regulators to take action while there is still time for it to be effective in reversing a bank's direction. Moreover, a number of sanctions, including insurance premiums, pass-through insurance coverage, use of brokered deposits, and interbank liabilities, are tied to these zones. By weakening the effectiveness of these sanctions, the incentives for banks to strengthen their capital or to reduce their risk are weakened. The carrot is offered far too easily, and the stick is threatened far too little.

In the General Accounting Office argued congressional testimony during the deliberations over FDICIA, that capital by itself, particularly when measured by book value, may be an inaccurate and lagging indicator of the financial health of an institution. As a result, Congress added supplementary provisions that both focus on noncapital measures, such as loan-loss reserves and the ratio of market to book value, and permit the regulators to downgrade an institution if it is of supervisory concern.[1] If properly implemented, these provisions, in effect, would raise the required book-value capital ratios in each classification zone.

Interest-Rate Risk Is Underestimated and Undercapitalized for in the Risk-Based Capital Standards. The act requires the existing risk-based capital standards to be revised to take adequate account of interest rate risk and concentration of credit risk. The failure to incorporate interest-rate risk (the primary cause of the recent S&L debacle) in the Basle risk-based capital standards has been a major weakness. It reflects poorly on the banking agencies that it took Congress to require inclusion of interest-rate risk. But the agencies still do not appear to take it as a major concern that requires capital protection.

The proposed regulations on interest-rate risk measure the risk poorly for commercial banks and require inadequate capital for both banks and thrifts. In contrast to the near state-of-the-art model developed by the Office of Thrift Supervision (OTS) for measuring interest-rate risk for savings and loan associations, the bank regulators constructed an ad hoc model that relies on numerous heroic and sweeping assumptions concerning option-adjusted durations. The model is justified on the basis of requiring minimum data. Not unexpectedly, it also generates output of minimum value either to the regulators or the banks themselves. Indeed, it requires less input data than many banks currently process for their own internal use.

The regulations proposed in early 1993 impose additional capital requirements only on institutions considered to be outliers, defined to be the 20 percent with the greatest interest-rate exposure. For banks, this represents institutions whose equity at the time had a duration longer than 12 years. (A duration of 12 years implies that an increase of 200 basis points would decrease a bank's capital by some 24 percent). Under the proposed regulations, a bank with an equity duration of 20 years would be required to hold only an additional 7.5 percent of capital, which would be absorbed by an interest-rate increase of only 38 basis points. Moreover, the regulations contain no provisions for replenishing the lost capital because the decrease in capital value will not be recorded. This accounting differs significantly from credit-risk accounting, where additions to loan-loss reserves reduce book-value capital. This lost capital must be replenished. As the Shadow Financial Regulatory Committee (1993a) noted, both consistency and good economics suggest at least the adoption of parallel interest-rate loss reserves to recognize reductions in capital values from adverse interest-rate shocks. In the absence of such reserves, the proposed regulations do not appear to carry out the intent of FDICIA.

Accounting Reforms Are Neglected.   Section 121 of the act requires the banking agencies to review the accounting principles currently used by depository institutions; modify those accounting principles that fail to reflect accurately the capital position of institutions and hamper effective supervision, prompt corrective action, and least cost resolution; include off-balance-sheet items; and develop techniques for introducing supplementary market value reporting "to the extent feasible and practicable."

The agencies were required to review these matters before the end of the first year of the act (December 19, 1992) and to make appropriate modifications to achieve the accounting objectives. As of mid-year 1993, no report had been released nor modifications proposed. Neither did the agencies release any new studies pertaining to these issues. At a minimum, this represents regulatory foot-dragging.

Future of FDICIA

As noted earlier, FDICIA provides for potential effective deposit-insurance reform, but does not guarantee it. The problem rests not so much with the legislation itself, although it is relatively weak, but with the bank regulatory agencies and the industry, which see themselves as under attack. The regulators view the reduction in their discretion and flexibility in dealing with troubled banks as a reduction in their power and visibility. This has adverse implications for their career advancement, as well as their self-esteem. Moreover, for a government sector in which the revolving door between regulators and the industry being regulated is at least as busy as for any other government agency, including the Defense Department, any such reductions also have adverse implications for the regulators' future career opportunities in the private sector. In terms of national visibility and prestige as well as their future career opportunities, bank crises are to regulators what wars are to generals.

But FDICIA does not eliminate regulatory discretion. As can be seen from table 7–1 the regulators maintain considerable discretion in the higher capital tranches. It is only when banks apparently do not respond to these actions and sink into lower tranches that the sanctions become less discretionary and more mandatory. Indeed, public-spirited regulators should welcome these provisions, as it protects them from political and industry pressures, such as were exerted on them during the S&L debacle. Since FDICIA, they can respond to those who attempt to exert pressure by saying, "Look, I would like to help you, but FDICIA ties my hands." Moreover, two students of regulation (Scott and Weingast, this book) have recently argued that FDICIA

> still relies heavily on the discretion of the banking agencies to take the proper action and make the proper judgments. . . . For example, the agencies have the authority but are not required to make the calculation of net worth in terms of market rather than historical accounting values. It remains to be seen how much, in actuality, has been accomplished.

They earlier concluded that discretion had not served the regulators, industry, or taxpayers well:

> By the time they [the agencies] move to resolve a large bank, its net worth is not zero but *hugely* negative. As taxpayer watchdogs, they get an F throughout recent history, down to and including the Bank of New England at the beginning of 1991 and Crossland Savings in early 1992.

The industry views FDICIA primarily as one more piece of legislation requiring massive additional regulations. And to an extent it is. The truth-in-savings regulations run nearly 300 pages. The prompt corrective action, interbank exposure, interest-rate risk, and other SEIR regulations are also long and complex. And they all come nearly at the same time. What appears to upset the industry most is what they perceive to be an increase in government micromanagement in the form of provisions that specify standards of internal controls, loan documentation, credit underwriting, asset growth, and executive compensation.[2] These are contained in section 132 of the act, entitled "Standards of Safety and Soundness." To the industry, enough is enough, and FDICIA is the last straw.

The fire underlying this sense of frustration is being fanned by regulators, who view this a tactic to help them modify or eliminate SEIR and recapture their discretionary authority, and by a regulatory lawyer and consultant nexus. These groups are uniting in appealing to the Clinton administration and Congress that repeal of many of the fundamental provisions of FDICIA is necessary if banks are to start lending again and help jump-start the economy. Because they do not fully understand SEIR, many banks are willing to throw out the baby of deposit insurance reform with the bath water of overregulation. But if they are successful and the banking situation deteriorates again to a point where the taxpayer is at risk, it is likely that Congress will engage in more radical legislative surgery that would be less favorable to the banking industry, such as narrow banking and increased government micromanagement.

Repealing much or all of FDICIA to reduce burdensome regulation is putting the cart before the horse. The industry is more likely to reduce its regulatory burden and gain greater freedom, including broader product and geographic powers, through first increasing its capital and financial strength to levels where it is not perceived to require taxpayer support. In part, banking has been a whipping boy for Congress because it has been weak and in a poor position to defend itself. As Congressman Henry Gonzalez has noted, "people on welfare always face rules." Similarly, Federal Reserve Governor Wayne Angell has concluded that "banks are overregulated because they are undercapitalized."

Ironically, through its carrot-and-stick approach, FDICIA provides banks with an opportunity to regain their strength and to unshackle themselves from burdensome regulation. Although far from perfect, FDICIA does represent a big step forward in correcting the perverse incentives imposed by deposit insurance within a market oriented framework. Its long-term effectiveness will be determined over the next few years and depend greatly on congressional resolve to withstand calls for prudential weakening from the regulators, industry, possibly the administration, and even some individual congresspersons.

To date, Chairmen Riegle and Gonzalez of the Senate and House Banking Committees, the legislative forces behind the act, have successfully resisted these pressures and encouraged the regulators to support the intent of SEIR. In addition, the combined effects of one year advanced warning that banks with less than 2 percent tangible equity would be resolved beginning December 19, 1992 and of sharply lower interest rates that increased bank profits worked to reduce greatly the number of banks caught in the so-called December surprise from the number predicted. Many marginal banks used the one-year grace period to raise capital and capital ratios. Thus, the version SEIR enacted in FDICIA passed its first major test. This may serve to demonstrate the general effectiveness of SEIR and satisfy some of the opponents that all banks will not be closed nor harmed. Nevertheless, further strengthening of the act and greater cooperation with the spirit and intent of the act by the regulators will be required before an avoidance of the recent bank and thrift debacles can be promised with a high degree of confidence.

Notes

1. Emperical support for such supplements to reported book capital measures is provided in Jones and King, 1992.

2. The requirement for standards for executive compensation was liberalized by Congress in late 1992. A creative and not burdensome way of viewing these requirements is suggested in Shadow Financial Regulatory Committee (1993b).

References

Benston, George J., R. Dan Brumbaugh Jr., Jack M. Guttentag; Richard H. Herring, George G. Kaufman, Robert E. Litan and Kenneth E. Scott, *Blueprint for Restructuring America's Financial Institutions*, Washington, D.C.: Brookings Institution, 1989.

Benston, George J. and George G. Kaufman, *Risk and Solvency Regulation of Depository Institutions: Past Policies and Current Options*, New York: Salomon Brothers Center, New York University, 1988a.

――――, "Regulating Bank Safety and Performance," in William S. Haraf and Rose Marie Kushmeider (eds.), *Restructuring Banking and Financial Services in America*, Washington, D.C.: American Enterprise Institute for Public Policy Research, 1988b, pp. 63–99.

――――, "The Intellectual History of the Federal Deposit Insurance Corporation Improvement Act," *Reforming Financial Institutions and Markets in the United States*, Boston, MA: Kluwer Academic Publishers, 1993.

Davies, Sally M. and Douglas A. McManus, "The Effects of Closure Policies on Bank Risk-Taking," *Journal of Banking and Finance*, September 1991, pp. 917–938.

Eisenbeis, Robert A. and Paul M. Horvitz, "The Role of Forbearance and Its Costs in Handling Troubled and Fall Depository Institutions," *Reforming Financial Institutions and Markets in the United States*, Boston, MA: Kluwer Academic Publishers, 1993.

Jones, David S. and Kathleen Kuester King, "The Implementation of Prompt Corrective Action," *Credit Markets in Transition*, Federal Reserve Bank of Chicago, 1992, pp. 68–100.

Kaufman, George, G. and Robert E. Litan, eds., *Assessing Bank Reform: FDICIA One Year Later*, Washington, D.C.: Brookings Institution, 1993.

Levonian, Mark E., "A Note of Caution on Early Bank Closure," *FRBSF Weekly Letter*, Federal Reserve Bank of San Francisco, November 20, 1992.

――――, "What Happens If Banks Are Closed 'Early'?," *Rebuilding Banking*, Federal Reserve Bank of Chicago, 1991, pp. 273–295.

McManus, Douglas A. and Richard Rosen, "Risk and Capitalization in Banking," *Rebuilding Banking*, Chicago: Federal Reserve Bank of Chicago, 1991, pp. 296–321.

Miller, Geoffrey, "Remarks of Senator Riegle," *Congressional Record*, March 5, 1991, p. S2650.

Scott, Kenneth E. and Barry R. Weingast, "Banking Reform: Economic Propellants, Political Impediments," *Reforming Financial Institutions and Markets in the United States*, Boston, MA: Kluwer Academic Publishers, 1993.

Shadow Financial Regulatory Committee, "An Outline of a Program for Deposit Insurance and Regulatory Reform" (Statement No. 41, February 13, 1989), *Journal of Financial Services Research*, August 1992, Supplement, pp. S78–82.

――――, "Rule Proposed by Bank Regulators to Control Interest Rate Risk" (Statement No. 87, September 14, 1992), *Journal of Financial Services Research*, January 1993a, pp. 101–102.

――――, "Standards for Safety and Soundness" (Statement No. 89, September 14, 1992), *Journal of Financial Services Research*, January 1993b, p. 104.

8 THE COLLAPSE OF BCCI: IMPLICATIONS FOR THE SUPERVISION OF INTERNATIONAL BANKS

Richard J. Herring*

Introduction

The collapse of the Bank of Credit and Commerce International (BCCI) in July 1991 captured media attention in a way matched by only the most lurid of financial scandals. Several books and more than a thousand newspaper and magazine articles describe allegations of gun running, money laundering, drug trafficking, international influence peddling, and blatant fraud. The principle focus of this chapter is the implications of the collapse of BCCI for the supervision of international banks. It reviews initial efforts to coordinate the supervision of international banks culminating in the Concordat of 1975 and examines the first real test of the Concordat, the collapse of the Banco Ambrosiano in 1982, and the revision of the Concordat, which followed in 1983. It then sketches the rise and fall of BCCI, emphasizing the way in which the bank took advantage of the gaps in the international supervisory network, and concludes with lessons to

* I am grateful to George Kaufman for comments on an earlier draft.

be drawn from the episode and options for improving the supervision of international banks.

The Concordat

The world economy was in trauma during 1974. The sharp increase in oil prices caused major economic dislocations, exacerbated inflationary pressures, and intensified exchange-rate volatility. Three internationally active banks failed—Bankhaus Herstatt of Cologne, the British-Israel Bank of London, and the Franklin National Bank of New York—but the closure of Herstatt had by far the most significant impact on the rest of the world.

Herstatt had been notorious for overtrading—taking foreign-exchange transactions that were very large relative to its capital. When the German authorities discovered that Herstatt had fraudulently concealed losses that exceeded half the book value of its assets, they closed the bank on June 26, 1974, at 4:00 P.M. (Dale, 1984). This was the end of the business day in Germany but still morning in New York. The closure of Herstatt aborted the settlement of millions of dollars of foreign-exchange contracts. Banks that had paid European currencies to Herstatt earlier in the day in the expectation that they would receive dollars at the close of the business day in New York suffered losses. When Herstatt's New York correspondent received word of the closure, it declined to honor $620 million in claims on Herstatt's account. This abrogation of foreign-exchange contracts caused a prolonged disruption in foreign-exchange trading (Morgan Guaranty, 1974).

Lack of information regarding the allocation of spot transaction losses and the anticipation of prospective losses on forward transactions with Herstatt also led to dislocations in the international interbank market. Although market participants believed that the magnitude of defaulted foreign-exchange contracts was large, they did not know the identity of the counterparties that would sustain losses. In the absence of reliable information, market participants took precautions against the worst outcome. They withdrew lines of credit from banks that were judged least able to sustain the losses if they were, in fact, counterparties to Herstatt's foreign-exchange contracts. Many banks that had relied on their ability to borrow at the London Interbank Offer Rate were obliged to pay a substantial premium above that benchmark rate. Some were unable to borrow at all (Guttentag and Herring 1985). Banks learned from this painful experience that even spot exchange contracts are subject to credit risk that must be monitored.

The disproportionately large spillover effects from the closure of Herstatt, a relatively small, privately held German bank, focused official attention on the growing interdependence of the international banking system. It also raised the question of whether banking supervision had kept pace with the expansion of international banking. After the collapse of Herstatt in 1974, the governors of the Group of Ten[1] established the Standing Committee on Banking Regulations and Supervisory Practices (the Basle Committee)[2], composed of representatives of the supervisory authorities and central banks of the Group of Ten countries plus Switzerland and Luxembourg. When the Basle Committee was formed, banks headquartered in these 12 countries accounted for roughly 90 percent of international banking activity. The Basle Committee met for the first time in February 1975 (Cooke, 1981a). The charge to the Committee included the establishment of broad principles for international coordination of banking supervision with which all supervisory systems might conform; the identification of gaps in the supervisory coverage of international banking; and the provision of opportunities for supervisors to exchange information and discuss best supervisory practices (Guttentag and Herring, 1983).

The Concordat, an agreement reached on September 26, 1975, was the first major accomplishment of the Basle Committee.[3] The Basle Committee agreed that the basic aim of international cooperation should be to ensure that no foreign banking establishment escaped adequate supervision. This required a demarcation of responsibilities among national supervisory authorities, since at least two supervisory authorities are intrinsically involved in any international banking transaction.

While recognizing that supervision was the joint responsibility of the host and parent supervisory authorities, the Committee allocated primary responsibility for supervision of solvency to the parent supervisory authority. This is the obvious solution for a foreign branch because the solvency of the foreign branch is inextricable from that of the parent. The role of the host supervisory authority is more important in the case of a subsidiary or joint venture, but the Basle Committee stressed that even when the foreign entity was separately incorporated, the parent bank should recognize a "moral commitment." This commitment would involve support of faltering corporate children, even though limited liability excused the parent bank from the *legal* obligation to provide additional resources. Consequently, the parent supervisory authority should monitor the insolvency exposure of the parent bank arising from the activities of its foreign subsidiaries and joint ventures.[4]

To facilitate cooperation between parent and host authorities, transfers of information were essential. This raised immediate difficulties. Many of the members of the Basle Committee were constrained by bank secrecy laws that prohibited exchanges of information relevant to judging the solvency of a banking entity (Kapstein, 1991). Over time, the Basle Committee has made some progress in modifying secrecy laws to ease the flow of information among supervisory authorities.

In 1978 the Basle Committee recommended adoption of the principle of consolidation—that banks' international business should be monitored on a consolidated basis—to improve the quality of information on international bank activities. Cooke (1981a) emphasized that this was a natural extension of the Concordat: "[Consolidated supervision] is an invaluable aid to parent supervisors in enabling them to fulfill in practice their responsibilities under the Concordat for the supervision of the solvency of their banks' foreign affiliates."[5]

The principle of consolidation is difficult to implement. Problems arise when the parent's ownership of a foreign entity is partial or if the entity engages in additional, nonbanking business. Differences in national accounting practices also impede meaningful consolidation. Moreover, the principle of consolidated supervision is not a panacea even if properly implemented.

Claims on affiliated banks are not legally binding claims on the parent bank. No host supervisor routinely insists that foreign parent banks fully guarantee the liabilities of their affiliates, and the comfort letters required by some host authorities have doubtful legal standing. Since parent banks are not legally responsible for claims on separately incorporated, foreign affiliates, the host country supervisor must be concerned about the solvency of resident foreign banking entities. Considered apart from the rest of the banking family with which it is affiliated, each entity must be solvent. Thus consolidated supervision offers little assistance to the local supervisory authorities unless they have complete confidence that the parent bank will honor the liabilities of the local affiliate without limit *and* complete confidence that the parent supervisory authority is monitoring the solvency of the consolidated banking group effectively.

For different reasons, the principle of consolidated supervision is of limited value to the home country authority. Local bankruptcy laws often discriminate in favor of local creditors, even if the entity in question is a foreign branch.[6] Thus the parent supervisory authority must be sure that the parent bank is solvent in its own right and on a consolidated basis. It must recognize that, in the event of trouble, assets in a foreign office may not be available to cover deficits in other parts of the banking family. As the Concordat recognizes, the solvency of a foreign banking entity is intrinsically mutual concern of both the parent and host supervisory authorities. The collapse of BCCI highlighted this fundamental point.

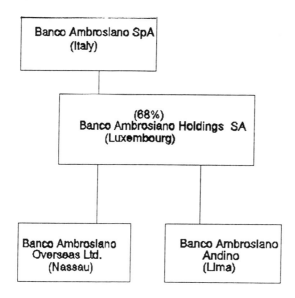

Figure 8–1. The corporate structure of Banco Ambrosiano.

The Revised Concordat

The Concordat dramatically flunked its first real test. When the Luxembourg subsidiary of a prominent Italian bank collapsed, it became clear that neither Italy nor Luxembourg—both members of the Basle Committee—had supervised the entity. They had failed to honor a fundamental principle of the Concordat. Clearly a foreign banking establishment had escaped supervision.

During the weekend of July 10–11, 1982, the Italian authorities orchestrated a rescue of Banco Ambrosiano SpA, the largest privately-owned bank in Italy. When the rescue attempt faltered, a compulsory liquidation of Banco Ambrosiano SpA quickly followed.[7] To protect the creditors of Banco Ambrosiano SpA, the authorities transferred claims on Banco Ambrosiano SpA to the newly organized Nuovo Banco Ambrosiano. The Bank of Italy and a consortium of Italian banks invested $450 million in Nuovo Banco Ambrosiano. The largesse of the Italian authorities did not, however, extend to creditors of the Luxembourg holding company in which Banco Ambrosiano owned 68 percent of the equity. Figure 8–1 displays a simplified diagram of the corporate structure of the Banco Ambrosiano Group.

Banco Ambrosiano Holdings SA (BAH) had been carefully situated in a gap in the international supervisory system. It was chartered in Luxembourg as a financial holding company. Since a financial holding company is not regarded as a bank in Luxembourg, the Luxembourg Banking Commission did not supervise the activities of BAH. Luxembourg's rigorous secrecy laws protect holding companies from foreign scrutiny, and so the Bank of Italy was unable to supervise BAH. Although BAH was not supervised as a bank, its major investments indicate that it was deeply engaged in a banking business. BAH owned Banco Ambrosiano Overseas Ltd., then the fourth-largest bank in Nassau—a jurisdiction well known for the rigor of its secrecy laws, but not for the quality of its supervision of foreign banks. In addition, it owned Banco Ambrosiano Andino in Peru, a jurisdiction in which foreign banks may not have been subject to any supervision whatsoever.

Although the activities of BAH were shrouded in secrecy, it was able to borrow more than half a billion dollars from 250 international banks. Clearly, these interbank placements were not made on the basis of rigorous credit analysis because even now, with the benefit of a decade of hindsight, little is known about what BAH actually did with the money. It seems likely that the banks that made deposits with BAH relied heavily on the evident connection of BAH with Italy's largest privately-owned bank, Banco Ambrosiano SpA, and on the presumption that the Italian authorities would recognize a moral commitment to protect creditors of the foreign subsidiary. The strategy of identifying offshore entities with the parent bank paid off handsomely for those who controlled Banco Ambrosiano; but it proved costly to the creditors of BAH.

The Italian authorities disclaimed any responsibility for BAH on grounds that it was technically not a bank and not under the control of the Bank of Italy. Luxembourg also refused to accept responsibility for BAH on grounds that it was licensed as a holding company and not a bank.

Spillover effects from the collapse of Banco Ambrosiano were limited mainly to six other Italian banks with similar organizational structures. Luxembourg demanded that these Italian parent banks transfer the controlling block of shares in bank subsidiaries from their Luxembourg holding companies bank to their Italian parent banks. Meanwhile, they were asked to guarantee unconditionally the solvency of their Luxembourg subsidiaries (Dale, 1984). The Italian government also experienced some resistance when it attempted to borrow in international capital markets. But these impacts were slight in comparison to the disruptions caused by the collapse of Herstatt.

Market participants learned an important lesson from the collapse of

Banco Ambrosiano: corporate structure matters. Although all the creditors of Banco Ambrosiano SpA were repaid promptly, creditors of BAH received only partial repayment after considerable delay (Guttentag and Herring 1985).[8] Disregarding the question of whether official supervision prevents bank failures, sophisticated market participants drew the inference that in the event of trouble, governments are unlikely to assist entities for which they do not have primary supervisory responsibility.

The Basle Committee learned that it was still possible for foreign banking establishments to escape supervision even when they were corporate children of a bank headquartered in a member country. The Committee responded in May 1983 (Committee on Banking Regulations and Supervisory Practices, May 1983) with revisions to the Concordat.[9]

The Committee (May 1983, p. 1) began by reminding practitioners that the Concordat set out principles "that are not necessarily embodied in the laws of the countries represented on the Committee. Rather they are recommended guidelines or best practices, which all members have undertaken to work towards implementing, according to the means available to them." The Basle Committee reaffirmed the principle of consolidated supervision that had been adopted in 1978. And it reemphasized the point that both host and parent authorities must collaborate in supervising foreign banking entities: host authorities are responsible for the foreign banking entities operating in their territories as individual institutions while parent authorities are responsible for these entities as part of the parent bank.

In addition, the Basle Committee adopted several new principles designed to close the gaps in the regulatory system revealed by the collapse of Banco Ambrosiano. First, the Committee recommended that if the entity is not classified as a bank by the host supervisory authority, then the parent supervisory authority should either supervise it or demand that it be closed. In the context of the Banco Ambrosiano case, this implies that since Luxembourg did not classify BAH as a bank, the Bank of Italy should have demanded the right to supervise BAH or require the parent to shut it down.

Second, the Committee recommended that if the host supervisory authority thinks that supervision by the parent authority is inadequate, it should either prohibit operations of the local entity or place stringent prudential restrictions on its operations. In the context of the Banco Ambrosiano case, this implies that if Luxembourg suspected that banking activity was being conducted by BAH and that supervision by the Bank of Italy was inadequate, it should have closed BAH or placed stringent conditions on its operations. More quixotically, it implies that if the authorities in the Bahamas or Peru believed that Luxembourg was not supervising BAH adequately, they should have closed the local subsidiaries or constrained their operations.

Third, the Committee recommended that if the parent entity is a holding company, supervisors of separate subsidiary banks should cooperate to supervise the holding company. In the context of the Banco Ambrosiano case, this has the highly impractical implication that the Bahamas and Peru should have cooperated in supervising the holding company protected by Luxembourg secrecy laws.

Fourth, the Committee recommended that if the holding company is a subsidiary, the parent supervisor should supervise the holding company and its subsidiaries or close it. This appeared to be a direct criticism of the behavior of the Bank of Italy. When the Bank of Italy found that it could not supervise BAH, it should have demanded that Banco Ambrosiano SpA close BAH.

The Revised Concordat appeared to be motivated by the collapse of Banco Ambrosiano. Indeed the Basle Committee's 1982 report (Committee on Banking Regulations and Supervisory Practices, March 1983, p. 4) referred to forthcoming recommendations based on "a close examination of the implications of the Ambrosiano case." Nonetheless, a participant in the meetings of the Basle Committee has stated that the Committee was also concerned about another international bank that was not subject to consolidated supervision—the rapidly growing Bank of Credit and Commerce International (Friedman and Waters, 1991).

The Rise and Fall of BCCI

Aga Hassan Abedi founded BCCI in 1972. His aim was to establish a new kind of bank that would finance trade with the Third World. Although many important managerial decisions were made in Pakistan, the bank was initially based in Abu Dhabi and incorporated in Luxembourg. The Bank of America greatly facilitated the international expansion of BCCI by investing $2.5 million in exchange for a 25 percent equity stake in the startup bank. BCCI's association with what was then the largest bank in the world gave it an aura of respectability that it could not otherwise have achieved so quickly. In return, the Bank of America hoped to gain a stronger foothold in the Arab world through its association with BCCI. By September 1973, BCCI had offices in Beirut, London, Luxembourg, and three of the Gulf emirates.

Over time the Bank of America became frustrated and concerned about the reluctance of BCCI to provide it with adequate information, and late

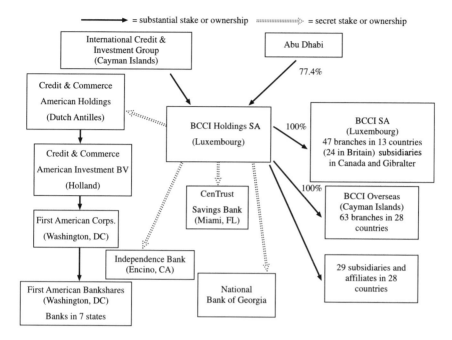

Figure 8–2. The structure of the BCCI circa June 1991.

in 1977 it began to sell its stake in BCCI. Over the next two years, "Abedi arranged for a wealthy Saudi Arabian associate to acquire some of the shares; others were moved into ICIC Holdings, the employee benefit fund" (Adams and Frantz, 1992, p. 44). But by this time BCCI had gained entry into nearly 70 countries. Indeed, by the mid-1970s it had more retail branches in the United Kingdom than any other foreign bank. During the 1970s Abedi carefully structured the bank to avoid consolidated super-vision. Although figure 8–2 shows the structure of the bank just before it was closed, the essential elements of the structure were in place by the end of the bank's first decade.

BCCI adopted a dual banking structure. The nonbank holding company established in Luxembourg in 1972 (BCCI Holdings SA) owned two separate banks that were licensed and supervised in two separate jurisdic-tions, well-insulated by bank secrecy laws: BCCI SA in Luxembourg and BCCI Overseas in the Cayman Islands. Although BCCI SA was registered as a bank in Luxembourg, its banking business was conducted through 47 branches in 13 countries but not in Luxembourg. BCCI Overseas did conduct a banking business in the Cayman Islands that controlled 63 branches in 28 countries. As the Shadow Financial Regulatory Committee (1991) noted, "BCCI's headquarters were established in countries with weak supervisory authorities, strong secrecy laws, and neither lenders of last resort nor deposit insurers who would have financial reasons to be concerned about the solvency of banks that are chartered in their jurisdiction."

Contrary to what the organizational chart seemed to imply, neither Luxembourg nor the Cayman Islands was the operational headquarters of BCCI. Instead, most managerial decisions were made in London with oversight from Abedi in Pakistan. This complex corporate structure virtually precluded consolidated supervision of the activities of BCCI. To further fragment external scrutiny of the bank, Abedi hired separate auditing firms for each bank: Ernst and Young audited the Luxembourg bank and Price Waterhouse, the Cayman Islands bank.[10] Thus, before the Concordat was officially published, BCCI had constructed a corporate structure that skillfully evaded the new supervisory principles. Indeed, once the Bank of America sold its stake, BCCI was not subject to comprehensive scrutiny by any external entity.

The refusal of the U.S. banking authorities to grant a banking license to BCCI in 1978 and 1980 was the principal obstacle to BCCI's global expansion. The U.S. authorities rebuffed BCCI's attempt to obtain a New York State banking license and its attempt to acquire the predecessor of First American Bankshares. U.S. authorities opposed granting entry to a foreign bank unless it had a home-country primary supervisor on whom they could rely for information (Heimann, 1991). This was an admission price that BCCI was unwilling to pay.

It seems likely that BCCI's attempt to gain a New York State license and its attempt to acquire the predecessor of First American Bankshares were intended to gain access to the Clearing House Interbank Payments System (CHIPS), the mechanism through which almost all large-scale, dollar-denominated transactions are cleared and settled (Herring, 1991). To participate in CHIPS a bank must have an office in New York City. For historical reasons, First American Bankshares and its predecessor bank had the unusual privilege of controlling an interstate network of banks that included a bank in New York City. Direct access to CHIPS would facilitate the secret movement of funds, and this may have motivated BCCI's persistent efforts to gain control of First American Bankshares.[11] Later BCCI achieved through indirect (and illegal) means what it could not accomplish openly.

Although BCCI continued to expand rapidly, its profitability is open to question. The managers of BCCI appear to have been clever at evading supervision but inept at banking. During 1985, BCCI incurred almost $1 billion in trading losses. Under pressure from the Bank of England, BCCI moved its treasury operations from London to Abu Dhabi (Lascelles et al., 1991).[12] About this time—perhaps to compensate for these and other losses—BCCI seems to have stepped-up its efforts to attract nontraditional sources of funds. The diversity of depositors at BCCI is notable. They included the Israeli intelligence agency, the Palestine Liberation Organization, Abu Nidal, Saddam Hussein, and Libya; the Sandinistas and the Contras; the CIA and many Eastern European intelligence agencies; the U.S. government and Manuel Noriega, the Mafia, and Colombian drug cartels; a variety of third world dictators; several Third World central banks; and, most poignantly, more than 1 million unsophisticated retail depositors in the United Kingdom and several less-developed countries.

By the mid-1980s BCCI appears to have become a full service bank in the most sinister sense of the term. In addition to offering the usual array of financial products, BCCI laundered money, and financed arms deals providing shipping, insurance, personnel and security as well. BCCI is also alleged to have operated a black network that functioned like a global intelligence service and enforcement squad (Beaty and Gwynne, 1991).

The supervisory authorities experienced frustration in their attempts to monitor the bank. Luxembourg lacked resources to oversee the worldwide operations of BCCI, and since BCCI conducted no banking business in Luxembourg, the Luxembourg Monetary Commission had slight incentive to assume the role of lead regulator. It urged that Bank of England to accept the responsibility because the operational headquarters were in London. The Bank of England, however, did not want the burden of supervising the global operations of a bank that it did not charter.

What of the Revised Concordat? Why didn't the members of the Basle Committee accept their obligation to see that a sizable international bank with total assets equal to roughly $20 billion in book value was adequately supervised? First, the Revised Concordat is a code of best practices, not an enforceable set of rules. It reflects the aspirations of the supervisory authorities, not their capabilities.

Second, BCCI had already entered most major markets before the revision of the Concordat in 1983. The supervisory authorities have much greater discretion over entry decisions than exit decisions. When a foreign bank seeks entry to a country, the local supervisory authorities have significant leverage in applying fit and proper tests. Once the foreign bank has received a license to conduct a banking business, most supervisory authorities must have evidence that a bank has committed serious violations of local laws or is insolvent before the license can be revoked. It is rarely sufficient to know that a bank is engaged in misconduct; since the supervisors are sure to be challenged in court, they must be able to prove misconduct beyond reasonable doubt.

Third, supervisory authorities are always reluctant to take actions that diminish prospects that depositors will be repaid. Public disciplinary action against BCCI would almost certainly have caused a run on the bank and inflicted losses on depositors. The authorities hoped that the bank would be recapitalized by its major shareholders. If BCCI were closed, depositors would almost certainly sustain losses; as long as BCCI remained open, depositors had some chance of being repaid.[13]

Because the supervisory authorities lacked the authority to compel BCCI to modify its corporate structure so that it could be supervised on a consolidated basis, they improvised a supervisory structure. In 1987 the supervisory authorities from Britain, the Cayman Islands, France, Luxembourg, Spain, and Switzerland formed a "regulatory college" to share information about the operations of BCCI. This sharing of information was consistent with the Revised Concordat but proved entirely inadequate for supervising BCCI.

BCCI entered the United States overtly from 1980 through 1984 by establishing state-chartered agencies and representative offices.[14] During 1988, BCCI's agency offices in Miami and Tampa were indicted for money laundering. BCCI did not contest the charges and paid a fine. But the supervisory net did not begin to tighten around BCCI until April 1990 when Price Waterhouse reported to the Bank of England that some of BCCI's accounting was "false or deceitful."[15] The Bank of England reacted by demanding that new management be introduced and that the bank be recapitalized. Abu Dhabi responded by investing an additional $1.2 billion in the bank, which lifted its ownership share from 30 percent to roughly 77 percent. The emirate also placed substantial additional deposits in the bank. The Bank of England commissioned Price Waterhouse to conduct a much broader investigation of the bank. Meanwhile authorities in the United States continued to investigate allegations that BCCI had covertly acquired control of four U.S. banks. On March 4, 1991, they ordered BCCI to divest its interest in the holding company of First American Bankshares.[16]

On July 2, 1991, supervisory authorities from several major countries met at the Bank of England to read a 45-page report prepared by Price Waterhouse. The report documented massive fraud at BCCI on a global scale. Regulators in 60 nations closed offices of BCCI on the weekend of July 5, 1991, in a carefully orchestrated operation.[17]

Later in July the U.S. Federal Reserve Board (Fed) took enforcement action against four individuals involved with BCCI's illegal acquisition of the Independence Bank in Encino, California. At the end of the month, the Fed accused BCCI of illegally acquiring control of the National Bank of Georgia, CenTrust Savings Bank (Miami), and the parent holding company of First American Bankshares (see figure 8.2). The Fed assessed a $200 million civil penalty against BCCI.

In December 1991, the fiduciaries appointed by courts in Britain, the Cayman Islands, and Luxembourg to administer BCCI's affairs entered into an agreement with the U.S. authorities whereby BCCI agreed to plead guilty to federal and state criminal charges and to forfeit its assets in the United States. Under the agreement, BCCI also consented to the Federal Reserve's civil money penalty action.

The government of Abu Dhabi, the principal shareholder of BCCI, and the court-appointed liquidators of the bank have reached a tentative settlement. Under terms of the proposed settlement, the assets of BCCI would be pooled along with $2 billion from the majority shareholders. In return, all creditors worldwide would be obliged to give up their rights to seek further legal redress against the majority shareholders. The net result is that depositors would realize from 30 to 40 cents per dollar deposited with BCCI (Reuters, 1992). Courts in the Cayman Islands and Britain have approved this agreement. Final approval from the court in Luxembourg is pending an appeal by some creditors.

Options for Improving the Supervision of International Banks

The European Community (EC) drew an important (though tentative) lesson from the collapse of BCCI. Like the Basle Committee, the EC has adopted the principle that the supervisors of parent banks are responsible for supervising the solvency of the banking family. One possible implication from the ineffectual supervision of BCCI is that regulators such as Luxembourg or the Cayman Islands, whose citizens have a negligible financial stake in the solvency of banks that they charter, may lack incentives to implement consolidated supervision rigorously. Concern for the reputation of a financial center may not be an adequate substitute for a financial stake in the solvency of chartered institutions. In the aftermath of BCCI, the EC produced a draft directive on deposit insurance that reversed the original allocation of responsibility for deposit insurance to the host country. Under the draft directive, the parent authority is to be responsible for providing deposit insurance to branches of all banks that they charter wherever the branches may reside within the European Community. Because this places supervisory and financial responsibility in the same country, it should enhance incentives to supervise solvency or to implement more rigorous fit and proper tests for granting and continuing a banking charter. During the December 1992 meeting of the finance ministers of the EC, the draft directive was tabled. Several countries feared that the draft directive would give a competitive advantage to banks headquartered in countries that offer comparatively generous deposit insurance protection (*Economist*, 1992).

The collapse of BCCI had negligible impact on international financial markets. Some regarded this as evidence of the faith of market participants in the ability of the regulators to manage a crisis (Heimann, 1991). A more cynical interpretation is that sophisticated market participants had disengaged from BCCI long ago.[18] Those who lost money at BCCI include retail depositors, some British local authorities, and a score of third world central banks. Very few international banks or institutional investors are on the list.

Indeed BCCI did not pose a systemic threat to international banking because large, sophisticated market participants were not exposed to BCCI. Apparently they and some supervisory authorities were keenly aware of BCCI's unsavory reputation.[19] This asymmetry of information raises troubling questions. Should the suspicions of sophisticated market participants and supervisors have been shared with unsophisticated depositors? Any disclosure of suspicions regarding BCCI would undoubtedly have set off a run that would have caused losses to existing depositors. Moreover, the authorities were understandably reluctant to act on the basis of unsubstantiated rumors. But the considerable delay before officials acted on their suspicions undoubtedly exacerbated the losses to many unsophisticated depositors.

The collapse of BCCI emphasized again the importance of consolidated supervision for monitoring the solvency of banks with foreign branches. Equally, it highlighted the difficulties of accomplishing effective consolidated supervision. As the Shadow Financial Regulatory Committee observed (1991), "Fraud is notoriously difficult for regulators to detect . . . [and] it is especially difficult to discover when fraudulent transactions cross national borders and can be concealed through the use of secrecy havens."

On July 6, 1992, the Basle Committee announced yet another attempt to strengthen the Concordat to prevent a repetition of the BCCI scandal (Basle Committee for Banking Supervision, 1992). The Committee added greater emphasis to the implementation of the Concordat by restating the key provisions as minimum standards, including the following:

1. All international banking groups and international banks should be supervised by a home-country authority that capably performs consolidated supervision;
2. The creation of a cross-border banking establishment should receive the prior consent of both the host-country supervisory authority and the bank's, and if different, banking group's home-country supervisory authority;
3. Supervisory authorities should possess the right to gather information from the cross-border banking establishments of the banks or banking groups for which they are the home-country supervisor; and
4. If a host-country authority determines that any one of the foregoing minimum standards is not met to its satisfaction, that authority could impose restrictive measures necessary to satisfy its prudential concerns.

The new feature is the authority of the host country to impose "restrictive measures" if it is uncomfortable with the quality of the home-country supervision of a local banking establishment. Such measures may range from setting a deadline for the bank and its home supervisory authority to meet acceptable standards, to obliging the banking establishment be restructured as a separately capitalized subsidiary, to closing the banking establishment. This emphasis implicitly recognizes the difficulties of harmonizing supervisory standards in a world where countries differ greatly in their supervisory traditions and in their capacities to monitor global financial institutions.

If these standards had been applied to BCCI, Luxembourg should have exercised consolidated supervision over BCCI because it chartered the parent of the banking group. If other countries were not satisfied with the quality of Luxembourg's supervision of BCCI, they should have taken restrictive measures against local offices. This example, however, points out a significant impediment in implementing the new guideline. Since Luxembourg is a member of the European Community, the Second Banking Directive prohibits other member states from discriminating against branches of Luxembourg banks. Moreover, restrictive measures are inherently easier to apply to banks seeking entry than to banks that may have altered their structure or conduct of business.

The Bank of England is seeking stronger powers (Peston et al., 1992). It wants the authority to shut down a bank "on the sole ground that an applicant authorized bank cannot be effectively supervised." In addition to the "restrictive measures" incorporated in the newly issued Concordat, the Bank of England wants to be able to withdraw authorization from a bank if it subsequently sets up branches in countries lacking an effective supervisor and if the nature of a bank's business changes—even though its ownership structure is unaltered. Such measures, if applied to a member of the European Community, would clash even more sharply with the EC's fundamental principle of mutual recognition. But they do address the difficult problem of dealing with a foreign bank after it has gained entry.

Congress has mandated that the Fed take a more active role in the establishment and termination of foreign bank offices in the United States. The Fed is currently implementing the Foreign Bank Supervision Enhancement Act of 1991, a subsection of the Federal Deposit Insurance Corporation Improvement Act of 1991.[20] The act applies not only to branches and subsidiaries of foreign banks but also to agencies and loan production offices. The Fed assumes primary supervisory responsibility for all foreign banking entities even if they hold a state charter. The Fed must determine whether home-country supervision is adequate with regard to five standards. The act provides a process to control the entry of foreign banks into the United States and to strengthen the authority of the Fed to regulate, supervise, and terminate foreign bank offices.

The Fed accepted comments on the proposed regulations until June 16, 1992. Predictably some state banking authorities objected to the extension of the Federal Reserve's power into their traditional domain. And foreign banks expressed concern about the increased regulatory burden and the cost of supplying different kinds of information to each host regulator.

Much depends on how the Fed administers the proposed regulations. The United States risks obtaining a safer banking system at the cost of diminished competition and efficiency. Ironically, the proposed regulations would not have prevented BCCI from gaining control of First American Bankshares. Even though the Fed strongly suspected that BCCI was seeking to gain control of First American Bankshares and made extensive investigations of the ownership structure of the holding company, it was unable to thwart BCCI. The Fed will continue to have difficulty determining who is really buying an American bank if the purchaser is intent on concealing its true identity.

Three fundamental options could improve the supervision of foreign banks: (1) centralized supervision by some supranational regulatory agency with full powers to implement consolidated supervision; (2) harmonization of international prudential standards among all major banking centers; or (3) greater autonomy for individual countries to apply their own standards to foreign banking entities. The political obstacles to the first option are overwhelming. Members of the Basle Committee still experience impediments in simply sharing information. The prospect of surrendering sovereignty to some supranational entity is virtually unimaginable.

The second option, greater harmonization of prudential standards, has been the traditional thrust of the Basle Committee; but the histories of BCCI and Banco Ambrosiano raise questions about whether harmonization—even among the relatively homogeneous countries of the Basle Committee—can be achieved. The success of the approach depends on agreement regarding prudential standards among all countries that host important banking centers. Moreover, these countries must have the willingness and capacity to implement the agreed standards. It is convenient to assume that all sovereigns are equal, but the assumption is demonstrably false.

The most recent revision of the Concordat recognizes that harmonization may be too difficult to achieve and provides greater scope for autonomous decisions by host countries. Supervision in the United Kingdom and the United States appears to be moving even more rapidly in the direction of the third option, greater autonomy. This approach may result in a safer international banking system, but not without cost. If each country applies substantially different supervisory standards, the costs of regulatory compliance will surely increase, the volume of international banking activity is likely to diminish, and the cost of financial services may rise.

Notes

1. The Group of Ten includes the ten leading capitalist countries—Belgium, Canada, France, Germany, Holland, Italy, Japan, Sweden, the United Kingdom, and the United States. The governors of the central banks of the Group of Ten meet regularly at the Bank for International Settlements in Basle, Switzerland.

2. While descriptive, the formal name of the committee proved so cumbersome that it was seldom used. Initially, most references to the committee used the name of the chairman—first the Blunden Committee, then the Cooke Committee. In order to discourage this practice, the Committee shortened its name to "The Basle Committee on Banking Supervision." For still greater brevity, I will refer to it as the "Basle Committee."

3. The Concordat was not officially disseminated until March 1981, when Peter Cooke (1981b), then chair of the Committee, made public a report to the governors by the Basle Committee.

4. The Concordat also allocated primary responsibility for supervision of liquidity to the host authority. The host authority was assumed to have a better capacity to judge the foreign bank's liquidity position in local currency transactions and a better incentive to insure its compliance with local monetary regulations. With regard to the management of liquidity in foreign currencies, the comparative advantage of the host authority was less clear. Indeed, "not all host authorities were willing to accept the same degree of responsibility" (Cooke, 1981b, p. 30).

5. This principle was noncontroversial in most member countries. Indeed, some countries had practiced consolidated supervision for several years. But in Germany, adoption of

the principle of consolidated supervision required a major, bitterly contested, legislative reform.

6. For example, for the purposes of French bankruptcy law the BCCI branches in France are considered to be a separate legal entity just as if they had been incorporated in France (Rowe, 1992).

7. The scandal surrounding the collapse of Banco Ambrosiano was comparable to that surrounding the collapse of BCCI. The chief executive officer of Banco Ambrosiano, Roberto Calvi, was found hanging from Black Friar's Bridge in London. In addition, the financial arm of the Vatican, the Institute of Religious Works, was alleged to be involved in several unsavory transactions with Banco Ambrosiano. The event has been fictionalized in at least two motion pictures and has generated several articles and books. See, for example, Cornwell (1983).

8. At least one bank rating agency provides two ratings for each bank: one based on the financial condition of the bank and a second based on the likelihood that the bank will receive official support.

9. The Revised Concordat was also adopted by the Offshore Group of Banking Supervisors.

10. In the mid-1980s Price Waterhouse demanded that it be named auditor for the entire bank. BCCI reluctantly agreed. The attempt of Price Waterhouse to audit the entire banking group ultimately led to the closure of BCCI.

11. The Federal Reserve (Mattingly, 1992) alleged that BCCI participated in certain management decisions of the First American Bank of New York, including the selection of the senior management of the bank. The Federal Reserve has reviewed all clearing transactions over $100,000 by the New York subsidiary over a two-year period from 1989–1991. All transactions greater than $1 million were analyzed by country of origin and country of disposition, but the Fed has not yet found evidence of impropriety.

12. Goldstein et al. (1992) note that the market risk underlying this loss was not addressed in the Basle Accord on Capital Adequacy. Neither was the concentration risk implicit in BCCI's subsequent $700 million loan to a single borrower.

13. This view weighs the interests of current depositors more heavily than those of future depositors. But since the authorities lacked objectively verifiable evidence that BCCI was insolvent, forbearance seemed a defensible (and attractive) option.

14. Although BCCI was never permitted to operate a branch in the United States or to openly control an insured bank, it did operate state-licensed agencies in New York, San Francisco, Los Angeles, Miami, Tampa, and Boca Raton. Agencies may hold credit balances from customers associated with international banking transactions but may not accept deposits from U.S. residents. BCCI also established representative offices in several U.S. cities, but such offices have severely limited powers (Mattingly, Taylor, and Corrigan, 1991).

15. Under U.K. banking law, auditors are permitted to share information with the regulators without their client's knowledge. Lord Bingham, in his report on the collapse of BCCI, has recommended that auditors should have a legal duty to report to the Bank of England in some circumstances (Donkin, 1992).

16. For a discussion of how the U.S. authorities finally detected the link between BCCI and First American Bankshares, see Mattingly (1991).

17. The supervisory authorities had clearly learned a valuable lesson from the closure of Herstatt: politically damaging spillover effects can be minimized when a bank can be closed during the weekend, reducing the disruption of routine clearing and settlement transactions. Nonetheless, one large Japanese bank did sustain a loss because it was awaiting a dollar payment in New York after it had delivered yen to the Tokyo branch of BCCI when the authorities closed BCCI. A gap of at least six and as much as 14 hours inevitably intervenes

between the time at which yen are paid in Tokyo and the time dollars can be received in New York (Goldstein et al., 1992).

18. The collapse of Banco Ambrosiano had revealed the risks inherent in a Luxembourg holding company structure. Moreover, the disreputable standing of BCCI among sophisticated market participants undoubtedly dissuaded some who might otherwise have placed deposits with the BCCI.

19. Robin Leigh-Pemberton, governor of the Bank of England, testified before the Commons Treasury Select Committee in July 1991 that the City had long had a nickname for the BCCI—the "Bank of Crooks and Criminals International" (Sampson, 1991).

20. Although this subsection is often interpreted as a response to the collapse of BCCI, it was also motivated by the fraud committed at the Atlanta office of Banca Nazionale del Lavoro.

References

Adams, James Ring and Douglas Frantz, *A Full Service Bank*, New York: Simon and Schuster, 1992.

Basle Committee on Banking Supervision, "Minimum Standards for the Supervision of International Banking Groups and Their Cross-Border Establishments," Basle, June 1992.

Beaty, Jonathan and S.C. Gwynne, "The Dirtiest Bank of All," *Time*, July 29, 1991, pp. 42–47.

Committee on Banking Regulations and Supervisory Practices, "Principles for the Supervision of Banks' Foreign Establishments," Mimeo, Basle, May 1983. This paper is reprinted in Dale (1984, pp. 188–194).

———, *Report on International Developments in Banking Supervision 1982*, Basle, March 1983.

Cooke, W. Peter, "Developments in Co-operation Among Banking Supervisory Authorities," *Journal of Comparative Law and Securities*, 1981a, pp. 55–64.

———, "Supervision of Banks' Foreign Establishments," in Richard C. Williams with G.G. Johnson et al., *International Capital Markets: Recent Short-Term Prospects, 1981*, Occasional Paper No. 7, International Monetary Fund, August 1981b, pp. 29–32.

Cornwell, Rupert, *"God's Banker,"* New York: Dodd, Mead, 1983.

Dale, Richard, *The Regulation of International Banking*, Cambridge: Woodhead-Faulkner, 1984.

Donkin, Richard, "Accountants Back Extra Legal Duties," *Financial Times*, October 23, 1992, p. 11.

Economist, "Deposit Insurance, Euro-Muddle," *The Economist*, December 19, 1992, p. 74.

Friedman, Alan and Richard Waters, "The BCCI Shutdown: Top Regulators' Worries Discussed a Decade Ago," *Financial Times*, July 25, 1991, p. 5.

Goldstein, Morris, David Folkerts-Landau, Mohammed El-Erian, Steven Fries, and Liliana Rojas-Suarez, *International Capital Markets: Developments, Prospects and Policy Issues*, World Economic and Financial Surveys, International Monetary Fund, September 1992.

Guttentag, Jack N. and Richard J. Herring, "Funding Risk in the International Interbank Market," in W. Ethier and R.C. Marston (eds.), *International Financial Markets and Capital Movements: A Symposium in Honor of Arthur I. Bloomfield*, Essays in International Finance No. 157, Princeton University, September 1985, pp. 19–32.

——, *The Lender-of-Last-Resort Function in an International Context*, Essays in International Finance No. 151, Princeton University, May 1983, pp. 1–26.

Herring, Richard J., "Pressures on the Plumbing of the International Financial System: The Threat of Systemic Risk," in Horst Siebert (ed.), *Capital Flows in the World Economy*, Institut für Weltwirtschaft an der Universität Kiel, Tübingen: J.C.B. Mohr (Paul Siebeck), 1991.

Heimann, John, "Don't Over Regulate After BCCI," *Wall Street Journal*, September 12, 1991, p. 18.

Kapstein, Ethan B., *Supervising International Banks: Origins and Implications of the Basle Accord*, Essays in International Finance No. 185, Princeton University, December 1991, pp. 1–34.

Lascelles, David, Richard Donkin, et al., "Behind Closed Doors," *Financial Times*, November 9–16, 1991.

Mattingly, J. Virgil, Jr., "Testimony Before the Subcommittee on Consumer and Regulatory Affairs of the Committee on Banking, Housing, and Urban Affairs," U.S. Senate, May 23, 1991.

——, "Testimony Before the Subcommittee on Terrorism, Narcotics, and International Operations of the Committee on Foreign Relations," U.S. Senate, May 14, 1992.

Mattingly, J. Virgil, Jr., William Taylor, and E. Gerald Corrigan, "Testimony Before the Committee on Banking, Finance and Urban Affairs," U.S. House of Representatives, September 13, 1991.

Morgan Guaranty Trust Company, *World Financial Markets*, July 16, 1974.

Peston, Robert, Ralph Atkins, and Andrew Jack, "Bank Criticized over Role in Supervision of BCCI," *Financial Times*, July 9, 1992, p. 8.

Reuters Ltd., "BCCI Caymans Liquidators Put Settlement on Hold," *Financial Report*, July 22, 1992.

Rowe, Michael, "Appeals Court Ruling Gives French Depositors Limited Hope of Recovering BCCI Investments," *Thompson's International Banking Regulator*, July 20, 1992, p. 6.

Sampson, Anthony, "A Man with Too Many Secrets," *The Independent*, August 29, 1991, p. 23.

Shadow Financial Regulatory Committee, "Statement on the Bank of Credit and Commerce International," Statement No. 74, September 16, 1991.

9 FINANCIAL MARKETS AND MANAGERIAL MYOPIA: MAKING AMERICA MORE COMPETITIVE*

Franklin R. Edwards

Introduction

In the Japanese bestseller, *The Japan That Can Say "No,"* Sony president Akio Morita and liberal democratic party member Shintaro Ishihara (1990) say, "We [Japan] are focusing on business 10 years in advance while you [the United States] seem to be concerned with profits 10 minutes from now. At that rate you may never be able to compete with us." Yotaro Kobayashi (1990), the president of Fuji Xerox, describes the Japanese view of U.S. managers this way: "It is one of people who love to plot takeover bids and play the mergers and acquisitions game, who have their minds on only short-term profits, and who readily lay off workers while rewarding themselves with fat bonuses."

In recent years U.S. managers and financial markets have come under increasing attack at home as well because of their perceived myopic

* The author wishes to thank the Smith Richardson Foundation, Inc. for its support, without which he would not have been able to pursue this topic.

behavior. Critics contend that the short-term investment horizons of U.S. investors are forcing corporate managers to focus on short-term earnings to the detriment of both the long-run interests of their firms and the United States. Corporate managers, it is alleged, forego long-run, value-enhancing projects out of a fear that a reduction in short-run earnings will cause their stock prices to plummet, exposing them to hostile takeover.

Critics cite several pieces of evidence in support of the view that stockholders are to blame. First, stockholders have become increasingly impatient. The trading of stock, as measured by annual turnover, increased sharply during the 1980s. Stocks are now held on average for just two years, as opposed to over four years in 1980 and seven years in 1960. The average holding period for institutional investors is even shorter: for pension funds and mutual funds it is less than two years (Froot, Perold, and Stein, 1991; Lorsch and MacIver, 1991). A decline in a firm's current earnings, it is argued, triggers an immediate sell reaction on the part of many investors. Critics also point to the increased stock market volatility during the 1980s, which they link to the increased turnover of stocks and to a pervading speculative mentality.

The impatient behavior of U.S. investors stands in sharp contrast to their counterparts in Japan and Germany. While the average turnover of stocks in Japan and Germany is much the same as in the United States, this statistic hides more than it reveals. In these countries a large portion of stock is held by long-term or "relationship" investors, who seldom trade the stock. For example, in Japan the average holding periods of corporate stockholders (which hold about 30 percent of total equity) and insurance companies are 7.4 years and 18.3 years, respectively. Overall, about 70 percent of total Japanese equity is held for an average of just over five years. In contrast, no single group of U.S. stockholders has an average holding period of more than five years (Froot, Perold, and Stein, 1991).

Second, the trend in the United States is clearly toward a growing presence of institutional investors, which, as stockholders, rank among the most impatient U.S. investors. During the last ten years, institutional ownership of stock has grown to over 50 percent of total stock outstanding in the United States, and this trend shows no sign of abating. A recent survey conducted by the New York Stock Exchange found that from 1985 to 1990 more individuals (14 million) added stock mutual funds to their investment portfolios than added shares of individual stocks (8.6 million people). By the end of 1990 there were more than 25 million holders of stock mutual funds, which was more than double the number just five years earlier. Thus, more investment power is being placed in the hands of professional money managers, whom business executives view as short-term oriented, ready to sell at the slightest hint of lower current earnings.

Third, the frequency of hostile takeovers during the 1980s, it is contended, reinforces the view that short-termism is prevalent. If impatient investors fail to appreciate the long-run strategies of companies, and instead push stock values to unrealistic low levels, takeover specialists can acquire the firm, oust management, and dismember the firm in order to realize its true long-run value. A hostile-takeover environment, therefore, encourages short-run managerial planning.

Those who hold these views point as well to Japan and Germany, where hostile takeovers are virtually impossible. Management in these countries, it is argued, is protected from precipitous ouster and is left free to pursue strategies that enhance the long-run value of their firms.

The evidence cited above, however, is subject to alternative interpretation. For example, the more active trading in the 1980s may simply have been a response to lower trading costs. Similarly, the advent of hostile takeovers and leveraged buyouts during the 1980s may have been a response to managerial inefficiency or myopia, rather than a cause of it. Critics may be confusing correlation with causality. The causality may run the other way: corporate myopia may have resulted in inefficient firms that investors sought to profit from by replacing underperforming management through hostile takeovers.

Despite the ambiguity of the evidence, there appears to be widespread agreement among business executives and financial managers that investor short-sightedness is a major cause of myopia in U.S. companies. A 1990 survey conducted by the Financial Executives Institute asked 2,000 of its members to list in order of importance the factors that inhibit the international competitiveness of U.S. firms. Institute members consist of top American financial executives, ranging from corporate financial officers to private pension fund managers. Their responses singled-out two factors as primarily responsible for America's competitiveness problems: the "shortsightedness of investors" and "the shortsightedness of corporate managers" (Jacobs, 1991, p. 8). Another survey of chief executive officers conducted by James M. Poterba and Lawrence H. Summers (1991, table 1) revealed that U.S. managers believe that U.S. firms have shorter planning horizons than do their foreign competitors. Further, there is some evidence that foreign CEOs in Japan, Germany, and the United Kingdom agree with this assessment.

Although these views have not yet found their way into public policy, several aborted legislative efforts have sought to reduce investor myopia by curbing short-term trading. In 1989 Republican senator Nancy

Kassebaum of Kansas introduced a bill that would impose a 10 percent tax on capital gains earned by pension funds on assets held less than 30 days, and a 5 percent tax on assets held less than 180 days. The cosponsor of the bill was no less than Senate minority leader Robert Dole. The Bush administration also considered introducing a similar tax bill. Such a bill, in the words of then Treasury secretary Nicholas Brady, would "encourage Americans to take the long-term view in their economic thinking" ("White House," 1989). Finally, and perhaps of more import today, in 1989 the Senate Finance Committee chair (and now Treasury secretary) suggested that he might propose a tax on short-term trades by pension funds ("White House," 1989). Still other proposals have been made to tax spot and derivative-market transactions in foreign exchange for the purpose of "increasing the weight that market participants give to long-range fundamentals relative to immediate speculative opportunities" (Tobin, 1992).

This chapter reviews the evidence related to the question of whether U.S. investors, both individuals and institutions, behave myopically. In general, this evidence is found to be inconsistent with the view that U.S. investors behave myopically. Second, it provides an alternative explanation for the existence of managerial short-sightedness in the past: U.S. firms have faced a higher cost of capital than have Japanese and German firms. Differences in the cost of capital between U.S. and foreign firms are partly due to the higher risk premiums demanded by American stockholders and lenders, which in turn appear to stem from differences in the structure of corporate ownership in the respective countries. In Germany and Japan financial institutions and institutional investors are able to take "large-owner" roles, and as a consequence are able to reduce the risk premiums they demand, resulting in a lower cost of capital for German and Japanese firms. Third, I propose that financial reforms be undertaken in the United States both to encourage long-term ownership by institutional investors and to enable institutional investors to take a more active role in corporate governance.

The United States' Competitive Decline and Its Link to Managerial Myopia

The genesis of the debate over corporate myopia in the United States is the widespread perception that the United States in general and U.S. firms in particular are losing out in the global struggle for markets and jobs. During the 1980s the United States' share of total world exports declined as Japan and Germany wrested a greater share of the world's economic pie. More alarming, perhaps, is that the United States' share of world exports of *manufactured* products declined from about 12.1 percent in 1982 to 11.8 percent in 1989. In 1986 the Japanese share of manufactured exports surpassed the United States for the first time.

The real wages of U.S. workers also fell during the last 15, years while the real wages of workers in many other countries were rising. Of the major countries, only the United States has seen the real hourly compensation of its workers fall. In the other countries real wages rose by substantial amounts: 40 percent in Germany, 22 percent in Japan, 42 percent in France.

Ironically, what has happened to U.S. workers stands in sharp contrast to that of the top U.S. business executives: during the last decade the compensation of U.S. CEOs has more than doubled. At a time when U.S. workers were losing out to their counterparts in Japan and Germany, the gap between the pay of top managers and workers in the United States was growing relative to that of leading competitor countries. In the United States the pay of top executives is more than 100 times the average U.S. worker's pay. In Japan this pay ratio is more like 17 times the average worker's wage, and in European countries is closer to 35 times the typical worker's pay (Jacobs, 1991). These glaring differences in compensation, not surprisingly, have raised questions about the determinants of managerial compensation in the United States and about whether the compensation of U.S. managers is tied closely enough to the performance of their firms.

Perhaps most disturbing of all, productivity growth in the United States has been consistently below that of our major competitors since the 1960s. Although U.S. workers are still 20 percent more productive than the workers of main foreign rivals, this lead is steadily eroding.

There is a widespread belief that managerial myopia is at the heart of this relative decline in productivity. Three factors largely determine worker productivity: labor quality, technology, and the amount of capital goods used per worker. These in turn are the cumulative results of past investments in, respectively, human capital, research and development (R&D), and plant and equipment (U.S. Department of Labor, 1989). Critics allege that U.S. firms are underinvesting relative to our foreign competitors because of the shortsightedness of corporate managers.

Defining and measuring investment on a consistent basis across countries is difficult, but the evidence we have leaves a distinct impression that U.S. firms are not investing as much as their foreign counterparts. The U.S. invests about half as much of its GNP in new plant and equipment as does Japan and about two-thirds as much as does Germany (Brooks, 1985). Recent estimates of *absolute* capital spending in 1990 indicate that U.S. and Japanese capital spending is almost identical—$586 billion versus $524 billion, although Japanese GNP is only half as large as the U.S.'s GNP ("Japan Seen Passing . . . ," 1992). Further, net domestic investment in the United States declined from an average of almost 7 percent of GNP during the 1960s to an average of 3.2 percent by the mid-1980s (Friedman, 1988). The relative difference in our investment pattern may be even more significant than the figures suggest because of a growing "vintage" gap: U.S. capital stock is older and is aging more rapidly than capital stock in foreign countries (Sunohara, 1990).

U.S. spending on R&D is also declining relative to our rivals. The July 1991 issue of the *Japan Economic Survey* stated that Japanese business in 1989 spent 9.60 trillion yen on research. At a market exchange rate of 135 yen to the dollar, that figure is equal to $71.10 billion dollars, compared to a 1989 figure of $71.77 billion for the United States ("Japan Seen Passing . . . ," 1992). Further, as a percent of GNP our *total* R&D spending is only slightly less than in West Germany and Japan, but if defense activities are excluded from total R&D spending in all countries, the gap between the U.S. and Japan and Germany widens considerably. The non-defense R&D/GNP ratio for the U.S. in 1987 was 1.7 percent, compared to 2.6 percent for West Germany and 2.8 percent for Japan. This is a large difference in total R&D spending, no matter how measured. In addition, the growth in spending on R&D in the United States appears to have slowed even more in recent years.

In future years a critical contributing factor to higher productivity is likely to be investment in human capital—educating and training the workforce. Industry has complained that the U.S. workforce lacks the requisite basic skills to make the United States more productive, and that the quality of U.S. education is dismal compared with that of other countries (Reich, 1988). Critics argue that U.S. firms are partly to blame for this. With longer horizons, they contend, firms would be willing to invest more in on-the-job training for employees and in improving the quality of the workforce.

Reliable estimates of the extent of U.S. worker training by U.S. firms relative to Japanese and German firms do not exist. The few available data we have, however, indicate that "competitor countries provide more training, take a much more systematic approach to training, provide government support for it, and train their workers to higher average standards" (U.S. Congress, 1990; Blinder and Krueger, 1992; Kochan and Osterman, 1992). Data on training programs in U.S. and Japanese automobile plants are suggestive. Figures 9–1a and 9–1b compare the annual hours of training per employee for U.S. and Japanese auto assembly plants: plants in Japan (J-J), Japanese-owned plants in the United States (J-U.S.), and U.S.-owned

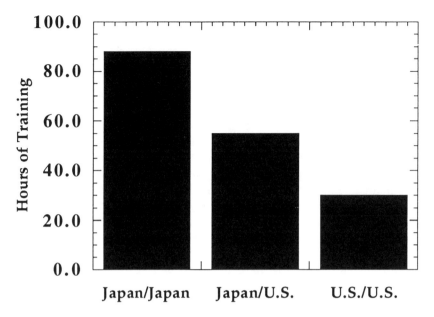

Figure 9–1a. Annual Hours of Training Per Employee, Automobile Assembly Workers.

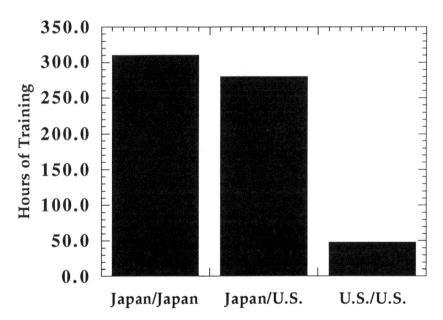

Figure 9–1b. Hours of Training, Newly Hired Automobile Assembly Workers.
Source: John F. Krafcik, *Training and the Automobile Industry: International Comparisons*, contractor report prepared for the Office of Technology Assessment under contract N3-1910 February 1990, pp. 8–9.

plants in the United States (U.S.-U.S.). Autoworkers in J-J plants get more than three times as much training each year as workers in U.S.-U.S. plants. Even more striking differences exist for newly hired workers: new employees in J-J plants get more than 300 hours of training in their first six months compared with fewer than 50 hours for U.S. workers in U.S.-U.S. plants (U.S. Congress, 1990).

Not all evidence, however, is supportive of the view that the United States has a competitive problem (Lawrence, 1991a). For example, U.S. firms themselves, as opposed to the United States as a geographical entity, have maintained their share of the world's export market. They have done this as multi-national firms, exporting from production locations throughout the world. U.S. multinationals' share of world exports of manufactured goods was 16.1 percent in 1989, compared to 17.3 percent in 1966, a rather small decline over 23 years. If U.S. firms have had incompetent, short-sighted, management, how have they managed to hold their worldwide market share so well?

Another piece of inconsistent evidence is that the United States continues to be a leading exporter of high-technology products—products made by research-and-development-intensive industries. U.S. multinationals operating from locations around the world account for 30 percent of total exports of high-technology products, and this share has been nearly constant for the last 15 years. It is difficult to understand how managers who manage only for the short-run could maintain a leadership role in an area requiring extensive long-run planning and expenditures on research.

Despite such inconsistent evidence, there persists a widely held view that short-termism on the part of U.S. managers has been a major cause of the United States economic decline. Further, this short-termism is seen as being the direct result of pressures on managers by U.S. investors and Wall Street money managers who care only about firms' current earnings. Corporate myopia, critics charge, is the business executive's response to myopic shareholders.

Are U.S. Investors Myopic?

Many corporate managers clearly believe that the stock market penalizes them for adopting long-run strategies. In a survey of 100 CEOs of major U.S. corporations, 89 said that Wall Street's preoccupation with quarterly earnings was a key reason for their failure to emphasize long-term investment ("Business Bulletin," 1986).

Do in fact firms that undertake long-run investments see their stock values decline? Studies that examine the stock market's response to announcements of various kinds of proposed corporate long-term investments generally find just the opposite: a positive reaction to such proposals. For example, a study of 634 "strategic" or investment decisions announced by 347 different companies operating in 81 different industries, over the period 1972 to 1984, found that in general there was a positive stock market reaction to such announcements (Woolridge, 1988). The announcements studied included those related to increased research and development spending, increased expenditures for expansion or modernization, joint ventures, and various new product strategies. Of particular note is that a company's stock value generally rose immediately following an announcement that it was undertaking new R&D projects or increasing plant and equipment expenditures.

In still another study of 658 corporate capital expenditure announcements over the period 1975 to 1981, McConnell and Muscarella (1985) found that increases (decreases) in capital budgets result in significantly positive (negative) abnormal stock returns for the companies making the announcements. In another study of 62 R&D expenditure announcements over the 1973 to 1983 period, Jarrell, Lehn, and Marr (1985) found that these announcements were generally associated with significant increases in stock values.

These results appear to contradict the common perception that stockholders do not care about the long-run prospects of companies (Hector, 1988). In fact, investors generally have looked favorably upon companies that have planned for the long-run, even at the cost of reduced current earnings.

Another way of analyzing the weight that stockholders put on the long-run prospects of firms is to determine what portion of a company's stock value is attributable to its current earnings as opposed to future (or expected) earnings. The current price of a stock should be equal to the present value of all of the future cash flows to investors. This includes both current dividends as well as future expected dividends, no matter when occurring and in what form. These expected cash flows are normally discounted by a rate that should reflect both the time value of money (the risk-free interest rate) and the risk of holding the specific security. This rate is investors' required rate of return on that particular security.

In a study by Woolridge, current earnings and dividends as well as five-year projected dividends' and earnings' growth rates are used to estimate companies' dividends and earnings over the next five years (Woolridge, 1988). These five-year cash flows are then discounted by an estimated required rate of return to determine what portion of a company's current stock price is attributable to its earnings over only the next five years. Whatever is not attributable to these cash flows must, of course, be due to dividends and earnings that are expected to occur subsequent to the five-year period—or in the long-run. Woolridge finds that, on average, about 80 percent of a company's stock value is dependent on its long-run *dividends*, or about 55 percent of its stock value depends on its long-run *earnings*.

Woolridge's results are similar to those of Alfred Rappaport, who examines the stocks of the 20 largest U.S. companies (Hector, 1988). He finds that from 66 to 89 percent of a company's stock price cannot be explained by projected dividend flows further out than the next five years. The inference, therefore, is that a considerable portion of a stock's value depends on the market's assessment of the firm's long-run prospects (or its earnings beyond a five-year horizon).[1]

The general inference to be drawn from these studies also is consistent with what we observe in the venture capital market, where investors pin their hopes entirely on the future prospects of a firm—often many years into the future. Highly innovative and successful companies such as Apple Computer, CML Group, Cray Computer, Data General, Digital Equipment, Federal Express, Genentech, Intel, Lotus Development, Microsoft, Sun Microsystems, and Teledyne all received early funding in the venture capital market. In 1989 an estimated 674 venture capital firms in the United States managed more than $33 billion in capital, up from $5 billion in 1980 (Venture Economics, 1990). In committing venture capital, investors are looking to the long-run success of their companies and not to short-term earnings.

The contention that U.S. investors generally take a long-run view is supported as well by responses to the recent survey of CEO's taken by Poterba and Summers (Porterba and Summers, 1991). They asked whether the firm ever decided to forego making a profitable investment out of fear that the stock market would penalize its share price. More than three quarters (81 percent of the respondents said that they had *never* passed up a profitable investment opportunity because of this fear, and fewer than 1 percent indicated that they passed up such opportunities frequently. These responses are consistent with the view that U.S. investors do not penalize firms for undertaking long-term investments. Indeed, firms undertaking such investments usually experience a rise rather than fall in their stock values.

Finally, it is often alleged that stockholders can be fooled by managers who manipulate accounting rules in order to inflate short-term earnings. The evidence, however, does not support this concern. In a study of 108 accounting policy changes where the effects of the changes on reported earnings were disclosed, Ball finds that there is no relationship between a firm's value and "cosmetic" changes in reported earnings (Ball, 1972). A firm's value changes only if there is an effect on the firm's real cash flows, either positive or negative.

In another study Kaplan and Roll (1972) examine the effects of changes in two accounting policies: a switchback to straight-line depreciation, and a switch from the deferral to the flow-through method of accounting for deferred taxes. Both of these changes affect reported earnings but do not affect tax liabilities. Thus, they do not affect real cash flows. Kaplan and Roll conclude that neither change has an effect on a firm's stock price. Stockholders are not fooled: they have their eyes squarely on real cash flows and not on reported earnings. Managers, therefore, do not appear to be able to boost stock values by cosmetic, short-term changes in current earnings: no one is fooled.

There is substantial evidence, therefore, that U.S. stockholders are not myopic. Although it is still possible, of course, that the statistical studies discussed above fail to capture some form of myopic behavior, those who allege such behavior have the burden of producing some evidence in support of this view.

Are Institutional Investors Different?

Another common perception is that the behavior of U.S. investors has changed in the last decade because of the increasing dominance of institutional investors. Institutional ownership—by pension funds, mutual funds, etc.—has skyrocketed during the past decade, putting more stock under the control of fiduciaries.

In 1950 institutional investors owned only 8 percent of the equity of U.S. corporations. By 1980 their holdings had risen to 33 percent of equity, and today they exceed 53 percent of all publicly-traded stock (see table 9–1) (Brancato and Gaughan, 1988). Institutions own on average 53 percent of the outstanding shares of the largest 100 U.S. corporations. In several of the companies their holdings are much greater: 82 percent in General Motors Corp., 74 percent in Mobil Corp., 70 percent in Citicorp, 86 percent in Amoco, and 71 percent in Eli Lilly & Co. (Brancato, 1990a). The 10 largest pension funds together with the ten largest (nonpension) professional money managers now control more than 15 percent of the stock of the largest 10 U.S. companies (Brancato, 1990b).

Institutional investors do appear to behave differently than individual

Table 9–1.   Changes in Institutional Equity Ownership, 1981 to 1990 (Percentage of Total U.S. Market Capitalization)

Institution	1981	1986	1990	Change from 1981 to 1990
Private pension funds	15.5%	16.7	19.9	4.4%
Bank trusts	10.1	10.1	9.2	−0.9
Public pension funds	3.0	5.1	8.3	5.3
Mutual funds	2.5	6.8	7.2	4.7
Insurance companies	5.7	4.8	6.9	1.2
Foundations/endowments	1.2	1.3	1.8	0.6
Total	38.0%	44.8%	53.3%	15.3%

Source: Brancato and Gaughan (1991, table 10). Brancato and Gaughan (p. 2) define *institution* to include pension funds, mutual funds, insurance companies, bank-managed trusts, and foundation and endowment funds. This definition excludes shares owned by investment banks, bank holding companies, and nonbank, nonpension trusts.

shareholders. The average annual turnover of institutional stock portfolios is about 50 percent. Turnover is only about 20 percent for individuals (Froot, Perold, and Stein, 1991). Thus, institutional investors hold a stock on average for about two years, as opposed to five years for households. Further, in the early 1970s the rate of turnover of the average share on the New York Stock Exchange (NYSE) was just 16 percent, which implies an average holding period of more than five years. Today, the average holding period for NYSE stocks is just over two years. The increase in trading activity during the 1980s appears to stem largely from the increased trading of institutional investors.

Many believe that the high turnover of institutional portfolios manifests the short-term investment orientation of professional money managers. However, the link between either institutional ownership or increased trading and the investment horizons of corporate managers is not obvious. In a world of perfect capital markets, in which there are no information asymmetries, stock values should reflect all information about the firm, including its long-run prospects. Thus, even traders with short horizons will not be reluctant to hold the stocks of companies with a long-run orientation. Stock values will accurately reflect all long-run as well as all short-run prospects immediately. Similarly, corporate managers who have attractive long-run investment opportunities will not be deterred from undertaking these investments even if their stocks are more actively traded, because stock values will reflect the long-run prospects of the firm accurately.

Froot, Perold, and Stein (1991) explore possible market imperfections that might lead to a link between increased turnover (or short investor trading-horizons) and corporate behavior. They examine, first, whether increased trading may cause excess volatility, or stock prices to respond to nonfundamental factors as well as to economic fundamentals. Excess volatility, arguably, could result in a higher cost of capital for firms, which would shorten their planning horizons and reduce long-term investment.

Second, they explore the possibility that an information gap (or information asymmetry) between managers and stockholders may exist that causes managers to emphasize short-run strategies out of fear that impatient stockholders will sell their stock when current earnings decline, even though the earnings decline is due to the firm undertaking long-run investment that will eventually enhance the firm's value.

Froot, Perold, and Stein conclude that there is no clear relationship between turnover and volatility, either in the stock market or in any other market. This conclusion is consistent with studies that find no correlation between volatility and institutional ownership. Indeed, there is some evidence that volatility is lower in the stocks of companies that have *greater* institutional ownership (Jones, Lehn, and Mulherin, 1990; Aggarwal and Rao, 1990). Thus, in the absence of a link between trading activity and excess volatility, there is no reason to think that the greater trading activity of institutional investors results in a higher cost of capital for firms.

A study by Lakonishok, Shleifer, and Vishny (1991) supports the view that trading by pension fund managers does not destabilize stock prices. They examine quarterly changes in the portfolio holdings of 769 all-equity pension funds between 1985 and 1989 to see if a trading pattern exists that is consistent with the view that institutional behavior causes price instability. The funds examined were managed by 341 different institutional money managers. Lakonishok, Shleifer, and Vishny find that although institutional investors pursue a broad spectrum of trading strategies, their trading does not exhibit the kind of herding or positive-feedback pattern that would increase stock-price volatility.

With respect to a possible information-gap link, the conclusion is less clear. Froot, Perold, and Stein (1991, p. 36) say that "because the theory is all about information problems and "invisible" investments, it is hard to assemble unambiguous evidence in its favor." In general, however, after examining various kinds of circumstantial evidence, they conclude that the existence of an information gap between managers and stockholders does not result in any obvious links between institutional stock holdings and shortened managerial horizons.

The results of this research are consistent with evidence garnered from survey data. Although a survey of CEOs, conducted by Poterba and Summers (1991, table 1), revealed substantial variation in the "hurdle rates" (or in the cost of capital) used by firms in deciding whether or not to undertake an investment, there appeared to be no relationship between the presence of institutional investors and the hurdle rates used by firms. More specifically, one-third of the firms used "real" hurdle rates below 10 percent, while more that 10 percent of firms employed "real" hurdle rates greater than 15 percent. Poterba and Summers attempt to explain these differences with both financial variables (P/E ratios, current ratios, etc.) and with variables representing the characteristics of a firm's stockholders—in particular, the fraction of stock held by institutions and the annual turnover of a company's stock. They could find no association between either institutional stock holdings or turnover and the hurdle rates used by firms. Thus, there is no evidence that either institutional ownership or trading affects the investment horizons of firms.[2]

Do Differences in the Cost of Capital Explain Short-Termism in the United States?

If myopic behavior by U.S. investors is not responsible for the shortened investment horizons used by U.S. corporate managers, what is? A possible explanation is that U.S. firms have faced a higher cost of capital. Several studies have concluded that the cost of capital for U.S. corporations has been significantly higher than for Japanese and German companies during the last 15 years (Hatsopoulos, 1983; Hatsopoulos, Krugman, and Summers, 1988).

If U.S. firms have faced a higher cost of capital than their foreign competitors, this could explain their shorter planning horizons. A higher cost of funds can have a significant effect of the calculation of the net present value of an investment project. Further, as the returns associated with an investment become more distant, a higher cost of capital on an investment becomes more significant. For example, an increase of two percentage points in the cost of capital (say, from 10 to 12 percent) will reduce the net present value of a return to be received in one year by only 2 percent. But the same increase in the cost of capital applied to an investment that will yield returns over 20 years will reduce the net present value of that 20-year investment by over 30 percent (Malkiel, 1991). Thus, if Japanese and German firms have had a cost of capital that was only one or two percentage points lower than that of U.S. firms, they would have been willing to undertake much longer-term projects than would U.S. firms, and would have appeared to have had much longer managerial horizons. In fact, using data for the 1977–1988 period, studies of the relative cost of capital have estimated the disparity in favor of foreign firms to have been much greater than two percentage points (Malkiel, 1991).

The standard definition of the cost of capital is that it is the minimum before-tax rate of return that an investment project must generate in order to pay its financing costs after tax liabilities. This rate of return is determined by the required payments to a firm's debt and equity holders (or the cost of funds), by the economic depreciation of the investment and the tax treatment of that depreciation, the taxation of corporate earnings, and any other fiscal incentives associated with investment (McCauley and Zimmer, 1989). It is obvious, therefore, that comparing the cost of capital in different countries requires a thorough analysis of both differences in financing costs and differences in tax burdens. Further, measuring the cost of capital is not straightforward. In particular, the cost of equity capital (or the rate of return demanded by equity investors) cannot be observed directly but must be inferred or estimated. As consequence, there is considerable debate about the proper methodology and assumptions to use when making such estimates.

Despite these difficulties, several carefully researched studies have provided us with what are viewed as reasonably accurate estimates of the cost of capital in different countries. These studies unanimously indicate that U.S. firms have in fact faced a higher cost of capital during most of the 1970s and 1980s. In general, these studies calculate the cost of capital for a firm as the weighted average after-tax cost of the debt and equity in the company's capital structure. Typically, debt costs are taken to be stated borrowing rates adjusted for taxes and any other factor affecting borrowing costs, while equity costs are inferred from adjusted earnings-to-price ratios.

Studies by McCauley and Zimmer, Ando and Auerbach, Bernheim and Shoven, and Malkiel all find that the cost of capital was considerably higher in the United States than in Japan and Germany during the 1977–1988 period (McCauley and Zimmer, 1989; Ando and Auerbach, 1988; Bernheim and Shoven, 1989; Malkiel, 1991). A particularly striking finding is McCauley and Zimmer's estimates of the real after-tax cost of funds in the three countries (shown in figure 9–2). Here the cost of funds represents the weighted average of debt and equity costs to firms, using the book value of debt and the market value of equity. During the 1980s, the cost of funds

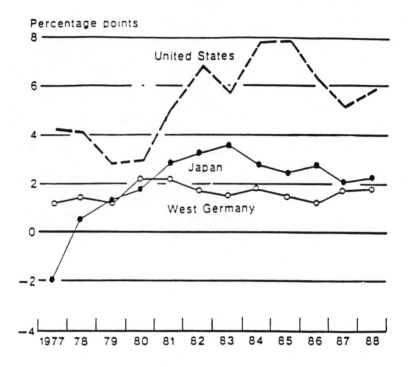

Figure 9–2. McCauley/Zimmer Estimates of the Real After-Tax Cost of Funds. Source: Robert N. McCauley and Steven A. Zimmer, "Explaining International Differences in the Cost of Capital," FRB, NY Research Paper No. 8913, August 1989.

in the United States was on average twice as high as in Japan and Germany. Although the cost of funds alone does not measure the cost of capital because it does not take into account differences in inflation, taxation, and depreciation conventions, McCauley and Zimmer show that even after adjusting for these factors there still existed a substantial cost of capital gap in favor of foreign firms.

To illustrate the effect of a higher cost of capital on long-investment decisions, McCauley and Zimmer (1989, table 2) estimate that in 1988 a U.S. firm would have needed to earn an 11.2 percent return on an investment in equipment and machinery with a life of 20 years before being willing to undertake such an investment, while Japanese and German firms would have needed to earn only about a 7 percent return on the same investment. Alternatively, in order to undertake an R&D project that would not yield returns for ten years, after which such returns would fall progressively over many future years, a U.S. firm would in 1988 have required a return of about 20 percent, whereas a Japanese firm would have required a return of only 8.7 percent and a German firm would have required a return of 14.8 percent (McCauley and Zimmer, 1989, table 2). Clearly, many more long-term projects would have been attractive for Japanese and German firms than for U.S. firms. In contrast, U.S. firms would have found it more profitable to concentrate on projects with a shorter life or a quicker pay-back. Such a strategy would have maximized the value of the firm.

The factors responsible for the higher cost of capital to U.S. firms are not obvious. Recent studies conclude that factors commonly blamed, such as the low U.S. savings rates and tax and depreciation differences, do not fully explain the cost of capital gap. The billions of dollars that flow across international borders every day makes it unlikely that real interest rate differentials can persist (Poterba, 1990). In addition, although comparing the relative tax burdens on capital in different countries is difficult, the consensus seems to be that tax disparities have worked in the direction of lowering U.S. capital costs relative to firms in foreign countries. McCauley and Zimmer (1989, p. 10), for example, find that although the nominal cost of debt (a weighted average of bank and bond debt) was considerably higher in the United States than in both Japan and Germany during the 1977–1988 period, when these figures are adjusted for both inflation and tax differences the effective real after-tax cost of debt was very similar in the U.S. and Japan. In Germany, on the other hand, firms have had a consistently lower cost of debt because of their greater use of bank loans, which have carried lower real interest rates.

The major source of the cost of capital gap appears to be due to the higher cost of equity to U.S. firms and to the fact that U.S. firms use more equity than debt financing relative to foreign firms. McCauley and Zimmer (1989, p. 12) estimate that the U.S. cost of equity capital has been much higher than in either Japan or Germany: it has often been more than double that in Japan and Germany (see figure 9–3). When this higher cost of equity is combined with the greater reliance of U.S. firms on equity financing (see figure 9–4), it is clear that U.S. firms must have a higher cost of capital: this cost is a weighted average of a firm's debt and equity costs (McCauley and Zimmer, 1989, p. 13).

These findings raise two questions. First, why is the cost of equity capital so much higher for U.S. firms than for either Japanese or German firms? Second, why do not U.S. firms simply use more debt (and less equity) financing and in that way reduce their cost of capital?

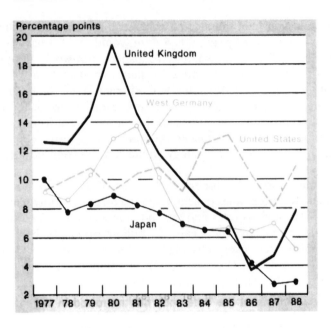

Figure 9–3. Cost of Equity.
Source: FRBNY Quarterly Review/Summer 1989, p. 12.

The answer to the second question is that U.S. firms have apparently used the level of debt that is optimal for them, *given* the supply of funds that they face. If they were to use more debt relative to equity, U.S. investors would perceive them to be more vulnerable to bankruptcy and would therefore demand a greater risk premium, thereby raising the interest rate on debt. More specifically, it has been estimated that in the United States during the 1977–1988 period a 10 percent increase in leverage was associated with a 29 percent rise in the fraction of corporate debt in bankruptcy (McCauley and Zimmer, 1989, p. 23). Thus, most U.S. firms may not be able to achieve a lower cost of capital by increasing their use of debt or their leverage.

McCauley and Zimmer (1989, p. 24) estimate that by doubling corporate leverage U.S. firms could only marginally reduce their cost of capital. For example, a corporation leveraging from a debt-to-equity ratio of one-to-one up to two-to-one on a book-value basis would typically be downgraded from a BBB to a B rating, and its interest payments would rise from 18 to 36 percent of its pretax cash flow. In 1989 B-rated bonds yielded

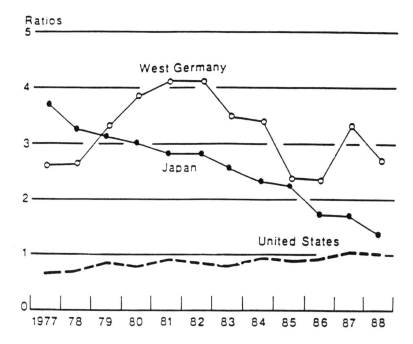

Figure 9–4.   Debt/Market Equity Ratios.
Source: McCauley and Zimmer, *op.cit.*

on average about 150 basis points more than BBB-rated bonds. (The rate spread ranged from 122 to 264 basis points during the year.) As a consequence, two-thirds of the firm's capital structure would become more expensive than before (even though interest costs are tax deductible). McCauley and Zimmer conclude, therefore, that because of the substantial risk premiums associated with greater leverage in U.S. capital markets, U.S. firms would have little to gain by increasing their use of debt relative to equity financing.

Thus, the question of why U.S. firms use relatively less debt than their foreign competitors is in fact a question about why U.S. lenders penalize U.S. firms so much more than foreign lenders penalize foreign firms for assuming greater leverage. The answer seems to be that the frequency of bankruptcy in Japan and Germany is less related to financial leverage than in the United States. Although Japanese and German firms must devote a higher proportion of their cash flows to interest payments, corporate bankruptcy rates in these countries are *lower* than in the United States

(McCauley and Zimmer, 1989, p. 22). Further, although corporate leverage is higher in Japan and Germany, the proportion of corporate debt in bankruptcy in the two countries is the same as it is in the United States (McCauley and Zimmer, 1989, p. 23). Thus, the risk premium associated with greater leverage in Japan and Germany appears to be less than in the United States.

A possible explanation for this difference is that Japanese and German firms rely to a much greater extent on banks for financing than do U.S. firms. In Japan, banks hold about 65 percent of total corporate loans and bonds (Prowse, 1990; Hamada and Horiuchi, 1987). Similarly, in Germany bank funding constitutes over 20 percent of corporate external funding. In contrast, in the United States bank financing is a relatively minor source of corporate funds.

Banks in Japan and Germany, it has been argued, are more willing to provide funding because they are better able to monitor borrowers than are most securities holders (Hoshi, Kashyap, and Scharf stein, 1989). In addition, Japanese and German banks have a greater incentive to be effective monitors: they usually own or control, either directly or indirectly, a substantial amount of stock in the companies to which they lend (Prowse, 1990; Mayer, 1989). For example, although banks in Germany own less than 10 percent of market equity, through the proxies they hold they control almost 60 percent of the total market value of equity. Further, in a survey of 66 large German companies, 51 had more than one banker on the board, and membership on these boards was concentrated among the top few banks (Bannock, 1991). Thus, the close relationship between banks and borrowers in Japan and Germany may reduce the agency and monitoring costs common to the lender-borrower relationship. Japanese and German firms are able to use relatively more bank debt than are U.S. firms without appreciably increasing their debt cost, resulting in a lower cost of capital for them.

Another reason that Japanese and German firms have had a lower cost of capital is that they have had a considerably lower cost of equity capital. While the precise sources of this cost advantage are debatable, it appears that it is at least partly due to a lower equity premium (Frankel, 1991). A common definition of the equity premium is the required rate of return on equity minus the risk-free interest rate. Thus, if there are significant differences in the cost of equity capital in different countries, they should occur because investors in the respective countries demand different equity premium.

Bernheim and Shoven (1989) use data on adjusted earnings-price ratios in 1988 to estimate for both Japan and the United States the required rates of return on securities of different riskiness, where a security's riskiness is defined to be its systematic or nondiversifiable risk with respect to the market portfolio. They find that required rates of return for a given risk-asset are much higher in the United States than in Japan (see figure 9–5), implying that U.S. investors demand a higher risk premium on equity.

Malkiel (1989) uses survey data of investors' expectations to arrive at the same conclusion. He shows that the required rate of return on equity can be estimated as the sum of the dividend yield (the anticipated yield for the next year) and the long-term growth rate of dividends. Dividend yields can be readily estimated, but long-term growth rates are more difficult to assess. For the latter, Malkiel uses the five-year forecasts of investors in the United States, Japan, and Germany for the years 1977 through 1989, obtained from survey data. His estimates of the cost of equity capital show that during the 1980s the real (adjusted for inflation rates) cost of equity funds in the U.S. was on average about two percentage points higher than in both Japan and Germany (see table 9–2).

Thus, equity capital, as well as debt capital, is subject to a lower risk premium in Japan and Germany. The explanation again may lie in the different institutional arrangements employed in those countries.[3] With respect to debt, we argued earlier that banks were more effective monitors because of their close ties to industrial firms, and because their equity participations in borrowing companies provided them with a greater incentive to monitor. A similar story can be told with respect to equity capital. In particular, "big ownership" of corporate equity, either directly or indirectly, is common in Japan and Germany, and big owners commonly have closer relationships with companies and have a much greater incentive to be informed and to monitor the firms in which they invest. Since big owners are more informed and are more able to exercise control over management, they are less subject to the kind of information asymmetries and agency costs that plague U.S. investors. Thus, there is less need for them to demand high equity premiums: their risk exposure is less.[4]

To summarize, studies of the cost of capital in the United States and in foreign countries generally find that U.S. firms have been subject to a higher cost of capital during much of the 1970s and 1980s. In response to this differential, it would have been rational for U.S. firms to have adopted shorter planning horizons and to have been less willing to undertake long-term investment and R&D projects. Similarly, it would explain why the managers of Japanese and German firms appear to be more long-run oriented, and why these firms have spent relatively more on capital improvements and R&D. The critical question is, why have U.S. firms had a higher cost of capital? An important part of the explanation is that U.S. investors have demanded a higher risk premium, on both debt and equity capital. Although the reasons for this are not clear, a possible explanation

Expected Monthly Return (% per month)

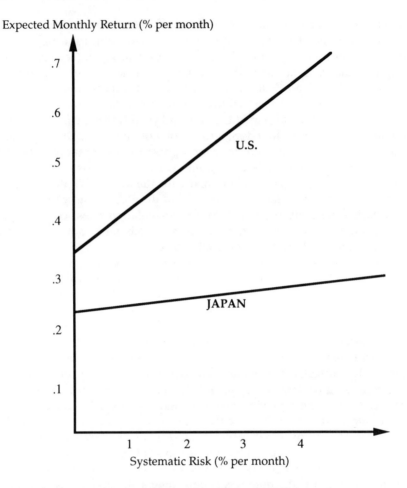

Figure 9–5.   Capital Market Lines: U.S. vs Japan—1988.
Source: B. Douglas Bernheim and John Shoven, "Comparison of the Cost of Capital in the U.S. and Japan: The Rates of Risk and Taxes", CEPR Publication No. 179, Stanford University, September 1989.

Table 9-2. Estimates of Cost of Equity Capital (k_0)

	Nominal			Real		
	United States	*Japan*	*Germany*	*United States*	*Japan*	*Germany*
1977	14.4%	11.4%	10.2%	6.2%	6.5%	6.3%
1978	14.9	10.3	9.6	6.8	6.1	5.9
1979	14.4	9.7	9.4	6.7	6.0	5.9
1980	13.4	9.1	9.2	7.7	6.3	6.0
1981	13.3	7.9	8.8	8.0	5.7	6.0
1982	13.7	7.2	8.7	9.4	5.6	6.4
1983	11.9	7.1	7.5	7.9	5.6	5.4
1984	12.1	6.8	7.1	8.3	5.5	5.2
1985	10.9	6.3	6.8	7.3	5.0	4.9
1986	10.0	6.2	6.3	6.2	4.7	4.2
1987	9.8	6.5	7.1	5.6	4.8	4.7
1988	10.5	6.7	7.8	6.3	5.0	5.2
1989	10.3	6.3	7.8	5.9	4.8	4.6
Average, 1980–89	11.6%	7.0%	7.7%	7.3%	5.3%	5.5%

Source: Malkiel (1991).

Note: $K_0 = \dfrac{D_0\,(1+g)}{P_0} + g$. D_0 is the dividend paid in the past year; P_0 is the current price of a share; and g is the constant long-term growth rate of the dividend.

is that institutional arrangements related to the ownership and control of corporations in Japan and Germany may lower the risk associated with both lending and equity ownership. In particular, the ability of investors in Japan and Germany to take large or controlling equity positions in companies may enable them to reduce the costs associated with resolving the agency and monitoring problems that are commonly associated with both lending and equity ownership.

Big Ownership and Relationship Investors in Japan and Germany

The term *big ownership* refers to stockholders with a large enough position in a company to be able to replace management. Such stockholders are presumed to be well informed about the companies in which they invest and to be active in evaluating and monitoring managerial performance.

Relationship investors, although not necessarily big owners in the sense that they own a large block of a company's stock, play a similar role. Together with other similarly oriented investors, relationship investors hold controlling positions in companies for the purpose of maintaining long-term business relationships with those companies. Usually they develop communal arrangements for monitoring the managements of companies, and through these mechanism exert an influence on corporate management similar to that of big owners.

In Germany, big ownership is more common and plays a dominant role in monitoring and directing corporate management. There is, to begin with, a greater concentration of equity ownership than in the United States. Banks, families, foundations, other companies, and even state entities own sizeable blocks of shares in many major companies. In 29 of the 40 largest German companies there are shareholders who own 10 percent or more of the company's stock. In contrast, in the United States only 8 of the largest 50 publicly traded companies have stockholders with positions greater than 10 percent (Lorsch and MacIver, 1991). An example of how big ownership works in Germany is Porsche, the well-known German automobile manufacturer. Porsche is owned by two families—the Pech and Porsche families—who together own all of the company's common stock and 40 percent of its preferred stock. This kind of ownership stake makes it imperative for owners to stay informed and to take an active role in determining company strategy. If hard times befall a company, owners cannot easily sell their stock and move on to a new investment. They must either sell the entire company or put the company back on track. In 1992, when Porsche's sales were faltering badly and the future of the company was in doubt, the big-owner families intervened actively. Although in this instance they ultimately agreed to retain the company's management, they were able to influence the company's future strategy and goals.[5]

A big-ownership role also is exerted in Germany through banks. German banks directly own a substantial share of the voting stock. In 1987 the ten largest German banks owned 25 percent or more of the stock of 33 large German companies (capitalized at more than one billion DM). But banks control much more stock through their trust and custodial accounts. As a consequence, it is common for banks to have representation on the supervisory boards of German companies and to take an active role in corporate affairs. For example, when a managerial dispute erupted at Daimler-Benz a few years ago, the Deutschebank intervened to settle it. The Deutschebank alone controls about 25 percent of Daimler-Benz's stock, some directly and some indirectly through its fiduciary funds and custodial accounts (Roe, 1991). Thus, German banks, in contrast to U.S. banks, play a direct role in the governance of German corporations.

In Japan, arrangements among relationship investors are the main vehicles through which control of corporate managers is exercised. The financial *keiretsu* lies at the heart of the Japanese industrial structure. At least 28 separate *keiretsu* groups presently exist in Japan (Flath, 1990). Typically, the *keiretsu* is characterized by extensive cross-holdings of stock among many companies and by the inclusion of a major (or main) Japanese bank that performs a centralized coordinating and monitoring function. These companies are bound together by long-term business relationships and by both social and financial ties. In addition, borrowing by member firms is commonly concentrated in the *keiretsu's* main bank so that the bank is not only a stockholder but a large creditor as well. As a consequence, key bank personnel often serve on corporate boards and may be put in top managerial positions in firms experiencing financial distress. Thus, although no single company in the *keiretsu* may own or control a substantial block of any company's stock, together the *keiretsu* member companies typically own more than enough stock in a company to permit effective monitoring and control of a company. It has been reported that about 70 percent of Japan's 1,500 public companies are at least 50 percent owned by related companies or financial institutions (Taylor, 1990).

A 1988 survey of the 300 largest manufacturing companies in both Japan and the United States by the Industrial Policy Bureau of MITI shows just how different the pattern of stockholding is in Japan and the United States. Almost 80 percent of Japanese corporate shares are held by relationship investors, while in the United States just the opposite is true. In the United States two-thirds of shares are held by purely financial investors, such as mutual funds and pension funds. Institutional investors in the United States have typically focused on financial returns and have not gotten involved in monitoring corporate management. Only in the last few years have public pension funds begun to take a more active role in corporate governance.

Table 9–3 shows the comparative ownership structure in Japan and the United States (Malkiel, 1991). In the United States passive institutional investors are clearly the dominant stockholders, while in Japan financial institutions with business relationships to the companies in which they hold stock are the dominant stockholders.

The role of relationship investors is manifested as well by the stock trading patterns in Japan and the United States. Data on stock trading on the Tokyo Stock Exchange show that while relationship investors own over two-thirds of the shares of Tokyo Stock Exchange companies they do

Table 9–3. Comparisons of Ownership Patterns of Equity Securities, United States and Japan, January 1988

	United States	Japan
Purely investment-return-oriented investors:		
Institutional investors (e.g., pension funds, mutual funds)	44%	15%
General public investors	19	3
Other	4	4
Total	67%	22%
Relationship-oriented investors:		
Financial institutions with business relationships (e.g., banks, life insurance companies)	12%	47%
Nonfinancial corporate holders	9	11
Parent and other group companies	3	17
Owner-founder	10	4
Total	34%	79%

Source: Industrial Policy Bureau of MITI from a survey of 300 of the largest manufacturing companies in the United States and Japan.

Note: Figures may not add due to rounding.

just over 25 percent of the trading (Malkiel, 1991). In contrast, passive institutional investors in the United States, while holding about half of the stock of New York Stock Exchange companies, do anywhere from 50 to 80 percent of the trading in these companies, depending on the year.

The long-term orientation of Japanese relationship investors also shows up in the longevity of their stock holdings. The top shareholders in 1978 in Japan's largest 181 corporations were still among the top five shareholders in the same company in 1988, ten years later. In addition, only 15 percent of the ten largest shareholders in 1978 had dropped out of the top 20 shareholders in the same company in 1988 (Futatsugi, 1990). Thus, control of Japanese companies commonly rests in the hands of relationship investors, who do not trade the company's shares frequently and who do not respond to the short-term financial vicissitudes of the company.

In both Germany and Japan, banks play a critical corporate governance role, although in somewhat different ways. In Germany their power comes from their ability to exercise influence through both the stock they own and the stock they hold in trust or custodial accounts. In Japan control is exercised through cross-holdings of stock and the main-bank structure.

Jonathan Charkham, advisor to the governors of the Bank of England, succinctly sums up the difference between the ownership structure in the United States and in both Germany and Japan: "In Germany and Japan the banks play a leading role in exerting influence because historically they are the main source of funds, often supplying a wide range of services: they have shareholdings and (in Germany) a seat on the supervisory board. In Japan associated companies, customers and suppliers (all of whom may be shareholders too) may exert influence. All of this is done quietly without public confrontation except in extremes" (Taylor, 1990).

In the United States neither big ownership nor relationship investing is an important feature of the corporate landscape. Consequently, U.S. stockholders generally do not have the same incentive to be informed and to stay informed and do not invest the same amount of time and effort in monitoring corporate management. Further, even if they wished to, they normally would not have the power to change the management. It is not surprising, therefore, that institutional investors in the United States "vote with their feet," selling a company's stock at the first sign of poor performance. This is often the only option open to them.

Thus, because U.S. stockholders are less informed about firms and the capabilities of management and are less able to influence management, they are subject to greater risk than are Japanese and German shareholders. A rationale response, therefore, is for U.S. stockholders to charge corporations a higher risk premium for the use of their funds, increasing the cost of capital to U.S. firms relative to Japanese and German firms.

Policy Implications for the United States

To the extent that managerial "short-sightedness" exists in the United States, it cannot be cured by easy solutions like a transactions tax on securities trading or a higher short-term capital-gains tax. Active trading by investors or a high turnover in financial markets is not the cause of managerial myopia; nor are leveraged buyouts and corporate takeovers the cause. If anything, it has been the relatively higher cost of capital to U.S. firms that has caused the shorter planning horizons used by U.S. managers. The remedy for U.S. short-sightedness, therefore, is to lower the cost of capital to U.S. firms.

This can be accomplished in two ways. First, by government providing a more stable macroeconomic environment in the United States and by providing incentives to increase private-sector savings. Second, by regulatory reforms to encourage more active participation by institutional stockholders in corporate governance. More informed equity ownership can reduce the risk premiums that shareholders demand and lower the cost of capital to U.S. firms.

To encourage long-term, effective, ownership, several reforms need to be undertaken. First, institutional investors should be permitted to take larger equity positions in companies. Specifically, banks should be permitted to take equity positions in commercial firms (which they cannot do now), and restrictions on ownership by institutional investors such as insurance companies and mutual funds should be relaxed.[6] With larger ownership stakes, the incentive to work closely with corporate management for the long-run good of the firm will increase. Second, the array of legal deterrences to large ownership should be relaxed. Examples are existing filing requirements for large owners under section 13(d) of the Securities Exchange Act, the short-swing profit rule of section 16(b) of the Securites Exchange Act, and the extra layers of taxation that discourage corporate crossholdings (Black, 1992). Third, obstacles to being an active shareholder should be relaxed or eliminated. Examples are the requirements for active shareholders to report their holdings and plans on Schedule 13D; costly filing requirements imposed by the Hart-Scott-Rodino premerger notification rules; and SEC proxy rules that make it difficult and costly for owners to choose directors and engage in proxy campaigns (Black, 1992). These are just some examples of what might be done. The key point is that we must rethink our rules and regulations with a view toward encouraging both long-run ownership and the active participation of institutional investors in corporate affairs.

If these reforms are made, it is likely that in the future institutional investors will play a more dominant and active shareholder role than they do now. We will be asking fiduciaries and money managers to monitor corporate managers: managers will be watching managers. Clearly, this arrangement is not without risks. We must be attentive to the incentives of our fiduciaries and money managers as well as to our corporate managers. Still, there is reason to believe that such a system will work better than the one we have at present (Black, 1992). The alternatives, in any case, are less attractive.

Notes

1. These studies, it should be recognized, do not take into account the possibility that there may be a considerable amount of unexplainable "noise" in the determinants of stock prices.
2. Some studies find that institutional ownership may encourage a longer managerial horizon. See, for example, Hansen and Hill (1991) and McConnell and Servaes (1990).

3. Although the United States has had a less stable macroeconomic environment than either Japan or Germany, it is not clear to what extent this has been responsible for the different risk premiums extracted by investors (see Lawrence, 1991b).

4. For a discussion of big ownership of corporate equity in Germany and Japan in comparison to the United States, and its implications, see Edwards and Eisenbeis (1993).

5. A story in the *Wall Street Journal* reports that "the Piech and Porsche families have always been quite ruthless in the past in changing chairmen who they don't feel are doing the job correctly" (see "Internal Struggle at Porsche," 1992).

6. For a discussion of the existing legal restrictions on institutional ownership and their historical origins, see Roe, 1991b.

References

Aggarwal and Rao, "Institutional Ownership and the Distribution of Equity Returns," *Financial Review*, vol. 25, May, 1990, pp. 211–229.

Ando, Albert and Alan J. Auerbach, 'The Cost of Capital in the United States and Japan: A Comparison," *Journal of the Japanese and International Economies*, vol. 2, 1988, pp. 134–158.

Ball, R., "Changes in Accounting Techniques and Stock Prices: *Journal of Accounting Research*, vol. 10, Spring 1972, pp. 1–38.

Bannock, Graham, "Banks and Industrial Management," *The British and German Banking System: A Comparative Study*, Economists Advisory Group, ch. 5, 1991.

Bernheim, B. Douglas and John B. Shoven, "Comparison of the Cost of Capital in the U.S. and Japan: The Roles of Risk and Taxes," Stanford University CEPR Publication No. 179, September 1989.

Black, Bernard S., "Agents Watching Agents: The Promise of Institutional Investor Voice," *UCLA Law Review*, vol. 39, 1992, pp. 401–486.

Blinder, A.S. and A.B. Krueger, "International Differences in Labor Turnover: A Comparative Study with Emphasis on the U.S. and Japan," Time Horizons of American Management Project, Harvard Business School and Council on Competitiveness, 1992.

Brancato, Carolyn Kay, "The Momentum of the Big Investor," *Directors and Boards*, Winter 1990a, pp. 38–39.

———, "The Pivotal Role of Institutional Investors in Capital Markets," paper presented at the Conference on the Fiduciary Responsibilities of Institutional Investors, New York, June 13, 1990b.

Brancato, C. and P. Gaughan, *The Growth of Institutional Investors in the U.S. Capital Markets*, Center for Law and Economics, Columbia University, November 1988.

———, "Institutional Investors and Capital Markets, 1991 Update," Center for Law and Economics, Columbia University, 1991.

Brooks, Harvey, "Technology as a Factor in U.S. Competitiveness," Bruce Scott and George Lodge (eds.), *U.S. Competitiveness in the World Economy*, Boston, 1985.

"Business Bulletin," *Wall Street Journal*, June 12, 1986, p. 1.

Edwards, Franklin R. and Robert A. Eisenbeis, "Financial Institutions and Corporate Investment Horizons: An International Perspective," in Michael E. Porter (ed.), *Investment Behavior and Time Horizon in American Industry*, Boston: Harvard Business School Press, 1993.

Flath, David, "Shareholding in the Keiretsu, Japan's Financial Groups," unpublished paper, North Carolina State University, May 1990.

Frankel, Jeffrey A., "The Japanese Cost of Finance: A Survey," *Financial Management*, Spring 1991, pp. 95–127.

Friedman, Benjamin M., *Day of Reckoning: The Consequences of American Economic Policy Under Reagan and After*, New York, 1988.

Froot, Kenneth A. and Andne F. Perold, and Jeremy C. Stein, "Shareholder Trading Practices and Corporate Investment Horizons," Time Horizons of American Management Project, Harvard Business School and the Council on Competiveness, 1991.

Futatsugi, Yusaku, "What Share Cross-Holdings Mean for Corporate Management," *Economic Eye*, Spring 1990.

Hamada, Koichi and Akiyoshi Horiuchi, "The Political Economy of the Financial Market," Kozo Yamamura and Yasukichi Yasuba (eds.), *The Political Economy of Japan: Volume 1. The Domestic Transformation*, Stanford: Stanford University Press, 1987.

Hansen and Hill, "Are Institutional Investors Myopic? A Time Series Study of Four Technology Driven Industries," *Strategic Management Journal*, vol. 12, 1991, pp. 1–16.

Hatsopoulos, George, "High Cost of Capital: Handicap of American Industry," study sponsored by the American Business Conference and Thermo Electron Corp., April 1983.

Hatsopoulos, George, Paul Krugman, and Larry Summers, "U.S. Competitiveness: Beyond the Trade Deficit," *Science*, July 1988, pp. 299–307.

Hector, Gary, "Yes, You *Can* Manage Long Term," *Fortune*, November 21, 1988, pp. 66–75.

Hoshi, Takeo, Anil Kashyap, and David Scharfstein, "Bank Monitoring and Investment: Evidence from the Changing Structure of Japanese Corporate Banking Relations," Finance and Economics Discussion Series, No. 86, Federal Reserve Board, August 1989.

"Internal Struggle at Porsche Centers on Chairman Bohn," *Wall Street Journal*, February 20, 1992, p. A10, col. 4.

Jacobs, Michael, *Short-Term America*, Boston: Harvard Business School Press, 1991.

"Japan Seen Passing U.S. in Research by Industry," *New York Times*, February 25, 1992, p. C1, col. 4.

Jarrell, Gregg, Ken Lehn, and Wayne Marr, "Institutional Ownership, Tender Offers, and Long-Term Investments," Office of the Chief Economist, Securities and Exchange Commission, April 19, 1985.

Jones, Jonathan, Kenneth Lehn, and Harold Mulherin, "Institutional Ownership of Equity: Effects on Stock Market Liquidity and Corporate Long-Term Investment," Bicksler and Sametz (eds.), *The Fiduciary Responsibilities of Institutional Investors*, New York: Dow Jones-Irwin, 1990.

Kaplan, R. and R. Roll, "Investor Evaluation of Accounting Information: Some Empirical Evidence", *Journal of Business*, vol. 45, July 1972, pp. 225–257.

Kaplan, Steven N., "The Effects of Management Buyouts on Operating Performance and Value," *Journal of Financial Economics*, vol. 24, 1989.

Kobayashi, Yotaro, "A Message to American Managers," *Economic Eye*, vol. 11, no. 1, Spring 1990, pp. 8–12.

Kochan, T.A. and P. Osterman, "Human Resource Development and Utilization: Is There Too Little in the U.S.?," Time Horizons of American Management Project, Harvard Business School and Council on Competitiveness, 1992.

Krafcik, John F., Training and the Automobile Industry: International Comparisons, contractor report prepared for the Office of Technology Assessment under contract N3: 1910, February 1990, pp. 8–9.

Lakonishok, Josef, Andrei Shleifer, and Robert Vishny, "Do Institutional Investors Destabilize Stock Prices? Evidence on Herding and Feedback Trading," NBER Working Paper No. 3705, 1991.

Lawrence, Robert Z., "Deindustrialization: Concepts and Evidence," paper presented at Columbia University's Conference on Deindustrialization, November 15–16, 1991a.

———, "Time Horizons of American Management: The Role of Macroeconomic Factors," Time Horizons of American Management Project, Harvard Business School and Council on Competitiveness, 1991b.

Lorsch, Jay W. and Elizabeth A. MacIver, "Corporate Governance and Investment Time Horizons," Time Horizons of American Management Project, Harvard Business School and the Council on Competitiveness and the Harvard Business School, 1991.

Malkiel, Burton, "The Influence of Conditions in Financial Markets on the Time Horizons of Business Managers: An International Comparison," Time Horizons of American Management Project, Harvard Business School and the Council on Competitiveness, December 1991.

Mayer, Colin, "Financial Systems, Corporate Finance and Economic Development, unpublished paper, 1989.

McCauley, Robert N. and Steven A. Zimmer, "Explaining International Differences in the Cost of Capital," *Quarterly Review*, Federal Reserve Bank of New York, vol. 14, no. 2, Summer 1989.

McConnell, John J. and Chris J. Muscarella, "Corporate Capital Expenditure Decisions and the Market Value of the Firm," *Journal of Financial Economics*, vol. 14, July 1985.

McConnell and Servaes, "Additional Evidence on Equity Ownership and Corporate Value," *Journal of Finance*, vol. 27, 1990.

Morita, Akio and Shintaro Ishihara, *The Japan That Can Say "No": The New U.S.-Japan Relations Card*, 1990.

Poterba, James N. "International Comparisons of the Cost of Capital: A Survey of Methods, with Reference to the U.S. and Japan," *Bulletin*, Federal Reserve of New York, October 1990.

Poterba, James M. and Larry Summers, "Survey of CEO's on Investment Behavior," Time Horizons of American Management Project, Harvard Business School and Council on Competitiveness, 1991.

Prowse, Stephen D., "Institutional Investment Patterns and Corporate Financing Behavior in the U.S. and Japan," Finance and Discussion Series, No. 118, Federal Reserve Board, January 1990.

Reich, Robert B., *Education and the New Economy*, Washington, D.C.: National Education Association, Professional and Organizational Development, 1988.

Roe, Mark J., "Institutional Fiduciaries in the Corporate Boardroom," in A. Sametz and J. Bicksler (eds.), *Institution Investors: Challenges and Responsibilities*, 1991a.

————, "Political and Legal Restraints on Ownership and Control of Public Companies," *Journal of Financial Economics*, Symposium on the Structure and Governance of Enterprise, vol. 27, September 1990.

————, "A Political Theory of American Corporate Finance," *Columbia Law Review*, vol. 91, no. 10, 1991b.

Sunohara, T., "The U.S. on Losing End of Factory 'Vintage Gap'," *Japan Economic Journal*, July 28, 1990, pp. 1, 12.

Taylor, William, "Can Big Owners Make a Big Difference," *Harvard Business Review*, September-October, 1990.

Tobin, James, "Tax the Speculators," *Financial Times*, December 22, 1992, p. 10.

U.S. Congress, Office of Technology Assessment, *Worker Training: Competing in the New International Economy*, OTA-ITE-457 Washington, D.C.: U.S. Government Printing Office, September 1990.

U.S. Department of Labor, *Productivity and the Economy*, Bureau of Labor Statistics, August 1, 1989.

Venture Economics, 1990, *Venture Capital Yearbook 1990*, Needham, Mass.: Venture Economics.

"White House Flirts with Pension Tax," *Wall Street Journal*, September 25, 1989, p. A1, col. 3.

Woolridge, Randall, "Competitive Decline and Corporate Restructuring: Is a Myopic Stock Market to Blame?," *Journal of Applied Corporate Finance*, vol. 1, no. 1, Spring 1988, pp. 26–36.

About the Authors

Richard Aspinwall is Senior Vice President and Chief Economist of the Chase Manhattan Bank. He previously was Director of Bank and Financial Market Research in Chase's economics department. Before joining Chase Manhattan Bank, he was a research economist at the Federal Reserve Bank of New York. He has also served as an adjunct professor in the Graduate School of Business at Columbia University.

Dr. Aspinwall has published widely in professional journals, and has edited a number of books, including *The Handbook for Banking Strategy* (John Wiley & Sons, 1985). He serves as an associate editor of the *Journal of Financial Services Research*. Aspinwall is a member of the Shadow Financial Regulatory Committee.

George J. Benston is the John H. Harland Professor of Finance, Accounting and Economics at Emory University, where he was also previously the Associate Dean for Research and Faculty Development in the School of Business. He has taught at the University of Rochester and the University of Chicago and has been a visiting professor at Oxford University and the London School of Economics. He has served as a founding member of the board of directors of the Federal Agriculture Mortgage Corporation, as an elected trustee of the College Retirement Equities Fund, as a consultant to the World Bank, and as a visiting scholar at the Federal Reserve Bank of Atlanta.

Professor Benston has published widely in professional journals and has authored/edited numerous books in finance, economics, and accounting, including *Financial Services; The Changing Institutions and Government Policy* (Prentice-Hall, 1983), *Perspective on Safe and Sound Banking* (MIT Press, 1986) and *The Separation of Commercial and Investment Banking*

(Oxford, 1990). He is co-editor of the *Journal of Financial Services Research* and an associate editor of the *Journal of Money, Credit and Banking, Contemporary Accounting Research, Journal of Financial Research*, and *the Journal of Accounting and Public Policy*. Benston is a member of the Shadow Financial Regulatory Committee.

Franklin R. Edwards is the Authur F. Burns Professor of Free and Competitive Enterprise and Director of the Center for the Study of Futures Markets at Columbia University. He previously served as an economist at the Federal Reserve Board and at the Comptroller of the Currency. He also served as vice-dean for Academic Affairs at the Graduate School of Business at Columbia University in 1979–81.

Professor Edwards has published widely in professional journals and has authored/edited a number of books including *Issues in Financial Regulation* (McGraw-Hill, 1979) and *Futures and Options* (McGraw-Hill, 1992). He is co-editor of the *Journal of Financial Services Research* and an associate editor of the *Journal of Futures Markets, and Managerial and Decision Economics*. He has testified in Congress on many occasions. He served as a public director of the Futures Industry Association and on the nominating committee of the American Stock Exchange. Edwards is a member of the Shadow Financial Regulatory Committee.

Robert A. Eisenbeis is the Wachovia Professor of Banking and Associate Dean for Research at the School for Business Administration of the University of North Carolina. He previously served as an officer at the Federal Reserve Board and the Federal Deposit Insurance Corporation and as a visiting scholar at the Federal Reserve Bank of Atlanta.

Professor Eisenbeis has published widely in professional journals and has authored/edited a number of books including *Perspectives on Safe and Sound Banking* (MIT Press, 1986), *Handbook of Banking Strategy* (John Wiley, 1983), and *Applications of Classification Techniques in Business, Banking, and Finance* (JAI Press, 1981). He is a co-editor of the *Journal of Financial Services Research*, and an associate editor of the *Journal of Banking and Finance* and the *Journal of Economics and Business*. He has testified numerous times before Congress. Eisenbeis is a member of the Shadow Financial Regulatory Committee.

Richard Herring is Professor of Finance and Director of the Wharton Financial Institutions Center at the Wharton School in the University of Pennsylvania. He is also the Academic Director of the Wharton Advanced Management Program for Overseas Bankers, and previously was Director of the Wharton Program in International Banking and Finance. He has served as a Visiting Professor at the Institute of Banking Lore at the Johann Wolfgang Goëthe University in Frankfurt, Germany.

Professor Herring has published widely in professional journals and authored/edited a number of books. He was co-author of the Brookings Study *A Blueprint for Restructuring American Financial Institutions* (1991). His articles have appeared in the *Journal of Financial Services Research, Contemporary Policy Issues,* the *Journal of Money, Credit, and Banking,* the *Journal of Finance,* and the *Journal of Political Economy.* He serves on the editorial boards of the *Journal of Financial Services Research,* the *Journal of International Financial Markets, Institutions and Money,* and *Columbia Journal of World Business.* Herring is a member of the Shadow Financial Regulatory Committee.

Paul M. Horvitz is the Judge James A. Elkins Professor of Banking and Finance at the University of Houston. He previously served as director of research at the Federal Deposit Insurance Corporation and as an economist at the Comptroller of the Currency. He also was a visiting scholar at the Federal Reserve Bank of Atlanta, a public director of the Federal Home Loan Bank of Dallas, and a director of four saving & loan associations and one commercial bank.

Professor Horvitz has published widely in professional journals and has authored/edited a number of books including; *Perspectives on Safe and Sound Banking* (MIT Press, 1986), *Commercial Banking and Interstate Expansion* (University of Michigan Press, 1985), *Sources of Financing for Small Business* (JAI Press, 1985), and *Monetary Policy and the Financial System* (Prentice-Hall, 6th edition, 1987). He is co-editor of the *Journal of Financial Services Research.* He has testified numerous times before Congress, has been a consultant to a number of financial services organizations, and was a columnist for the *American Banker.* Horvitz is a member of the Shadow Financial Regulatory Committee.

Edward J. Kane is the James F. Clearly Professor in Finance at Boston College and a research associate in the National Bureau of Economic Research. He previously taught at Ohio State University Princeton University, and Iowa State University. He has also served as visiting professor at Arizona State University, Simon Fraser University and Istanbul University, as a visiting scholar at the Federal Reserve Bank of San Francisco and the Federal Deposit Insurance Corporation, and both an elected and appointed trustee of the Teachers Insurance and Annuity Association.

Professor Kane has published widely in professional journals and authored/edited many books including the *Savings & Loan Insurance Crises: How Did It Happen?* (Urban Institute Press, 1989), *The Gathering Crises In Federal Deposit Insurance* (MIT Press, 1985), and *Perspectives On Safe And Sound Banking* (MIT Press, 1986). He is a co-editor of the *Journal of Financial Services Research*, and an associate editor of the *Journal of Banking and Finance, Journal of Money, Credit and Banking, Journal of Financial Research*, the *Journal of Empirical Finance*, and the *Pacific-Basin Finance Journal*. He has testified numerous times before Congress. He has been honored by his peers by being elected President of the American Financial Association in 1977. Kane is a member of the Shadow Financial Regulatory Committee.

George G. Kaufman is the John F. Smith Jr. Professor of Finance and Economics at Loyola University of Chicago. He previously taught at the University of Oregon and was an economist at the Federal Reserve Bank of Chicago. He has been a visiting professor at Stanford University and the University of California at Berkeley, a visiting scholar at the Federal Reserve Bank of San Francisco and the Comptroller of the Currency, and also served as Deputy to the Assistant Secretary for Economic Policy at the U.S. Treasury Department. He is a member of the board of directors of the Rochester (NY) Community Savings Bank and was an elected trustee of the College Retirement Equities Fund.

Professor Kaufman has published widely in professional journals and authored/edited many books including; *The U.S. Financial System* (Prentice-Hall, 5th edition, 1992), *Perspectives on Safe and Sound Banking* (MIT Press 1986), *Deregulating Financial Services* (Ballinger, 1986) *Restructuring the Financial System* (Kluwer, 1990), and *Assessing Bank Reform* (Brookings, 1993). He is a co-editor of the *Journal of Financial Services Research* and an associate editor of the *Journal of Money, Credit, and Banking,* the *Journal of Financial Research* and *Contemporary Policy Issues*. He has testified numerous times before Congress. He has been honored by his peers by being elected President of both the Western Finance and the Midwest Finance Associations. Kaufman is co-chair of the Shadow Financial Regulatory Committee.

Kenneth E. Scott is the Ralph M. Parsons Professor of Law and Business at the Law School of Stanford University. He was formerly the general counsel of the Federal Home Loan Bank Board in 1963–67 and chief deputy savings and loan commissioner of the State of California in 1961–63. He serves on a number of committees of the American Bar Association and the State Bar of California and on the board of the National Center on Financial Services at the University of California at Berkeley.

Professor Scott has published widely in professional journals and has authored/edited a number of books including; *Economics of Corporation Law and Securities Regulation* (Little, Brown and Company, 1980), and *Retail Banking in the Electronic Age: The Law and Economics of Electronic Funds Transfer* (Allanheld, 1977). He has testified many times before Congress and has served as a consultant to a number of bank regulatory agencies and law firms. Scott is a member of the Shadow Financial Regulatory Committee.

Barry Weingast is Professor of Political Science at Stanford University and a Senior Fellow at the Hoover Institution, where he serves as Associate Director of the Program for Public Policy. He previously taught at Washington University (St. Louis) and was a research associate at their Center for the Study of American Business.

Professor Weingast has published widely in professional journals and books. His articles have appeared in the *Journal of Political Economy* and *The American Political Science Review*, among other journals.

Index